AFRICAN AMERICAN FIRSTS
of
WINSTON-SALEM/FORSYTH COUNTY
NORTH CAROLINA

Photos on the cover: Top (left to right): KBR Doctors and Nurses, Spurgeon Ellington, Tuskegee Airman, 1903 First Slater Graduation class. Bottom (left to right):LaFayette Theater, East Winston Library and Safe Bus Jitney. *(Courtesy* of Winston-Salem African American Archive)

Cover designed by Chenita B. Johnson

Copyright © 2020 by Chenita B. Johnson
ISBN: 978-0-578-83414-6 (Paper Back)
Library of Congress Control Number: 2021902334

All rights reserved. No part of this book may be reproduced, stored in a retrieval system, or transmitted in any form, or by any means, electronic, mechanical, photocopying, recording or otherwise, without prior written consent and permission of the author excepting brief quotes used in reviews and other noncommercial uses permitted by copyright law. For permission requests, write to the publisher at the listed address.

Printed in the United States of America
First Edition, 2020

Text OFL open font license

Published by:
Chenita B. Johnson
2411 N. Patterson Avenue
Winston-Salem, N.C., 27105
chenitajohn@hotmail.com

AFRICAN AMERICAN FIRSTS
of
WINSTON-SALEM/FORSYTH COUNTY
NORTH CAROLINA

Pioneers who greatly impacted this city, this county,
this nation and the world

Researched, extracted and compiled by

Chenita B. Johnson

Dedication

I dedicate this book to my mom, Ms. Jacquelyne Beatrice Barber, who was also a remarkable African American of firsts.

A graduate of the Star Stenographic School of Business, in 1965, at the age of twenty-four she became the first permanent African American employee hired at the Social Security Administration Office in Danville Virginia.

In 1974 she was promoted to the position of Claims Representative and became the first African American Claims Representative at the Social Security Administration Office in Parkersburg, West Virginia.

My mom taught me to persevere and to stand strong in what I believe, what I think, and not to waiver, regardless of the perception of others. She also said, "Never fear the unknown, because God has not given us the spirit of fear, but of love, power and a sound mind."

Table of Contents

Preface /vi
Introduction /ix
Chapter 1 Early Documentation and Religion /1
Chapter 2 Education and Educators /19
Chapter 3 Social and Community Activism /67
Chapter 4 Municipal Officials and Elected Representatives /99
Chapter 5 Businesses and Entrepreneurs /157
Chapter 6 Banks and Financial Institutions /193
Chapter 7 Attorneys /201
Chapter 8 Medical Institutions and Physicians /209
Chapter 9 Real Estate /231
Chapter 10 Communication Institutions /251
Chapter 11 Transportation /269
Chapter 12 Community Institutions /277
Chapter 13 Military /293
Chapter 14 Entertainment /309
Chapter 15 Sports /339
Notes /373
Bibliography /383
Index /435
About the Author

Preface

The beginning and completion of this book could not have happened without the consistent encouragement of my mom, Jacquelyne B. Barber. She was always with me whenever possible at the library pouring through various dusty documents, microfilm, books and she accompanied me when interviewing individuals. She also was a bountiful source of historical information and knowledge.

Although mom was unable to finish this journey with me, I have felt her in every jot and tittle of old newspapers, documents and with every stroke of the computer keyboard, and I thank her for her unceasing support.

I also thank the N.C. Room research librarian at the Forsyth County Central Library in Winston-Salem, for urging me to document this information and write this book when information on African Americans in Winston-Salem and Forsyth County was not readily available for another research project I was working.

The gap between information concerning African Americans in Forsyth County was such that if information was available it had to be sought in various uncoordinated publications.

Names and individuals were mentioned, but there was no direct connection between them and the history of Forsyth County. There was a need to compile, coordinate and connect this information.

My mom always said, "when a need presents itself to you, you are the one to fulfill that need." Thus, I began my trek documenting firsts of African Americans of our county from 1763 with the hired woman named Franke, through 2018, with Bobby F. Kimbrough, Jr., Lord High Sheriff of Forsyth County.

I am grateful for my supportive family; my husband Paul, my son Brandon, my daughter Braeden and my daughter in law Susanna, who put up with my long research hours across the county, and the piles of papers in our cars, in our living areas and taking up much computer space.

Thank you to my uncles, James Maurice Barber, Sr. and Michael L. Friday, who were conduits to those who could help me with information. And I greatly appreciate my son Dr. P. Brandon Johnson, PhD, Miss Latala Payne and "Auntie," Rev. Dr. Yvonne H. Hines, PhD for taking time from their very hectic and busy schedules to help edit my manuscript. Last but certainly not least I thank Mr. Lester S. Davis, Mrs. Linda Dark, and Mr. Billy Rich, archivists of The Winston-Salem African American Archive, Thomas Flynn, archivist of my alma mater Winston-Salem State University, and the archivists at Wake Forest University.

I am thankful to the families for their consent of family photographs, and elders in the Winston-Salem community, such as Dr. Harvey Allen, Sr., MD and Mrs. Wilhelmina Lash, who when they learned about my project expressed much interest in sharing, and once again experiencing a glorious time that I understand as history, but for them, reflection of a time they remember as yesterday and a time that should never be forgotten.

This book is not the definitive authority of African American Firsts of Winston-Salem/Forsyth County. It is a beginning of documentation of these events, and to the best of my knowledge these are the firsts acknowledged in print throughout the county and various publications.

It should be recognized that throughout the historical documentations, African Americans are interchangeably described as Black, Colored, and African American.

Knowledge is power, and I hope this book will not only provide knowledge of the rich history and contributions of African Americans of Winston-Salem/Forsyth County, but also will encourage you to want to obtain greater knowledge of the history in the city and county where you live.

Chenita B. Johnson

Introduction

The history of African Americans in Winston-Salem Forsyth County is extremely deep and rich; yet, information about African Americans in this county is limited.

While African American labor was a foundation of and contributed greatly to the growth and prosperity of Winston-Salem and Forsyth County, there is virtually nothing that connects the African American community with any of the county's history.

Many African American neighborhoods, institutions and businesses have been obliterated due to urban renewal and gentrification, leaving their names to exist only in fond memories and recollections of elder residents.

When many are asked about the builders and history of this county, they immediately think of the Reynolds, Babcock, Gray and Nissen families but never the Jones, Clement, Scales or Cash families.

African Americans in Winston-Salem Forsyth County not only dug the foundations for this county, they have sealed it with great integrity, and perseverance through a time of forced servitude, to disfranchised laws, yet still progressed and remained intact as a community.

The African American community has been an integral part of Forsyth County, almost from its birth. While most believed that African Americans arriving in Forsyth County were tied to R.J. Reynolds Tobacco factories the earliest documented arrival of African Americans in Forsyth County were as enslaved people tied to the Moravians, German immigrants from Pennsylvania, who settled Bethabara (now Old Town) in 1753.

At first, "individual Moravians were not permitted to own slaves; they were owned by the Moravian Church, which rented them to whites."[1] The Moravians believed that slaves would make their community become slothful, yet, it became difficult for them to resist the pressure from within and outside their community. They eventually succumbed and allowed individual ownership of slaves and these enslaved people became indispensable to the Moravian community.

"During the 1770's the Moravians brought Black slaves from the Caribbean to Salem to work for them. The operation of the Salem Tavern depended on a slave named Jacob. He was prized as one of the few people in the region who was bi-lingual in German and English and served as a liaison between the mostly English clientele and the German proprietors."[2] Jacob was not an anomaly in Winston-Salem Forsyth County history. There were many firsts by African Americans that have been lost or buried in faded documents, and some in plain sight, throughout the county. Even today they are rarely mentioned, giving the impression that progression for blacks came only during contemporary modern history.

After the Civil War, African Americans in Forsyth County had a low but stable population in the 1870's and 1880's. However, their population exploded during the 1890's as they left farms in surrounding areas and moved to town with the prospect of better paid labor in the new tobacco, and cotton mill factories and as domestic workers.

The transition from enslaved individual, to sharecropper, to paid laborer was difficult, yet, "making their way within the oppressive and discriminatory conditions typical of the post-Reconstruction South, a number of black individuals achieved some success and prominence"[3] forever entrenching themselves and greatly impacting this county, this country and the world.

Top to bottom: United States slave trade, 1830 (*Free Image*); Black cotton farming family c. 1890's (Public Domain); Domestic Nettie Johnson and her charges *(Courtesy of the McCollum Family Reunion)* and tobacco stemmers *(Courtesy of the Bradshaw Estate, Winston-Salem African American Archive and Lester S. Davis)*

"Those who have no record of what their forebears have accomplished lose the inspiration which comes from the teaching of biography and history."

Dr. Carter G. Woodson

Chapter One

Early Documentation and Religion

First Documentation of African Americans in Moravian Records

There is little information concerning the life and or the existence of African Americans in early Forsyth County. The village of Bethabara, a stockaded fort that was the first established community in Forsyth County existed for ten years prior to any mention of Blacks in the Moravian records. The first was documentation of the hiring of a black enslaved woman named Franke, a day laborer in the tavern in Bethabara, with her master receiving financial compensation for her work. The diarist wrote that on August 22, 1763, "Br. Gammern has hired a Negro woman, to serve as a maid in the tavern for 3 years. She came to Bethabara from James Blackborn, on Town Fork."[4] This may have been Rev. Abraham von Gammern who hired this woman.

There are various stories surrounding the hired woman Franke and her stay in Bethabara and possibly in Salem. One mentions her wanting to become a part of the Moravian community in Bethabara through baptism but there is no record of this occurring.

It is unclear if this is the same Franke, but it is mentioned "she was later purchased in 1773 by the same family that owned Oliver."[5] In 1774, Franke now working in the Salem Tavern asked to become part of the Salem congregation, but the *lots cast* were all inconclusive and some say she never became a part of the Moravian Brotherhood. At this time, there is no other known information of her that exists, and this woman has disappeared and has become a footnote into Forsyth County history.

Notable Moments

Oliver was a laborer and potter in Salem who later joined the Moravian Church and christened Peter Oliver. He later emancipated himself by purchasing his own freedom. The family of Dr. Raymond Oliver including Oliver Gibson, Cecil Oliver, Dazelle Benbow Jones and NBA Player Chris Paul, of Winston-Salem are descended from Peter Oliver.

Religion

View of Negro (St. Phillips) Moravian Church on South Church Street in 1860's the wood building on the far right is the first church built in 1823. The brick building (center left) was built by the congregation in 1861 photo. *(Courtesy of Old Salem Museums & Gardens)*

Before 1801, African Americans baptized into the Moravian faith worshiped with the Moravians; however after 1801, there was a change concerning the Moravians and these African American congregants. This was caused by the contention between the Moravians and their surrounding communities that treated African Americans and enslaved African Americans differently.

Moravians still allowed African Americans to worship in the Moravian church but confined them to the back of the churches or to the balconies. At the beginning of the 19th Century African Americans were not allowed to worship at all, in the Moravian church.

There were many in Forsyth County who continuously tried to maintain control over African American congregates and their participation in religious services throughout the decades. "Immediately following the Civil war, white southerners attempted to keep blacks in the balcony of white churches as they had been before the war. Much to their dismay, however, Negroes took the first opportunity to organize their own churches"[6] to control and to express their freedom of worship.

The First Purchased Enslaved Person and the First African American Moravian Convert

In 1769, a skilled cattle herder and teamster named Sam, "was purchased by permission of the Lord for £120, North Carolina currency"[7] becoming the first enslaved person bought by the Moravians. According to the North Carolina State Archives, this equals to about $2,995.77. Though quite a remarkable sum, it was consummate pay for skilled workers who were at a premium in the Bethania and Bethabara area. Although he had worked for years in Bethabara, originally Sam came to Wachovia (the name for the Bethabara settlement) in 1765 at age fifteen. He was rented to work as a slave at the Bethabara stock yard where he would work as a teamster for much of his adult life.

Sam was such a good worker as a teamster, that he was later chosen and trusted, to drive a wagon train on an expedition to Pennsylvania.

In 1771 Sam became the first African American in North Carolina to be baptized into the Brotherhood of the Moravian Church and was christened Johann Samuel. Within ten years of his conversion, he married a woman named Ida.

According to the *St. Phillips Church Museum at Old Salem* Johann Samuel and Ida had two sons named Johann Christian Samuel, and Jacob Samuel, and a daughter born in 1781 they named Anna Maria.

That same year Sam also became one of the first Wachovia residents to receive an inoculation for smallpox, when there was great apprehension about this type of treatment. In 1788 Sam became superintendent of the community farms in Bethabara, placing him in authority over white and enslaved workers on the community farms in Friedberg, Friedland and Hope.

In 1801 thirty-two years after he was purchased, Sam was freed by the church that bought him. He and his wife, who had been earlier emancipated, along with their family, leased a farm from the church outside of Bethabara in Hope or in Friedberg.

The First African American Church School Teacher

Israel Clement was the first Negro Church School teacher among early church and day schoolteachers."(8) He was a member of the Methodist Episcopal Church. He later became the first black town commissioner (Alderman) in Winston (see chapter 4).

First African American Preacher in the Area

Bethania A.M.E. Zion Church was organized in 1875 by Rev. A.T. Goslen, who is believed to have been the first African American pastor in the region.

The church was formed by black Moravians who had worshipped together since 1824 and built their own church in 1850. This congregation decided to leave the Moravian Church and form under the A.M.E. Zion Church because they wanted to have their own full-time pastor. Originally called the Bethania Negro Church, Bethania A.M.E. Zion Church is now located at 2120 Bethania Rural Hall Road in Forsyth County.

Bethania A.M.E. Zion Church
(Courtesy Lester S. Davis. Winston-Salem African American Archive)

The First African American Nun to enter the Sisters of Mercy of North Carolina

Sister Larretta Rivera-Williams, RSM
(Global Sisters Report: a project of National Catholic Reporter)

The first African American woman to enter the Sisters of Mercy of North Carolina is Sister Larretta Rivera-Williams. Originally from Winston-Salem, Larretta Rivera-Williams entered the Sisters of Mercy in 1982 and later became one of four African American Sisters within the Sisters of Mercy of the Americas, Inc. Her ministries have included her work as an elementary, secondary, and divinity school educator.

Sister Larretta Williams became an Associate Chaplain at Wake Forest University in Winston-Salem, North Carolina and later become coordinator of pastoral care at St. Leo the Great Catholic Church in Winston-Salem, NC.

First African American to Preside over the Episcopal Church

Bishop Michael Bruce Curry
(Winston-Salem Chronicle. Courtesy Winston-Salem African American Archive vertical file)

Bishop Michael Bruce Curry of the Diocese of North Carolina and formally Deacon in Charge at St. Stephen's Episcopal Church in Winston-Salem was installed as the presiding bishop of the Episcopal Church November 1, 2015. He was elected by a landslide at the Episcopal General Convention June 27, 2015 in Salt Lake City. He is the first African American in the United States to lead the Episcopal Church.

Bishop Curry studied at Yale Divinity School. He served churches in Winston-Salem, North Carolina, Lincoln Heights, Ohio, and was rector of St. James Church in Baltimore when he was elected 11th bishop of the Episcopal Diocese of North Carolina in 2000. He was the Deacon in Charge at St. Stephen's Episcopal church in Winston-Salem, North Carolina from 1978-1982.

Notable Moments

On May 19, 2018 Bishop Curry delivered a sermon at the Wedding of Prince Harry and Meghan Markle at Windsor Castle. His sermon of love and his drawing from the roots of American history of enslavement and quoting Dr. Martin Luther King, Jr. had a tremendous impact on the millions watching around the world.

Churches

The First African American Church

Early log church restored
(Courtesy of Lester S. Davis.. Winston-Salem African American Archive)

Before 1801, Blacks worshipped in church services together with White Moravians. However, this situation changed due to the pressure of the surrounding white community. By 1789 just eighteen years after Sam was baptized to become Johann Samuel, blacks were segregated from the white congregation and relegated to the back of the church, and by 1800 these baptized enslaved individuals of the Moravian brotherhood were no longer allowed to attend the Moravian church. This continued until 1822, when the nation's oldest black Moravian Congregation and the oldest surviving African American Church in North Carolina was established with help by the Salem Female Missionary Society. The black congregation held its first meeting "March 24, 1822 at the home of two slaves named Budney and Phoebe in the "*Negro Quarter, Salem Plantation.*"[9] According to the *St. Phillips Church Museum at Old Salem*, the Negro Quarter was the Wachovia administration farm about two miles from Salem.

"The little congregation had 14 regular members; 3 communicants, 2 baptized, 5 members and 4 others."[10] The minister for these black congregants was Brother Abraham Steiner, a white Moravian. Work began on a church building September 27, 1823. It was a log structure located on Church Street in Salem next to the African American and Stranger's Graveyard. The Salem diary noted, "30 Negroes gathered to lay up the logs for the Church for Negroes. The Female Missionary Society has with pleasure undertaken to bear the expense. All went well."[11] It was also noted by the Moravian Congressional Council on the building of the church, concerning the congregants that "all precautions will have to be taken that they go home right after service and not loiter around and talk together."[12]

The church was completed and was consecrated December 28, 1823. On March 4, 1827, the Female Missionary Society began a Sunday school at the church to teach the children to read, but due to the Nat Turner Rebellion in Virginia, the State of North Carolina passed a law making it illegal to teach black slaves to read and this was discontinued.

The black congregants worshipped in the log church until 1860 when they had outgrown the structure. In 1861, they built a brick structure large enough to accommodate the increasing congregation, north of the original log structure. It was in this new brick structure on "May 21, 1865, Rev. Seth G. Clark, the Chaplain of the 10th Ohio Cavalry, read General Orders 32 from the pulpit of the African Moravian Brick Church at 911 South Church Street in Salem. The orders announced the end of slavery."[13]

The church continued to grow and by 1890 two classrooms and a choir loft were added. This brick church existed for fifty-two years without a formal name. Prior to 1913, it was known simply as the *Negro Congregation* or the *Colored* Salem Moravian Church. The church was formally named St. Phillips Church, December 1, 1913 at the ceremonies conducted by Moravian Bishop Edward Randthaler. "Evidence suggests that the church was named for Phillip, the evangelist, an early Christian convert who baptized an Ethiopian."[14] The Ethiopian was the Nubian eunuch mentioned in the bible in the book of Acts 8:26-40.

For almost 100 years the congregation worshipped under white ministers until Dr. George Hall assumed leadership of the church in 1947.

Under his leadership the church relocated three times; twice in Happy Hill Gardens to reach more African Americans, and finally to Bon Air Avenue in 1967.

St. Phillips "is the only black church in North Carolina built before the Civil War still known to be standing."[15] The original old St. Phillips Moravian Church still stands on Church Street in Winston-Salem and the present St. Phillips Moravian Church is still located on Bon Air Avenue in Winston-Salem.

St. Phillips restored.
The brick building is where the chaplain of the 10th Ohio Calvary Regiment read the Emancipation Proclamation in 1865.
(Courtesy of Lester S. Davis, Winston-Salem African American Archive)

Early African American Churches in Winston

Two of the earliest churches in Winston were begun by John Fries and Harry Fries, two ex-slaves of the Francis Fries Family of Salem."[16] These men, with no known relationship other than servitude with the Fries family, moved next door to each other in Waughtown shortly after the Civil War, and began prayer and religious services in their homes. These services were on alternate evenings and never conflicted with the other.

John Fries was a worker at Fries Wool Mill. He and his wife Paulina, though very religious and able to read, had their prayer service conducted in their cabin in the evenings by a black minister "named Andrew Wilburn who had a little farm between Thomasville and High Point."[17]

These services began the Baptist movement in Winston, later becoming the First Baptist Church for African Americans in Winston. Eventually the congregation became too large for the small cabin. This lack of space caused the congregation to move three times all over the south side and Salem area. First to an old school building, later, to Happy Hill where they held service under a brush arbor, a crude wooden structure with wooden benches, and finally to Hinshaw's Hall, a community building on Fourth and Chestnut Streets in Winston.

"Harry Fries began the Methodist movement"[18] in his home. In time his congregation also moved from Waughtown to Winston. "The Reverend Isaac Wells preached for them under a bush arbor in front of a small log house on North Liberty Street. They finally built their church, Methodist Episcopal Church North, at Seventh and Chestnut Streets on the present site of the Warehouse of the Brown Rogers Dixon Hardware Company on Seventh Street near the railroad."[19] The current church was erected by Reverend George Morehead and was completed by Reverend Shamberger.

First Church in Winston

The first organized church for African Americans and the first organized church in the town of Winston is St. Paul Methodist Episcopal Church. Begun in the home of former slave Harry Fries in Waughtown shortly after the Civil War, Reverend Isaac Wells preached for them. The congregation eventually moved to Winston and held regular worship services under a brush arbor near Liberty Street in May 1871, the white First Baptist Church organized September 22, 1871. The official name of the congregation became Methodist Episcopal Church North. In 1879, the church built its first church building on the corner of Chestnut and Seventh streets near the railroad. It was often referred to as the "*church on the railroad*" because of its location.[20]

St. Paul United Methodist Church
(Winston-Salem)

St. Paul Church
(Courtesy of Winston-Salem African American Archive)

The church merged with Mt. Pleasant Methodist Church in 1967 and according to St. Paul's church history, in 1968 the Methodist Church and the Evangelical United Brethern Church merged to become the United Methodist Church.

St. Paul United Methodist Episcopal Church is now located at 2400 Dellabrook Road in Winston-Salem, North Carolina.

St. Paul United Methodist Church - 1871
Winston-Salem, North Carolina

Current St. Paul Church
(Courtesy of Winston-Salem African American Archive)

First African American Baptist Church

The first black Baptist Church in Winston, North Carolina was founded by Rev. George Washington Holland, a formerly enslaved and ordained Baptist minister from Danville, Virginia. After organizing thirty-five churches in Virginia, he began preaching to blacks in Winston and conducting early baptisms at Belo's Pond, near the former site of Union Baptist Church on Northwest Boulevard.

In 1879 with the assistance of Rev. Henry A. Brown, a white pastor of the Winston Baptist Church and pastor at large of the town, Rev. Holland organized the congregation into the first black church of the Baptist denomination in Winston. The congregation purchased a lot at the corner of Sixth and Chestnut streets, from the United Brethren of Salem for $75.00, July 23, 1879. In 1882 they built a wooden church on the property that faced Sixth Street. This formally designated it as the First black Baptist Church in Winston, and officially gave Winston two First Baptist Churches. Due to the growth of the congregation, a brick structure with stained glass replaced the wood structure and was dedicated Sunday, July 27,1902. It was one of the most modern churches at the time and was built completely by African American artisans and builders. According to Jane Steele, in *Key events in the African American Community 1870-1950,* this First Baptist Church is regarded as the "mother church for black Baptists in the county." [21]

The First Baptist Church also housed the first school for black children in the city.

In the latter part of the 20th century, the church initiated a housing development for senior residents. The church honored the memory and leadership of Rev. Holland by naming their housing development the George W. Holland Homes after him. Rev. G. W. Holland was Pastor of the First Baptist Church in Winston-Salem, NC, for 28 years. The First Baptist Church is presently located on Highland Avenue and Seventh Street in Winston-Salem, NC.

First Baptist Church ca.1902
A History of the Negro Baptists in North Carolina by J. A. Whitted, Raleigh: Edwards & Broughton Printing Co., 1908. *(North Carolina Collection, University of North Carolina at Chapel Hill, The Louis Round Wilson Special Collections Library. University of North Carolina at Chapel Hill)*

First Baptist Church ca.1955
(Courtesy of the Bradshaw Estate)

RELIGION 15

REV. G. W. HOLLAND,
Pastor First Baptist Church, Winston-Salem.
N. C., for Twenty-eight Years.

Image of Rev. G. W. Holland, Pastor First Baptist Church,
Winston-Salem, N. C. A History of the Negro Baptists in North Carolina by
J. A. Whitted, Raleigh: Edwards & Broughton Printing Co., 1908.
*(North Carolina Collection, University of North Carolina at Chapel Hill,
The Louis Round Wilson Special Collections Library. University of
North Carolina at Chapel Hill)*

Notable Moments
Rev. Holland also co-founded the Negro Orphanage along with Annie (Addie) Morris of Waughtown and Rev. Pinckney Joyce. It was an orphanage that gave aid and shelter to black children in Winston. He was also instrumental in the organization of various Baptist churches in the city including Mt. Zion Baptist Church, Shiloh Baptist Church, West End Baptist (now part of United Metropolitan), and New Bethel Baptist Church in Winston-Salem, which is located on Trade Street.

First African American Church with Community Services

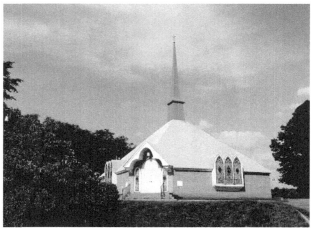

Wentz Memorial Congregational Church
(Courtesy of Lester S. Davis, Winston-Salem African American Archive)

The first church in the city whose purpose was to be community oriented, and created a variety of community services for the African American community was the Wentz Memorial Congregational Church of Christ. The church was organized by Dr. Samuel Wentz October 21, 1921 as the People's Congregational Church.

It began with 35 members and was housed at the Depot Street school building until a lot was purchased at 1508 East Fourteenth Street in the city. The building of the new church began in October 1923. During the building of the church Dr. Wentz died and the new church was named in honor of him. The church was finished and opened Sunday June 8, 1924 with a newly elected pastor.

Programs at the church included a social service program, playgrounds and a daycare. For years, parents who worked at the tobacco factory could leave their children in safe hands until their shift was over. As of today the church has a Social Justice Ministry, Annual Health Fair, and a kitchen ministry.

Wentz Memorial United Church of Christ is now located at 3435 Carver School Road in Winston-Salem.

The First Catholic Church for African Americans

St. Benedict the Moor Catholic Church on 12th Street
(Courtesy of the Catholic Dioceses of Charlotte and St. Benedict the Moor Catholic Church)

St. Benedict the Moor Catholic Church is the first Catholic Church established to service the African American community in Winston-Salem. The church was founded by Bishop Eugene McGuinness, Bishop of the Catholic Diocese in Raleigh, North Carolina. It was placed in one of the prominent East Winston neighborhoods, on the corner of Fourteenth Street and Hattie Avenue. The property was purchased on April 26, 1940 from the estate of Bishop Lynwood Westinghouse Kyles of the AME Zion Church. It was put under the control of the Franciscan Friars, with Father Ronald Scott O.F.M as pastor, aided by local African American Attorney Hosea V. Price, his wife, and eleven black Catholics in the area. The first Mass was celebrated November 24, 1940 at Robinson Funeral Home.

The parish was named after Benedict Manasseri, the black Italian Franciscan Friar from Sicily who lived a life of prayer and charity. He also served as a healer, guardian and novice master until his death in 1589. St. Benedict the Moor became the patron Saint of African Americans.

St. Benedict the Moore Catholic Church, at this time is located at 1625 E. 12th Street in Winston-Salem, North Carolina.

Notable Moments

St. Benedict the Moor was born to enslaved Africans Cristoforo and Diana Manasseri. In 1526, his parents converted to Christianity and because of their loyal service Benedict was freed at birth. According to Winston-Salem's Architectural Heritage, Catholic records say a Franciscan hermit saw Benedict being racially teased and noticed his calm demeanor, and he invited him to join the order. In 1743 Benedict was venerated as a Saint in the Catholic Church, being beatified by Pope Benedict XIV and canonized in 1807 by Pope Pius VII.

St. Benedict the Moor *(1526-1589)*
(Image Ownership: Public Domain. blackpast.org)

Chapter Two

Education and Educators

According to the book, *African Americans in Winston-Salem Forsyth County A Pictorial History*, the Female Missionary Society in Salem began to instruct young slaves to read and write, though the language was in German. However, due to the Nat Turner Rebellion in Hampton, Virginia, a state law was passed, making such instructions to slaves illegal. Nat Turner was an enslaved man who, with permission of his owner, had been instructed in reading, writing and religion. He grew to become a deeply religious man who read and studied the bible, prayed and fasted. Turner later became a preacher. He believed God chose him to lead black slaves out of the evil bondage of slavery. On August 21, 1831, he led a violent revolt in Southampton County, Virginia that ended with the death of more than 55 white men, women and children. He was eventually caught, tried in court and was hanged on November 11, 1831.

The Nat Turner Rebellion caused a fear among white southerners, but not enough to want to free the slaves. Their fear caused harsher laws against African Americans and made educating slaves illegal. It was not until after the Civil War that a school for African Americans was established in Forsyth County.

Drawing of Nat Turner's capture
(blackpast.org Image Ownership: Public Domain.)

The book, *History of Winston-Salem State University: 1890-1995* by E. Louise Murphy says, on September 29, 1865, less than six months following the civil war, *Negroes* of the state petitioned for legislation to assure compensation for labor and to enable them to educate their children. In 1866, under the Friends Freedmen Aid Association formed by the Quakers to help educate newly freed slaves, Forsyth County had established eight schools with a total of 350 students. One such school was in Waughtown. "In 1867, the state passed an ACT to incorporate the Colored Educational Association of North Carolina with the power for the purpose of establishing schools and encouraging and promoting general education among colored children of the state. Apparently, the passing of such an act was due largely to the activity of the newly freed Negroes whose contemporary intense concern for his own education was but the outgrowth of his antebellum desire." [22] This caused a fear among whites of forced integration. But integration was not mentioned in the constitution adopted at the 1867 Convention. "The first law passed under it provided for separate schools of 4 month terms." [23] Under the direction of State Superintendent of Public Instruction S. S. Ashley, and Assistant Superintendent of Public Instruction Bishop James W. Hood, an African American, a provision for separate schools for blacks and whites was made through the legislative Public-School Law in 1869. It would be 84 years before the United States Supreme Court would strike down this and other Jim Crow segregation laws in North Carolina and across the Country, and 103 years before Forsyth County North Carolina officially desegregated and integrated its educational system.

Image of Bishop J. W. Hood Asst. Superintendent NC schools. The History of the Negro Church by Carter Godwin Woodson, D.C.: The Associated Publishers, 1921 (*Rare Book Collection, University of North Carolina at Chapel Hill, The Louis Round Wilson Special Collections Library. University of North Carolina at Chapel Hill*)

First African American Educators and Administrators

First Depot Street School Graduate

Robert Washington Brown, Sr.
(Courtesy of Winston-Salem African American Archive)

Robert Washington Brown, Sr. (b. 1875 - d. April 1, 1941) was from Rockingham County, North Carolina but attended public school in Winston. "In 1894 he was the first graduate of Depot Street School and received his diploma from the principal Professor Simon Green Atkins, the soon to be founder of Winston-Salem State University."[24]
After graduation from the Depot School, Brown studied at the "Agricultural and Mechanical College for the Colored Race (now N.C. A&T)"[25] in Greensboro. After completion of his studies at the college he went to Charlotte, North Carolina and began teaching. In 1917, he pursued graduate studies at the University of Pennsylvania. Returning to Winston, he became a co-founder of the Winston Mutual Insurance Company and began teaching at the Woodland Avenue Colored Grade School which was later re-named Brown Elementary School in his honor.

Brown Elementary located at 1124 N. Woodland Ave.
(Courtesy of Winston-Salem African American Archive)

First Hired African American Principal

Simon Green Atkins
(WSSU Archives-University Photograph Collection. Winston-Salem State University Archives-C.G. O'Kelly Library)

On July 1, 1890, Simon Green Atkins (b. June 11, 1863- d.1934) became the first African American principal hired in Winston when he was elected principal of the Depot Street School. Atkins was offered the position through the efforts of John J. Blair, then superintendent of schools in Winston.

The son of former enslaved parents in Chatham County, Atkins was a graduate of St. Augustine's Normal Collegiate Institute (St. Augustine's College), in Raleigh in 1884. After graduating he became head of the grammar school department at Livingstone College in Salisbury, N.C. from 1884 -1890. He held that position until 1890 when he accepted the position of principal at Depot Street School in Winston, N.C.

Atkins served as principal of the Depot Street School until 1895 when he resigned to concentrate on The Slater Industrial Academy. He later received an honorary degree of Doctor of Laws from Howard University in Washington, D.C. during commencement services on June 7, 1928.

First African American Woman Principal

Lillian McLester Mebane
(Courtesy of the Bradshaw Estate)

During the early 1920's, Mrs. Lillian McLester Hayes Mebane became the first African American woman to be appointed principal in the Winston-Salem School System. She was a graduate of Slater Industrial Academy May 4, 1899, and Slater Industrial and Normal School May 22, 1902.

Lillian Mebane worked as an educator for years in Winston before she became Assistant Principal to Dr. Simon Green Atkins at Columbian Heights Primary School. In 1922, a new brick building was built on Bruce Street due to the increasing elementary school enrollment. She was Assistant Principal in direct charge of the Elementary Department. "After her death, the school was named Mebane Intermediate School in her honor."[26]

Mebane Intermediate School
(Courtesy of the Bradshaw Estate)

First to Establish the Kindergarten Program in North Carolina

Louise Smith
(Courtesy of Winston-Salem State University Archive)

Louise Smith was an education pioneer who established the first kindergarten program in North Carolina.

A native of Winston-Salem and a 1946 graduate of Winston-Salem Teachers College, Smith became the first director of public-school kindergartens for what later became the Winston-Salem/ Forsyth County School System.

First African American School Administrator

Palmer Gill Friende
(Courtesy of Society for the Study of Afro American History SSAH-calendar: Winston-Salem Forsyth County School Officials)

In 1963, Palmer G. Friende was appointed director of the audiovisual department of the Forsyth County school system. This appointment was the first time an African American administrator had authority throughout the entire school system. Mr. Friende joined Anderson Junior High School as a teacher in 1957. In 1959 he became a guidance counselor, and by 1960 he was principal of Anderson Junior High School. He became director of secondary education in 1966, an Assistant Superintendent in 1971 and an Associate Superintendent in 1978 and later interim Superintendent of the Winston-Salem/Forsyth County School System 1989-1992.

First African American Faculty Member at Clemmons School

In 1964, Daisy Chambers became the first African American teacher on staff at Clemmons School. She later became Assistant Superintendent of the Winston-Salem Forsyth County schools from 1994 until 1996.

Daisy R. Chambers
(Courtesy of Society for the Study of Afro American History SSAH-calendar: Winston-Salem Forsyth County School Officials)

First African American Supervisor of the County Schools

Dollie Patterson

According to the Society for the Study of Afro American History in Winston-Salem / Forsyth County, Dollie Patterson became the first Black Supervisor of County Schools.

Longest Teaching Career in Forsyth County

According to the Winston-Salem Chronicle newspaper, Mary McCurry had the longest teaching record in Winston-Salem/Forsyth County. She served 45 years in the Forsyth County school system before retiring in 1973.

Originally from King County, Virginia, McCurry moved south in 1928 and began teaching at Woodland Avenue School (Brown Elementary) in Winston-Salem with two years of training from a Normal School.

Mary McCurry
(Winston-Salem Chronicle November 8, 1980. Courtesy of Winston-Salem African American Archive-vertical file)

While at Woodland school she received her bachelor's degree from Winston-Salem Teachers College, and later received her master's degree from N.C. A & T State University. Her teaching career in Forsyth County includes, 23 years at Brown Elementary, 19 years at Skyland Elementary and three years at Walkertown Elementary schools.

First African American President of Hampton Institute

Raphael O'Hara Lanier
(Winston-Salem Journal Sentinel January 24, 1943. North Carolina Room Forsyth County Central Library)

R aphael O'Hara Lanier, became the first black President of Hampton Institute in Virginia. He assumed this position January 20, 1943 following the departure of then President Dr. Malcolm S. MacLean. Prior to this position, Lanier was the Dean of Instruction at the school. He later became the first president of Texas State University for Negroes in 1948.

Notable Moments

Lanier was born in Winston-Salem on April 28, 1900, was the son of Attorney James. S. Lanier. Lanier received his bachelor's degree at Lincoln University in Pennsylvania, and his master's degree from Stanford University. He was also a Rosenwald Fellow at Harvard University from 1931-32. He later was appointed to a two-year term as minister to Liberia. It was the first time this position was offered to a black man since 1893. In his local career, Lanier was the first editor of the Negro daily column in the Winston-Salem papers.

First African American President of a Non-Historically Black Institution

Dr. H. Douglas Covington
(*WSSU Archives-University Photograph Collection. Winston-Salem State University Archives-C.G. O'Kelly Library*)

Dr. H. Douglas Covington, a native of Winston-Salem, became the first African American to lead a non-historically black public College or University in Virginia. He became President of Radford University in the Commonwealth of Virginia in 1995, retiring in 2005. Afterward, he served as interim President of Emory and Henry College in Virginia. Prior to his position at Radford University, Dr. Covington served as Chancellor of Winston Salem State University for 8 years (1977-1984).

First African American Educator and Physicist on a National Weapons Development Project

Dr. Jasper Jeffries
(Winston-Salem Sentinel October 13, 1981. Courtesy of Winston-Salem African American Archive-vertical file)

Dr. Jasper Jeffries was born in Winston-Salem in 1912 to Brown and Edna Jefferies. He attracted acclaim for his research as a physicist with the Manhattan Project during World War II. This project led to the development of the atomic bomb. At that time, he was a professor of physics at Westchester Community College in New York.

Notable Moments

Jeffries was a 1928 graduate of Columbian Heights High School; he earned his bachelor's degree from West Virginia College in Institute West Virginia and earned his master's degree in physical sciences in 1940 from Chicago.

First African American and Student to Design the Forsyth County Seal

Willie H. Johnson, Jr

Carver student, Willie H. Johnson, Jr at Forsyth County Centennial Celebration, 1949 with James G. Hanes, unknown and William B. Simpson. Johnson is presented a copy of the resolution proclaiming a new seal for Forsyth County, which he designed.
(Courtesy of Forsyth County Public Library Photograph Collection, Winston-Salem, N.C.)

In 1949, Carver student Willie H. Johnson, Jr. won the design contest for the county seal during the Forsyth County centennial celebration. He received $20.00, a resolution proclaiming the new seal for Forsyth County and his design was buried in the time capsule under the now former courthouse building. The capsule was removed when the courthouse expanded in 1958 and will be opened in 2049. His design displayed the Forsyth County heritage of agriculture, manufacturing and Moravian history. It included the motto *Animis Opibusque Parati*- "Prepared in Mind and Resources." [27] However, due to an error during an early artist rendering it incorrectly reads *Animis Opibusque Patri*.

Johnson's design of the county seal is displayed at county facilities including outside the Board Meeting Room of the Forsyth County Commissioners, and on county publications.

Forsyth County seal
(County of Forsyth. Public image:)

First African American Student to Integrate Winston-Salem/Forsyth County Public Schools

Gwendolyn Bailey
(Black and Gold R.J. Reynolds High School Year Book, 1959-public photo)
http://library.digitalnc.org/cdm/singleitem/collection/yearbooks/
id/7915/rec/31

Three years after the "Brown Decision" of the United States Supreme Court, Gwendolyn Yvonne Bailey, the daughter of Rev. and Mrs. E.E. Bailey of 1732 N. Thurmond Street in Winston-Salem, broke the color barrier in the Winston-Salem Forsyth County School System, when she entered R.J. Reynolds High School September 4, 1957. She became the first black student at R.J. Reynolds High School and was "the first black to attend any previously all white school in the county where blacks and whites had been previously taught separately."[28]

Gwendolyn Bailey was part of a coordinated effort of public-school integration in North Carolina with Greensboro students Josephine Boyd at Greensboro Senior High School and Brenda Florence, Jimmy Florence Russell Herring, Elijah Herring, and Harold Davis at Gillespie Park Elementary School. While there was no outright violence towards Gwen Bailey that first day of school, there was some unrest and protest concerning this integration of Reynolds High School as someone had written "Black Nigger" in large white letters on Hawthorne Road in front of the school, and a black doll was hanged in effigy from the school flag pole. These were removed before her arrival at the school, and Claude "Pop" Joyner, then principal of Reynolds High School, "made it clear to teachers and to students that he would not stand for any racial incidents."[29]

Gwen Bailey did register without incident, but she was ostracized at school and those in Winston-Salem against the school integrating drove past her house with guns and taunted her and her family. Regardless of this disruption, she did graduate from R.J. Reynolds High School June 5, 1959.

Notable Moments

Integration began to slowly move throughout the Winston-Salem Forsyth County school system. The Winston-Salem Forsyth County schools later consolidated but it was not until 1971 that the school system completely desegregated.

The First Elementary School to Integrate

Easton Elementary School was the first elementary school to integrate in 1958. The students were Kenneth Richard Cooper, Norma Ernestine Corley, Roslyn Dianne Cooper.
In 1962, the county schools integrated when a black first grader attended Clemmons School. The Winston-Salem Forsyth County schools consolidated one year later, but it was not until 1971, 17 years after the Brown Decision that the school system completely desegregated.

Easton Elementary Students
Left to right: Mrs. Lovie Cooper, Kenneth Richard Cooper, Norma Ernestine Corley, Roslyn Dianne Cooper and Mrs. Ernest Corley.
Photographer Frank Jones is in the foreground.
(Courtesy of Forsyth County Public Library Photograph Collection, Winston-Salem, N.C.)

First Housing Management Degree in the Country

Earline Parmon became the first person in the country to graduate with a degree in housing management. She successfully completed the program and graduated from Winston-Salem State University December 15, 1976, with a degree in business administration with a concentration in housing management. "The program is funded by the Department of Housing and Urban Development"[30] to train competent, efficient housing managers for public and subsidized housing. Programs were also at Howard University in Washington, D.C., Temple University in Philadelphia, Pa., Southern University in Baton Rouge, La., and Southern Texas University in Houston, TX.

Notable Moments

Mrs. Parmon later became a community activist for education, and politically active in Winston-Salem. She became the first African American and first woman to be elected chair of the Forsyth County Democratic Party (see chapters 3 and 4).

She was later elected to the North Carolina State House of Representatives District 72 and to the N.C. State Senate.

Mrs. Earline Parmon
(Winston-Salem Chronicle January 22, 1977. Courtesy of Winston-Salem African American Archive-vertical file)

Schools and Institutions

First African American Student to Attend Salem Academy and to Live in the Single Sisters House

The Moravians opened Salem Academy, a school for local girls in Forsyth County in 1772, making it one of the oldest schools for girls in the United States. "The first African American student admitted into the school was Anna Maria Samuel, daughter of North Carolina's first baptized Moravian, Johann Samuel."[31]

Anna Maria was born December 24, 1781 and baptized into the Moravian church. She grew up bilingual speaking both English and German and was known for her love of singing and participation in church life, which included foot washing services, Love Feasts and assignments such as caring for the sick.

Anna Maria Samuel
Interpretative portrait of Anna Marie Samuel at the Single Sister's House in Old Salem. Public viewing in museum. Unknown artist; not mentioned or listed in posted documentation.
(Courtesy of the Single Sister's House. *Photo taken by Chenita B. Johnson)*

According to the book, *North Carolina Women Making History*, Anna Maria attended congressional school with white Moravian girls and at age eleven, became a part of the Salem Older Girls Choir and moved into the Single Sisters House in Salem. She lived there five years.

She and others of the Moravian community witnessed the visit of President George Washington to the Moravian village in 1791.

There were other African American children allowed to attend Moravian schools, including a young enslaved girl of Adam Schumacher, named Hannah, who was given permission to attend the school with Anna Maria, but Anna Maria Samuel is the first African American admitted to Salem Academy and the only one known to have lived in the Single Sisters House.

In 1797, she and her siblings were freed by the courts after the Moravian church emancipated her mother. After she left Salem Academy, Anna Maria Samuel moved to Bethabara where she worked in the communal kitchen. She died soon afterward and was buried in Bethabara in God's Acre. Her death in 1798 was documented in *Death notice of Anna Maria Samuel, Bethabara Church Book 1798*.

First African American Undergraduate of Wake Forest University

Ed Reynolds
(Wake Forest "Howler" Year Book. Courtsey of Wake Forest University)

In 1964 Edward Reynolds became the first Black student to graduate from Wake Forest College, (now Wake Forest University), in Winston-Salem.
A transfer student from Shaw University he enrolled at Wake Forest College in 1962 as a regular undergraduate student. Reynolds stayed in the dorms, and though his experience was considered pleasant, there were two racial encounters; one involved a picture of a gorilla mailed to him, and the other concerning his grades in a course at the school. A professor gave him a Grade of B in a course which he excelled with A's. Questioning his grade, he was informed by the professor that a B was a good grade for a Negro.

Ed Reynolds enrollment ended segregation at the college and was considered by Wake Forest to be a quiet revolution of peaceful integration.

Wake Finds a Way Amid Civil Rights Strife

Ed Reynolds in bottom photo on the right
(Wake Forest "Howler" Year Book. Courtsey of Wake Forest University)

First African American Woman Undergraduate from the University of North Carolina-Chapel Hill

Karen L. Parker
(Yackety Yack yearbook-University of North Carolina-Chapel Hill [1965])

The first African American woman to attend and graduate from the University of North Carolina at Chapel Hill (UNC- Chapel Hill) as an undergraduate student is Karen L. Parker. She graduated from UNC- Chapel Hill in 1965 with a BA in Journalism. Born in Salisbury, North Carolina to Mr. and Mrs. F. D. Parker, she grew up in Winton-Salem at 924 20th Street, N. W.

Parker was a graduate of Atkins High class of 1961. After graduation she attended the Woman's College in Greensboro (now UNC-Greensboro) and in 1963 she transferred from the college to the University of North Carolina at Chapel Hill, becoming the first Black woman to enroll at the university. She did not know of this distinction until she found herself placed on the top floor of the Cobb dormitory in a double room with no roommate. She became friends with a white student named Joanne Johnston-Francis who lived in another part of the dormitory building, who also had no roommate. They decided to room together after approval of their parents.

Karen Parker was journalism major, and was active in local and national civil rights movements, participating in sit-ins and marches and chronicling these experiences in a diary. Some of her entries included her observations in Chapel Hill to the assassination of President John F. Kennedy, descriptions of her civil rights experiences including her arrests due to protests and her involvement with the Congress of Racial Equality (CORE). She donated this diary in 2006 to the Southern Historical Collection in the Manuscripts Department of the UNC library.

During her senior year, Karen Parker was named the editor of *The Journalist*, a news publication of the School of Journalism and Mass Communications. She was also chosen to participate in UNC's exchange program with the University of Toronto.

Notable Moments
After graduating from UNC, Karen Parker had a successful career in journalism, including being copy editor for the Grand Rapids Press in Grand Rapids Michigan, the Los Angeles Times, and other newspapers before returning to Winston-Salem to work for the Winston-Salem Journal, where she retired in 2010.

In 2012 she was inducted into the North Carolina Journalism Hall of Fame.

First African American Woman Graduate from Wake Forest University

Patricia Smith

In 1966, Patricia Smith became the first black woman graduate, from Wake Forest University. She later became a Data Systems supervisor with AT&T.

First African American to Earn a PhD in Library Science

Dr. Eliza Atkins Gleason
(Courtesy of the Eliza Atkins Gleason Estate)

Eliza Valeria Atkins Gleason (b.1909-d.2009) was born in Winston-Salem, North Carolina in 1909, to Dr. Simon Green and Oleana Pegram Atkins. Her father was the founder of Slater School, now Winston-Salem State University, and her mother was also an educator.

Eliza Atkins Gleason was the first African American to earn a PhD in Library Science and the first African American to become a Dean of a library school. She attended Fisk University, where she graduated with a B.A. degree. After graduating from Fisk University, she attended and graduated from the University of Illinois with a B.A.S degree in library science.

Her sister Oleona (Ollie) Atkins Carpenter was the first African American college trained Librarian in the state of Kentucky. Eliza followed her sister to Kentucky and began her career at the Municipal College for Negroes, (Louisville Municipal college), where she replaced her sister in less than a year as the head librarian. For 20 years she also taught classes for African Americans in Kentucky along with the Louisville Western Colored Branch Library which were the only classes for African Americans in Kentucky.

In 1936, she earned her master's Degree from the University of California at Berkeley. One year later she married physician Maurice F. Gleason and completed her PhD in 1940. Her dissertation, *"The Government and Administration of Public Library Service to Negroes in the South"* was published as a book *"The Southern Negro and the Public Library."* After earning her PhD, she moved to Atlanta, Georgia and became the dean at Atlanta University where she organized a school of Library Science, becoming the first African American to become Dean of a library school. By 1986 this program trained 90 percent of all African American Librarians.

Eliza Gleason was also the first African American to serve on the board of the American Library Association, serving 1942-1946. She left Atlanta in 1946 to aid her husband in setting up his medical practice in Chicago, but she continued her career in library science, becoming an associate professor in library science at the South Chicago branch of the Illinois Teachers College. Later she was appointed to the Chicago Public Library Board and became the executive director of the Chicago Black United Fund.

In later years she returned to Kentucky where she lived until she passed away on her 100th birthday. According to her wishes, she was interred with her family in Winston-Salem, North Carolina.

Notable Moments

Eliza Atkins Gleason has been honored by the American Library Association which awards the triennial Eliza Atkins Gleason Book Award for the best book written in English in the field of Library History.

The First School for African American Children Built by African Americans

After the end of the Civil War, the first school for black children in Forsyth County was founded and built in 1867 by blacks in Old Salem and formed with the help of the Northern Quakers Friends Association for Relief of Colored Freedmen. The school was built on a lot "provided rent free by the Board of Trustees of the Salem Congregation of the Moravian Church. The lot was provided on the condition that the land was used for a school and the title to the property remains with the

EDUCATION

The first school for black children in Forsyth County
Built in 1867 and located in what is now Happy Hill Gardens.
(Courtesy of Old Salem Museums and Gardens)

Moravian Church." [32] The lot was located on a hill south of Brothers Spring in Salem and East of Waughtown, in what is now the Happy Hill Gardens. "The building was a one-room school with board and batten siding, louvered window shutters, a shingled roof and a brick chimney." [33] The school staff consisted of two or three black and white teachers and had 20 to 30 students. The superintendent was "Alfred Lind, a black teacher and missionary from Barbados, who briefly ran the school Spring 1870 until October 1871. In 1892, the school moved to a new location on East Liberty Street." [34]

First Tax Supported School for African American Children

The first tax-supported school for African American children in Winston began in 1882, in the basement of the First Baptist Church on Sixth Street. With little money on hand, and nominal concern for the building of a schoolhouse for black children, the Winston School Board arranged with First Baptist church trustees General Barringer, Henry Pendleton and Peter Martin to house the school. Other churches in the African American community were later used for this purpose.

On October 14, 1884 Dr. Calvin H. Wiley, chairman of Winston's first school board and North Carolina's first superintendent of schools, issued a colored school bulletin which was attached on the doors of the Baptist and Methodist churches used as schools. This bulletin listed specific days of registration for the children, six to 21 years of age. Registration was Thursday, Friday and Saturday morning and the term lasted six weeks.
Renting rooms from churches, such as First Baptist Church, Lloyd Presbyterian Church, and St. Paul Methodist Episcopal Church, for school space continued until the completion of the Depot Street Colored Industrial School in 1887.

Early School Sites
Left to right-Lloyd Presbyterian, St. Paul Methodist Episcopal *(Courtesy of Lester S. Davis, Winston-Salem African American Archive)* First Baptist Church ca. 1902. A History of the Negro Baptists in North Carolina by J. A. Whitted, Raleigh: Edwards & Broughton Printing Co., 1908. *(North Carolina Collection, University of North Carolina at Chapel Hill, The Louis Round Wilson Special Collections Library. University of North Carolina at Chapel Hill)*

First Public School for African American Students

Depot Street Colored Graded and Industrial School
(Courtesy of the Bradshaw Estate)

The first public school for African American students in Winston, North Carolina was completed and opened December 1887. Named the Depot Street Colored Graded and Industrial School, it was built on a lot on the corner of 615 Depot (now Patterson Avenue) and 7th Streets where the Allegacy Credit Union ATM is currently located. The lot was "purchased at a cost of $1,250, for location of the colored school, but resources was not made available. The school board commissioners collected $524 from Northern cities" [35] to help to build the school. The school was built and opened at a final cost of $8,500 which included building, grounds and furniture. According to the Historic Marker Program, the school opened with eight classrooms and large halls with rooms that could be adapted for a library and an office.

The school offered African American students in Winston, a primary education and limited industrial training. Samuel Waugh was appointed principal of the school and his sister Sallie Waugh was hired as a teacher. The students resented her reserved, yet superior demeanor and she resigned.

The school needed a change, and on July 1, 1890 Simon Green Atkins, an African American educator, was elected and hired as principal. Three years later, under his leadership, an auditorium and three additional classrooms were added designating the school as Winston's first African American High School. The school accommodated 257 students. "At this time the Depot Street School was the largest and most important public school for negroes in the state." (36) The school building was later sold to the YMCA in 1926.

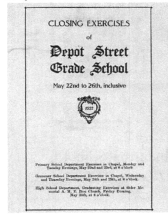 

Top left: Depot Street School graduation program 1922. *Above right: Depot Street School 9th grade graduation, 1922. (Courtesy of Winston-Salem African American Archive)*

First Public School for African Americans with the Largest Student Population

According to the Twin City Sentinel article dated May 4, 1935, the Fourteenth Street School had the unique distinction of having the largest enrollment of pupils and teachers of any black city public schools, elementary or high schools, in the state of North Carolina at that time. The school became a fixture in the African American community for decades. It was promised that the school would be renovated, but instead it was demolished in 1973 and never rebuilt. This created a lasting bitter memory as many in the African American community still remember it as a betrayal of their elected officials concerning their schools, their neighborhoods and their community.

EDUCATION

Fourteenth Street School
(Courtesy of Winston-Salem African American Archive)

Fourteenth Street School Cameron Ave. view and some students-1929
(Courtesy of Winston-Salem African American Archive)

Some Fourteenth Street School Faculty, 1929 *(Courtesy of Winston-Salem African American Archive)* and The Fourteenth Street School marker (Photo taken by Chenita B. Johnson)

First Organizational Structure of Students

Original Kimberley Park Elementary School on Cherry St.
(Courtesy of the Bradshaw Estate and Lester S. Davis, Winston-Salem African American Archive)

One of the first schools in the state, and the first in Winston-Salem, to adopt the Platoon Plan of organization for students was Kimberley Park Elementary School, which opened in 1925 with an enrollment of more than nine hundred pupils for the first day.

According to the Encyclopedia of American Education, this program was introduced in 1907 in Gary, Indiana, to double school capacity by dividing the school population into two groups or platoons. It allowed the school to accommodate more students with the same number of teachers with little additional cost. While one group attended academic studies in classrooms, the other group used non-classroom facilities, such as the gymnasium, art rooms, and shops.

The elementary school was in the Kimberley Park neighborhood which was named after the Kimberley Diamond Mines in South Africa. It was "a county school for Negroes located in Boston." [37] According to Black Business, Ink., Boston Cottages is an African American subdivision in Winston-Salem that was originally located outside of the city limits. It includes what is now Fourteenth Street North, Twentieth and Twenty-Third Streets, Grant, Washington, Harrison, Lincoln, and Garfield.

The Winston-Salem Journal (October 28, 1957), records that Mr. John Walter Paisley became principal of the new Kimberley Park Elementary

School in 1925. Prior to that appointment, he had been principal of the Oak Street Colored Grade School since 1918. Under his direction at Kimberley Park Elementary, the "Platoon Plan" was adopted.

Walter Paisley was principal at Kimberley Park Elementary school for 15 years.

The Winston-Salem School Board changed the name of a school that was constructed in 1957 to John Walter Paisley Sr. High School and dedicated it in his honor at a ceremony on April 28, 1958.

John Walter Paisley and Oak Street school
(Courtesy of the Bradshaw Estate)

Paisley High School named for Walter Paisley
(Courtesy of Winston-Salem African American Archive)

First African American Private School for Total Child Development

Nelson Preparatory School
(Winston-Salem Journal December 26, 1926. *North Carolina Room Forsyth County Central Library-vertical file*)

Professor Charles Calvin Nelson (b.1873 - d.1940) opened the Nelson Preparatory and Industrial School in 1904. It was a private school on "Hampton Road in Clemmons, North Carolina, near the present-day VFW Post." (38) This private school was the first of its kind in Forsyth County. It operated not only as an academy, but also as an orphanage and reformatory. According to the Winston-Salem Journal (December 26, 1926), students came from various walks of life, some were even sent by juvenile courts of various counties.

Professor Nelson was a community leader who also helped to organize many local churches including Capernaum Church of Christ in Clemmons, of which he was the first pastor. Reportedly, he had a reputation for straightening out wayward students and improving their overall academic performance.

C.C. Nelson School Reunion article
(Courtesy of Winston-Salem African American Archive-vertical file)

Nelson Preparatory School. Professor Nelson is looking to the left
(Courtesy of Capernaum Church, Clemmons, N.C.)

First Catholic School for African Americans

Kyles Heights, former St. Anne's Academy
(Winston-Salem Chronicle. Courtesy of Winston-Salem African American Archive-vertical file)

The first Catholic School for African Americans in Winston-Salem was St. Anne's Academy. It was opened by the sisters of St. Francis of Allegany N.Y. on property purchased from the estate of Bishop Kyles, located at the corner of Fourteenth Street and Hattie Avenue. The school opened September 7, 1946. It was dedicated September 29, 1946. It was followed in 1950 by St. Benedict that opened a grammar school with 116 students.

When St. Anne's Academy and St. Benedict Grammar School closed, the buildings were used to provide services to the community. The Kyles Heights Apartments is on the former site of St. Anne's Academy and Convent and the St. Benedict Grammar School became the Franciscans Day Care Center.

St. Benedict Elementary School
(Courtesy of Winston-Salem African American Archive-vertical file)

High Schools

First Designated High School for African American Students

Depot Street High School
(Courtesy of the Bradshaw Estate)

EDUCATION

In 1893 the Depot Street School, with the addition of an auditorium and three additional classrooms was designated as the first African American High School in Winston. Originally opened in 1887 as the first public school for blacks in Winston, it became the largest and most important public school for blacks in North Carolina.

Depot Street School graduation 1921 and Faculty: School Principal U. S. Reynolds seated in the front center 1921.
(*Courtesy of Winston-Salem African American Archive*)

Depot Street School marker located on the corner of Seventh Street and Patterson Ave. *(Photo taken by Chenita B. Johnson)*

First Accredited High School for African American Students

Columbian Heights High School
(Courtesy of the Bradshaw Estate and Winston-Salem African American Archive)

In 1928, the Columbian Heights High School was the only accredited High School for blacks in North Carolina. The school had three basic areas of study: Latin, Science and Industrial Training.

Columbian Heights H.S. Senior Class 1930
(Courtesy of the Bradshaw Estate)

The First Modern High School for African Americans

Atkins High School
(Twin City Sentinel. April 1931. North Carolina Room Forsyth County Central Library)

Winston-Salem Negro High School," [39] the state's first modern high school for African Americans, opened in 1931. The school was ready for occupancy that fall school semester. The opening of the school was celebrated by the Winston-Salem community at a dedication ceremony April 2, 1931, which included various dignitaries such as Mayor George Coan Jr.; A. H. Eller, Chairman of the School Board; Rev. H. D. Denson, President of the Negro Ministers Union; Rev. D. Clay Lilly, Pastor of Reynolda Presbyterian Church; and keynote speaker Frank Graham, President of the University of North Carolina and advocate of public education. Principal J. A. Carter accepted the building for the faculty and Hannah Mae Benjamin accepted for the student body. The great surprise of the community event was the naming of the school as Atkins High School, named for prominent local African American education pioneer, Dr. Simon Green Atkins. The name had been selected months prior and held in secrecy until this event. Dr. Simon Green Atkins was in attendance.

Located at 1215 Cameron Avenue on a 30-acre site, Atkins High School was designed by Harold Macklin. Built of common bond brick with a Neo-classical Revival vernacular, it was the first school building in the city built with a structural steel frame. The school was equipped with workshops, science labs, sewing rooms, study halls and 27 classrooms. The building, equipment and grounds were valued at $400,000.

It had been built with a cooperative effort of bonds from the city and a $50,000 donation from the Rosenwald Fund.

The original Atkins High School building is now listed on the National Register of Historic Places and is still standing on Cameron Avenue. It is now the Winston-Salem Preparatory Academy. A new Atkins High School was built and opened fall 2005 as a technology magnet school concentrating in biotechnology, computer technology and pre-engineering. It is the district's first dedicated magnet high school. This new school is located at 3605 Old Greensboro Road in Winston-Salem.

Notable Moments

The Rosenwald Fund was started by philanthropist Julius Rosenwald, then President of Sears Roebuck and Company. Rosenwald had been "influenced by the biography of William H. Baldwin, Jr., a railroad executive who influenced the funding of the Urban League and Booker T. Washington's autobiography "Up from Slavery". Washington's belief in hard work and personal initiative strongly impressed Rosenwald, and as a result, he actively provided for the improvement of black education and facilities through The Rosenwald Fund." [40] *To receive funding from the Rosenwald Fund, communities "were required to make their own monetary contribution, maintain the structures, and the schools were to be incorporated into the local school systems. In this way, Rosenwald hoped to foster a better relationship between the black and white communities uniting them in a common cause."* [41] *This fund not only sponsored the construction of Atkins High School but more than 5,000 schools for African Americans in the south.*

EDUCATION

Dedication program of Atkins High School, 1931
(*Courtesy of Lester S. Davis, Winston-Salem African American Archive*)

Later photo of Atkins High School
(*Courtesy of Winston-Salem African American Archive*)

New Atkins School building
(*Winston-Salem Forsyth County Schools: Public photo*)

The First County High School for African American Students

Carver School 1938
(Winston-Salem Journal. Courtesy of Winston-Salem African American Archive-vertical file)

Carver High School began at the Oak Grove Elementary School in Forsyth County. It was a two-room elementary school for black students in the county at the turn of the 20th Century. Edward Everett Hill became Principal of the school in 1930. In 1936, five years after the opening of Atkins High School, Oak Grove Elementary School opened the 1936-1937 school year with added rooms and became the Oak Grove Junior High School.

With great encouragement from Mr. Hill, African American parents and students in the county, the Forsyth County Board of Education headed by Superintendent Cash, created a high school for the county's African American students. Prior to this, there were no high schools for African American students in the county. Their only choice was to pay tuition to attend Atkins High School, attend in other cities or not at all.

The school expanded in 1938 to include high school extracurricular activities and a faculty of 16, which included six fulltime high school teachers, nine elementary teachers and the principal. The school was named Carver High School, for African American Scientist George Washington Carver. Many of the county schools were consolidated into this one school. This consolidated school was, a "six-room frame building on Mickey (now Carver Road) Road."[42] Although it meant a three-hour bus ride for some students to attend Carver, the first class of 18 students graduated May 12, 1939. Twelve years after the first graduating class and with the help of a $1.3million grant, the new Carver Consolidated school opened January 2, 1951 on what is now Carver School Road. This new consolidated school, for grades first through 12th, contained an auditorium with a 1,600-seat capacity, 60 classrooms and a cafeteria. There were 1,300 students and it was staffed with 56 teachers.

Carver High School students
(Courtesy of Winston-Salem African American Archive)

Edward Everett Hill *(Courtesy of the Bradshaw Estate)* Carver High School-present *(Courtesy of Winston-Salem African American Archive)*

First African American High School to Integrate

Atkins Senior High School in Winston-Salem became the first African American school in the system to enroll white students. On August 29, 1966, two white students registered with 950 black students. According to the Twin City Sentinel, the students had been assigned to the school under the Board of Education's policy, which requires that students be assigned first to the attending area in which they live.

First Time African American Senior High Schools Disappear

After the end of the 1970-71 school year, Winston-Salem Forsyth County schools desegregated, causing the reduction and near disappearance of black teachers, administrators and the end of black Senior High Schools.
It had been 17 years since the Brown Decision, and the Winston-Salem Forsyth County School system, which slowly moved toward desegregation and integration was now under court orders to quickly comply with the law. This caused African American Senior High Schools, that served grades ninth through 12th to become expendable. "Atkins, Paisley, Anderson (formally Columbian Heights Junior High), and Carver were demoted to ninth through 10th grade schools,"[43] and for the first time since 1893, there were no traditional black senior high schools in Winston-Salem Forsyth County.

The original Atkins High School converted into a middle school, is now the Winston-Salem Preparatory School. Paisley is a baccalaureate magnet school, and Anderson is a conference center on the campus of Winston-Salem State University. The new Atkins High School, built on Old Greensboro Road, opened in 2005 as a magnet high school.
Carver later became a high school once again, leaving it as the only traditional high school in the African American community in Winston-Salem and Forsyth County. These historic High Schools for blacks in Winston-Salem have become affectionately known as the Big Four.

African American school Principals and Coach Gains. Left to Right: D.C. Hobson (Skyland Elem); Albert Anderson (Kimberly Park); (center) Clarence Bighouse Gains; A.B. Reynolds (Columbia Heights Elem); and J.D. Ashely (14th St. School) *(Courtesy of the Bradshaw Estate)*.

(Top)Anderson High School-formally Columbian Heights Junior High School *(Courtesy of the Bradshaw Estate)*
Atkins High School, Carver High School Present, and Paisley High School *(Courtesy of Winston-Salem African American Archive)*

University

"African Americans are the only nonwhite ethnic group in America which has established institutions of higher learning in large numbers with the expressed purpose of educating its people."[44]

First Slater Industrial Academy and State Normal School
Graduating class, 1903
*(WSSU Archives-University Photograph Collection. Winston-Salem State
University Archives-C.G. O'Kelly Library)*

First African American Institution of Higher Learning to Grant Elementary Education Degrees

The first African American institution of higher learning in the nation to grant degrees for teaching in the elementary grades is Winston-Salem State University. It is the only public institution of higher learning in Winston-Salem, North Carolina. Founded by Dr. Simon Green Atkins, the school opened in Columbian Heights as Slater Industrial Academy on September 28, 1892. It was named after John Fox Slater, a white philanthropist from New York who established the John F. Slater Fund in 1882, with an initial gift of one million dollars. The object of this fund was "the uplifting of the lately emancipated population of Southern States and their posterity by conferring upon them the blessings of Christian education."[45] Slater donated money to the school along

First Slater Buildings
(WSSU Archives-University Photograph Collection. Winston-Salem State University Archives-C.G. O'Kelly Library)

with $2,000 from the African American townspeople and $500 donated by R.J. Reynolds.

The Slater Industrial Academy began with 25 students and one teacher, in a 20ft by 40ft one room, wood frame structure at the corner of what later became Stadium Drive and Atkins Street in Columbian Heights. The first members of the board of trustees were J. S. Hill, E.P. Mayo, W.A. Blair, H.R. Starbuck, Thomas H. Sutton, J.C. Alston, C.B. Cash, L.N. Grandson, and S.G. Atkins.

The school was recognized by the State Department of Education for a State Normal School in 1895. On March 6, 1897, the name of the school changed to the Slater Industrial and State Normal School. "In 1925, the General Assembly changed the name to Winston-Salem State Teachers College. The school became the first Negro institution in the United States to grant degrees for teaching in the elementary grades." [46].

February 1948 Winston Salem Teachers College became the first Black institution to achieve accreditation from the American Association of Colleges for Teacher Education. The name changed to Winston-Salem State College in 1963, and in 1969, a statute designating Winston-Salem State College as Winston-Salem State University received legislative approval. On July 1, 1972, the university became a constituent institution of the University of North Carolina system, yet maintains its identity as a (H.B.C.U) Historically Black College and University.

Notable Moments

As the only public institution of higher learning in Winston-Salem, Winston-Salem State University (WSSU) has always been open to anyone wanting to achieve success through quality education. The school graduated its first white student, Patricia Johansson of Tobaccoville, NC in 1968, and its first male nursing student, Gilbert Hill, in 1978.

Throughout its history, Winston-Salem State University has consistently influenced many people through the work of its outstanding alumni who have affected the city, county, nation and world, taking to heart the motto, "Enter to Learn Depart to serve."

This includes a track student on scholarship, named Louis Eugene Walcott now known as Louis Farrakhan. He entered Winston-Salem Teachers College in 1951. Although an athlete, Walcott was a violinist and sometimes sang with the school choir. He left in 1953 to professionally perform as a calypso musician. Two years later he joined the Nation of Islam, later becoming its leader.

Stephen Anthony Smith, better known as Stephen A. Smith, is a Sports Journalist and a host on ESPN's "First Take." While attending WSSU he was a basketball player under legendary Coach Clarence "Big House" Gains.

Theodore (Ted) Blunt is an educator, former athlete and retired elected official. An outstanding basketball player under Coach "Big House" Gains, he graduated from Winston-Salem Teachers College with a Bachelor of Science degree in Elementary Education. He received his master's degree in Social work from Rutgers University. With his passion for public service he began working as a juvenile gang worker for the Crime Prevention Association and worked with Temple University as a group therapist for the mentally challenged. He continued his public service after moving to Wilmington, Delaware where he worked with various school districts to improve lives through education. He later ran for and was elected to the City Council where he served for over 20 years.

Another alum is Luke Torian, a pastor at First Mount Zion Baptist Church and a co-president of Eastern Prince William County Ministerial Association. Torian is also a member of the *Virginia House of Delegates, representing District 52. He was elected in 2009 and was re-elected running unopposed, to a new term in 2017.*

(Top) Simon G. Atkins, (Above) Slater Industrial Academy and State Normal School graduation class of 1908, (Below) Alum Louis Eugene Walcott now known as Louis Farrakhan *(WSSU Archives-University Photograph Collection. Winston-Salem State University Archives-C.G. O'Kelly Library)*

First Motorsports Management Program in the United States

In 2007, Winston-Salem State University (WSSU) became the first public university in the nation to offer a Baccalaureate major in Motorsports Management with a Bachelor of Science degree. As the only Historically Black College or University in the nation to offer a degree in motorsports management WSSU became a part of NASCAR's Drive for Diversity program to include more women and minorities in the higher levels of motorsports.

Chapter Three

Social and Community Activism

"Power concedes nothing without a demand. It never did, and it never will. Find out just what any people will quietly submit to, and you have found out the exact measure of injustice and wrong which will be imposed upon them, and these will continue till they are resisted with either words or blows, or both. The limits of tyrants are prescribed by the endurance of those whom they oppress."

Frederick Douglas

R.J.R. workers on strike. Local #22 Union strikers on the picket line at R. J. Reynolds Tobacco Company 1947
(Winston-Salem Journal. Courtesy of Winston-Salem African American Archive-vertical file)

Forsyth County, and the rest of post-Civil War North Carolina and other former Confederate states, did not quite know what to do with the newly freed population, so Black Codes were passed. The intent of these Black codes was to restrict the freedom of African Americans. In 1865, newly freed African Americans were assisted with help from the Freedman's Bureau. The creation of this federal agency ended the Black Codes, passed by the former Confederate states.

These codes were outlawed in 1868 by the 14th amendment.

During Reconstruction the Civil Rights Act of 1875 was passed. It entitled equal treatment of all citizens in public accommodations and jury selection, but it later was declared unconstitutional. After the Civil Rights Act of 1875 was declared unconstitutional by the United States Supreme

Court in 1883, white citizens across the state of North Carolina tried to control the freedmen through separation, intimidation and threats, but unfortunately, many across the state also resorted to violent acts, such as lynching's. "Over a 5-year period, from 1889-1894, 12 Negroes died at the hands of lynch mobs." [47] These acts were considered deplorable by the contemporary newspaper editors of the time across the state, and due to their influence, and with the persistence of national African American Civil Rights activists such as journalist and educator Ida B. Wells, North Carolina passed an anti-lynching Law in 1893, however, it was dormant for over a decade.

The first federal bill aimed at lynching was introduced in 1900 by George H. White, an African American congressman from North Carolina. This bill along with similar bills died in committee until 1922 when a bill that made it to the floor for a vote was filibustered.

African Americans in Winston-Salem Forsyth County were often aided by white citizens who wanted to see them matriculate into post-Civil War society as full citizens. But due to the prevalence of "Black codes", and later Jim Crow laws, African Americans had to depend on each other to keep themselves and their families' safe while demanding equitable treatment for their community.

Early Empowerment

First Relief Program for Freedmen

In 1869, "the Friends Association for the Relief of the Colored Freedmen was created in Salem to help the former slaves deal with their sudden freedom." (48)

The First Strike in Winston

The first workers strike in Winston, North Carolina occurred in 1889 and was against the tobacco industry. It was a culmination of the organization from the Negro Knights of Labor and African American workers upset about their wages being cut by the tobacco factories. The Knights of Labor was a racially integrated union organization that came south and opened chapters in southern industrial areas, including Winston in 1886. While this caused some fear among whites across North Carolina of the urban workers readily joining this union, in 1889 manufactures in Winston followed other industrial companies and considerably reduced the wages of their tobacco rollers by seventy-five cents per hundred pounds. The tobacco rollers were among the highest paid workmen in Winston and with such a deep cut in their wage, they were concerned about their families surviving during the winter at the close of the production season.

The tobacco workers met at Knights of Labor Hall in East Winston to organize. In response, the tobacco factory raised the wage of the prize workers. The prize workers packed the tobacco in the factory for shipping. They were not as well paid as the rollers, and due to this pay increase some of them returned to work. In April 1889, at the beginning of the new production season the tobacco rollers walked out on strike in a public protest. Behind a large bass drum and fife, they marched through the streets of Winston. After several days of protest, factory managers responded to the strikers by showing that they were the highest paid in comparison to the factory workers in Virginia and other North Carolina towns. With that information, the strike ended, and they returned to work.

While this strike did not change the wage structure, it allowed African American workers to see how they could organize and not be afraid to challenge the tobacco factories and the oppressive demands on them that existed through Jim Crow laws. The tobacco industry and white society could no longer ignore African Americans as they had the previous generation. This knowledge helped create the opportunity for the increase in black businesses, black professionals, and a fire department.

Notable Moments
> *Although there were increases in black participation in the community, including the election of eight black commissioners, there still lacked a comprehensive political voice for the growing African American community. This voice would not be heard for another fifty-eight years. But the 1889 strike was a precursor of the coming political change.*

The First Riot

Events leading to Winston's first race riot began May 18, 1895 when a white police officer named Michael M. Vickers was said to have been shot and killed by a 19-year-old black youth named Arthur Tuttle, the son of Charles and Margaret Tuttle of Middle Fork.

"When police officer H.H. Dean, who was with Vickers, ordered a group of blacks to move off the sidewalk to let a white woman pass, all did except Tuttle whom Dean said told him, he would move when he damn well got ready." [49] Arthur's older brother Walter had been murdered by a police officer a year prior. Although the officer was indicted for the murder, which was the first for a white man against a black man in the town, the police officer was found not guilty at trial by an all-white jury.

Arthur had no kind thoughts towards the police and when physically shoved and hit with billy clubs, they had a scuffle, Vickers was shot, and Tuttle was taken into custody. Michael Vickers died the next day, causing concern about Tuttle's safety, so he was moved by train to Greensboro to be jailed. There, it is said, 400 blacks armed to defend him met the train. He was later sent to the Mecklenburg County jail.

Rumors of a lynching began when Tuttle was returned to the Forsyth County jail for trial. When a report reached all the black churches at about 9 p.m. that a group of whites were going to lynch Tuttle, it is said about 300-500 blacks marched in front of the jail on August 11, 1895 to protect Tuttle from being lynched. The sheriff's department called out the Forsyth Rifles, a militia unit from the civil war, to disperse the crowd of blacks protecting Tuttle. When they did not disperse, the militia fired into the crowd and an undetermined number of blacks were killed.

As blacks in the crowd defended themselves against the militia a riot ensued and lasted about eight hours.

The next day, August 12, 1895, A. B. Gorrell, the mayor of Winston, called a meeting and was "authorized to request of the City of Charlotte to lend a Gatling gun to the City of Winston and send a man to operate same at once." [50] The riot was over by the time it arrived, and the gun was not used. Subsequently, Tuttle was not lynched, due to a state law (passed two years earlier in 1893) differentiating between first and second-degree murder and stipulating the death penalty could not be imposed in cases of second-degree murder. The Union Republic newspaper in Winston stated, "But for the 1893 law Tuttle would have ended up on the gallows." [51]

Tuttle received 25 years of hard labor in the state penitentiary. What happened to him during or after he served his sentence is unknown at this time.

Notable Moments

This riot had a far-reaching impact. It was reported as far away as California in the San Francisco Call newspaper dated August 13, 1895.

The First Mission House for African Americans

Addie Morris, a local Missionary to Africa, opened the first known Mission House for blacks in Forsyth County. Born enslaved on a Forsyth County farm on June 4, 1855, Addie Morris later went to Philadelphia and worked as a cook. Returning to North Carolina in 1886 she attended Shaw University. Her concern about the future of young blacks led to her constructing a mission house. Through her efforts she raised $1,175.45 from Philadelphia, and $96.00 from Winston for its construction. The Mission was located at 202 E. Sixth Street in Winston.

Addie Morris
(Courtesy of the Bradshaw Estate)

The First Orphanage for African American Children

The first orphanage in North Carolina, organized and paid for by African Americans to help orphaned African American children, was the Colored Baptist Orphanage. It opened in 1905 in the Belview section of Waughtown (Winston-Salem). Belview was an integrated suburb of Waughtown, which was just outside of Salem in Forsyth County. Many prominent African Americans resided in Belview. Concerned about the amount of African American orphans living on the streets, local African Missionary Addie Morris, (who opened the first known Mission House for African Americans in Forsyth County), along with her brother-in-law Pinckney Joyce, Rev. G.W. Holland (chapter 1) and others, sought to create a safe place for these children and teach them life skills. They began raising funds for the orphanage in 1903 which helped to build dormitories and various other buildings. The orphanage grew into a working farm of 28 acres. The children worked on the farm, attended the Belview School and worshipped at First Waughtown Baptist Church.
After various changes, the orphanage merged in 1929 with the Memorial Industrial Institute and moved to Baux Mountain Road. At that time, The

Memorial Industrial Institute was considered one of the finest pieces of welfare work being done for African Americans anywhere in the south. The Memorial Industrial Institute is now located near Horizons Park in Winston-Salem on Memorial Industrial School Road.

The First Group Home for Young African American Women

Phyllis Wheatley Home for Young Women
(Winston-Salem Journal, 1927. North Carolina Room Forsyth County Central Library-vertical file)

During the early part of the 20th century, young women, as well as men, were coming to the city of Winston from surrounding areas in search of employment and financial freedom.
The Phyllis Wheatley Home for Young Women was an institution created to protect these young women and girls coming into the town.
This institution was organized and founded by a group of 23 African American women on March 12, 1918. One of its founders, and the first president was Mrs. Lena B. Neal.
In addition to boarding and meals, it also offered diverse activities for these young women such as night classes, domestic art and home economic courses, stenography and book clubs. The 10-room house on Maple and Fourth Streets was dedicated December 14, 1919. It had a value of about $12,000 and on average, 10-20 girls and women regularly resided in the home As of January 2, 1927, the Winston-Salem Journal estimated that 1,500 girls and women had made their home at the Wheatley House.

SOCIAL AND COMMUNITY ACTIVISM

First NAACP in the state with the Largest Membership

In 1946 the Winston-Salem Branch of the National Association for the Advancement of Colored People (NAACP) had a membership of 1,991 which at that time was the largest Branch membership in the state of North Carolina.

The First Community Program of Intervention for Children

Mrs. Dorothy Graham
(The Chronicle, January 10, 1991. Courtesy of Winston-Salem African American Archive-vertical file)

The Best Choice Center of Winston-Salem was founded in 1988 as an intervention program for children of parents with substance abuse. The first of its kind in Winston-Salem, its Executive Director was Dorothy Graham.

In 2001 the Best Choice Center became a part of the YWCA, and has expanded its program, by providing after school care, academic and enrichment activities for children including a summer camp for kindergarten through eighth grade. Youth intervention services are still provided through the Teen Court Program and the Work and Earn It Program, for youth that have been involved with the juvenile system.

First Union Strike that Unified the African American Community and Caused Political Change

Local No.22 of the United Tobacco Workers Union was organized at R.J. Reynolds Tobacco Company, from the strike on June 17, 1943. This union was integrated, but most of the workers on strike were led by and were black women who wanted better wages, a safe work environment and better working conditions.

R.J. Reynolds Local #22 strike in 1947. Workers celebrating end of strike
(Courtesy of Winston-Salem African American Archive)

Most of them were stemmers in the leaf houses. A stemmer removed tobacco leaves from the stems by hand. These tobacco workers worked in a dust filled area doing work unchanged since the beginning of the tobacco industry. African American workers were abused and there was no compassion.

African American women were under the constant threat of sexual harassment and physical abuse by white supervisors in the factory. A widow was physically abused because she slowed down on the job on the same day James McCardell, who showed support for the striking women, fell dead in the factory of a cerebral hemorrhage at thirty-eight years of age. His death was believed to have been caused by the abusive work environment.

SOCIAL AND COMMUNITY ACTIVISM

Left to right: Velma Hopkins *(Courtesy of Society for the Study of Afro American History SSAH Calendar 1995)* Theodosia Simpson *(Winston-Salem Journal. Courtesy of Winston-Salem African American Archive-vertical file)*

Notable leaders of this Union included women such as Theodosia Simpson and Velma Hopkins.

Under their leadership, in 1944, the union negotiated a contract empowering African American tobacco workers in the factory with increased wages, vacation time, and replaced arbitrary hiring with seniority. It also established a grievance procedure that allowed African American union stewards to resolve grievances with foremen and supervisors.

In 1947, another major strike occurred at R. J. Reynolds Tobacco Company. On April 27, 1947, after nine weeks of stalemate in the contract negotiations, thousands of workers of the United Cannery Agricultural Packinghouse and Allied Workers of America walked out of the factory and congregated at the Woodland Avenue School to discuss the possibility of a strike against R.J. Reynolds Tobacco Company. Union member Glenn Jones said "It was time to make the company take notice. It was time to strike. Ford Hand seconded the motion and almost everyone approved."[52] The strike began May 1, 1947 and lasted for 38 days ending on June 7, 1947. The union strike not only unified the African American workers at R. J. Reynolds, it unified the African American community in Winston-Salem. "Rallies were held almost every Sunday at the Shiloh Baptist
Church where Rev. Robert Pitts, considered the greatest pulpit orator in the city at that time, inspired the crowd."[53]

There were voter registration drives sponsored by the union, increasing voter rolls from 300 to 3,000 registered voters. However, with allegations of Communist infiltrators of union leaders, along with harassment by the federal government, the union was discredited, "gradually lost its power, and was decertified in 1951"[54] but the strike was successful in creating better working conditions and economic advancement in R. J. Reynolds for black workers. , and due to the increase of black registered voters, black political strength increased. This allowed African Americans in Winston-Salem to change the face of politics in the city by electing Kenneth R. Williams, the first black since reconstruction, into office as Alderman. They also helped to elect a white populist named Marshall Kurfees as Mayor in 1949. Kurfees served the longest tenure of any mayor at that time and set forth a progressive agenda for the city that included the African American community.

According to Dr. William E. Rice (chapter 12), who joined the picket lines as a high school student and later became a professor at Winston-Salem State University, "the purpose of the union, was to try and get blacks organized and registered to vote. Through that effort, we got the first alderman and eventually blacks on the school board and what have you. It was through that arena that blacks became more visible."[55]

Rev. Pitts (right) with K. R. Williams (left)
(Courtesy of the Bradshaw Estate and Winston-Salem African American Archive)

Top: Women Stemmers of a tobacco plant 1938. Notice the supervisor (back right center) watching the workers. Above: Piedmont Leaf Strike, 1944. Notice the sign carried by protester in the front right, " Fat Back .75, Our labor .50: We can't make ends meet." *(Courtesy of the Bradshaw Estate)*

The First Sit in Victory in North Carolina

Sit In at counter. Carl Mathews (in the center)
(*Winston-Salem Journal. Courtesy of Winston-Salem African American Archive-vertical file*)

North Carolina is noted for the beginning of the Sit In Movement connected with the Greensboro Four, the students at NC A&T State University protesting at the Greensboro Woolworth, but Winston-Salem also had a Sit in Movement and became the first community in North Carolina to nonviolently desegregate its lunch counters.

Winston-Salem's first Sit-Down Strike began at noon, February 8, 1960, at the S. H. Kress Company, by Carl Mathews, a graduate of Winston-Salem Teacher's College. Inspired by the Greensboro Four Sit In at Woolworth's, he sat at the counter of the S. H. Kress Company in Downtown Winston-Salem and waited to be served, but was refused service. Inspired by Mathews' continuous actions, 11 students from Winston-Salem Teachers College, 10 students from Wake Forest and Atkins High School student Patricia Tillman joined Carl Mathews in a Sit in at the Woolworth store near the corner of Fourth and Liberty streets "on February 23, 1960. They were arrested on misdemeanor trespassing charges. "[56] The guilty verdicts were subsequently changed to prayer for judgment continued.

The students arrested from Winston-Salem Teachers College were Royal Joe Abbitt, Everette L. Dudley, Deloris M. Reeves, Victor Johnson Jr., William Andrew Bright, Bruce Gaither, Jefferson Davis Diggs III, Algemenia Giles, Donald C. Bradley, Lafayette A. Cook Jr. and Ulysses Grant Green. Those arrested from Wake Forest College were Linda G. Cohen, Linda Guy, Margaret Ann Dutton, Bill Stevens, Joe Chandler, Don F. Bailey, Paul Watson, Anthony Wayland Johnson and George Williamson, and Jerry Wilson. Undaunted by the arrests, picketing and protests continued at the downtown lunch counters, which led Winston-Salem Mayor Marshall Kurfees to appoint a committee of 10 black citizens and 10 white citizens that included local clergy and downtown businessmen to solve this growing issue.

Within three months, on May 23, a desegregation agreement was announced by city officials, abolishing the Jim Crow law prohibiting blacks and whites to be served together, and desegregating Winston-Salem's downtown lunch counters. The first black person to be served at the Kress counter was Carl Mathews.

Larry Womble (former State House representative from district 71) said "Winston-Salem was one of the first cities to desegregate nonviolently our lunch counter." [57]

Carl Mathews (back left) released on bail. Left to right: Dr. F.W. Jackson, Bob Scales, and Robert Shoaf
(Winston-Salem Journal. Courtesy of Winston-Salem African American Archive-vertical file)

First Black Panther Party in the Southeast

The Winston-Salem Chapter of the Black Panther Party was the first to organize in the Southeast. Formed in 1969 during a turbulent time in the United States and North Carolina history, the Black Panthers asserted black empowerment by diverting from the doctrine of nonviolence that was stressed by others of the period and encouraged self-determination through cultural knowledge.

While considered by some to be a militant organization, the Panthers stepped in at a time when most in the Black community felt unserved by their government and did not trust their local police.

Not only did the Panthers create Black Pride in the community, they strongly defended the rights of African American residents.

The group also initiated social programs such as a free breakfast program for poor children, screened for sickle cell disease and the operation of an ambulance service for people in neglected areas.

The ambulance service was supported by a $35,000 grant from the National Episcopal Church to The Winston-Salem Chapter of the Black

Winston-Salem Chapter of the Black Panther Party Historical Marker
(*Photo taken by Chenita B. Johnson*)

Black Panther Office opens, 1969
(Winston-Salem Sentinel. Courtesy of Winston-Salem African American Archive-vertical file)

Panther Party. It included a van for transporting the invalid, and a station wagon for transporting non-emergency and emergency cases to the hospital, clinic, or to doctor's offices.

The death of Mrs. Maggie Watson an African American woman exemplified the need for this service in the community. Watson was a welfare recipient who died after she was refused service by white county ambulance attendants because she did not have the required $20 fee.

The Black Panther Party's influence loomed large, in Winston-Salem Forsyth County, with members such as Dr. Larry D. Little, Nelson Malloy, and Hazel Mack-Hilliard.

(Above left to right) Hazel Mack-Hilliard *(Courtesy of WFU Law Women's Center-Wake Forest University).* Dr. Larry D. Little and Nelson Malloy *(Winston-Salem Chronicle. Courtesy of Winston-Salem African American Archive-vertical file)*

Larry Little and Nelson Malloy were elected as Aldermen. Little, a graduate of Wake Forest University School of Law later became a professor at Winston-Salem State University. Hazel Mack-Hilliard became an attorney with Legal Aid of North Carolina and founded the Carter G. Woodson Charter School.

The Black Panther Party of Winston-Salem was presented with a historic marker October 14, 2012 at the corner of Martin Luther King, Jr. Blvd and Fifth Street in Winston-Salem, near the group's original headquarters.

Notable Moments
The Larry D. Little Fitness Course at Kimberley Park on Burton Street is named for him.

Larry Little stands behind Polly Graham in this 1970 photo. Little was protesting Graham's eviction.

Black Panther's Free Ambulance Service

Larry Little protesting to keep Polly Graham from eviction, 1970. *(Winston-Salem Journal. Courtesy of Winston-Salem African American Archive-vertical file)* Black Panther's Free Ambulance Service *(Courtesy of Winston-Salem African American Archive-vertical file)*

First African American and First Woman to Chair the Forsyth County Democratic Party

Earline Parmon was the first African American and the first Woman to be elected Chairperson of the Forsyth County Democratic Party.

Earline Parmon
(Courtesy of Winston-Salem African American Archive)

First African American Political Organization of the Forsyth County Democratic Party

The African American Caucus of the Forsyth County Democratic Party is the first and oldest AAC Chapter in North Carolina. It was voted on as a resolution of the Forsyth County Democratic Convention by Executive Committee members acknowledging and recognizing the establishment of the Forsyth County Caucus as the African American Caucus of the North Carolina Democratic Party in Forsyth County. The African American Caucus of the North Carolina Democratic Party the Forsyth County Branch was organized with the help of Harold Lee Hairston and Albert Porter of Forsyth, (who were part of the original 39 who co-founded the AAC-NCDP at the State Executive Committee meeting in Raleigh, NC), with Jacquelyne Barber and other local African American democrats in April 2003, at the Forsyth County Democratic Convention. This gave Forsyth County the distinction of having the first local African American Caucus in the state. It is the first organized auxiliary of a political party in the county to specifically and continually address all political problems, community concerns issues, and discussions of African Americans in Forsyth County.

The AAC of Forsyth held its first meeting to elect officers on April 29, 2003 at the East Winston Library now named the Malloy/Jordan Heritage Center.

Harold L. Hairston and Jackie Barber on CAT-TV (Community Access Television) program in Winston-Salem *(Courtesy of African American CaucusFCDP-Jacquelyne Barber Branch and Chenita B. Johnson)*

The meeting was attended by Albert Porter, Charles Reynolds, Chenita Johnson, Dorothy Brown, Evelyn Terry, Felicia Mack, Frank Williams, Harold Lee Hairston, Jacquelyne Barber, Josie Shirley, Joycelyn Johnson, Mabel E. Johnson, Marjorie Gregory, Odert Thompson, Phillip Carter, and Toni L. Jones. The officers elected were Harold Lee Hairston (East Ward), Chairperson; Evelyn Terry (Southeast Ward), Vice-Chairperson; Chenita Johnson (Northeast Ward), Secretary; and Phillip Carter (East Ward), Treasurer. The next meeting was held May 27, 2003 at the Winston Lake YMCA and added new members Mrs. Randon Pender, Paul Brandon Johnson, Rev. Lizzie Green, Mrs. Emma Ingram (Winston Lake precinct), Mr. Robert Leak (Easton Association), Doris Bines (Mother Wit) Dr. Irene Phillips (NAACP), and Ciat Shabazz. Later exo-ficio members included Councilwoman DeeDee Adams, NC Representative Larry Womble, NC Senator Earlene Parmon and NC Senator Paul Lowe.

On May 14, 2007, President Harold L. Hairston made a motion for an addendum to the name of the organization to posthumously honor the dedication of co-founding African American CaucusFCDP member, Vice-President Jacquelyne B. Barber. The motion was seconded and approved by unanimous vote of the membership. It is now African American Caucus of the Forsyth County Democratic Party-Jacquelyne Barber Branch, leaving intact the name African American Caucus and the county as approved by the African American Caucus of the North Carolina Democratic Party.

SOCIAL AND COMMUNITY ACTIVISM

Notable Moments

The auxiliary sponsors voter registration drives and education forums, and it sponsored a successful weekly local CAT-TV broadcast program. The AAC also met with Mayor Allen Joins to discuss and successfully gained more representation and appointments of African Americans to the local Boards and Commissions, spearheaded precinct organization, initiated and organized successful candidate's forums in various wards, initiated the first community forums in local barbershops called AAC Shop Talk, and sponsors the Jacquelyne B. Barber Excellence in Community Leadership Award which is presented to community advocates and activists. Named for co-founding African American CaucusFCDP member Jacquelyne B. Barber, this award spotlights positive, productive, and evidence-based community leadership.

Left photo front row (l to r): Mable Johnson, Emma Ingram, Marjorie Gregory. Backrow-Braeden Johnson and Jackie Barber. Right photo l to r: Charlie Reynolds, Larry Womble and Robert Leake.
(Courtesy of African American CaucusFCDP-Jacquelyne Barber Branch and Chenita .B. Johnson)

 MLK, Jr. Parade- holding the banner are Jemmise Bowen(l) and Braeden Johnson (r) *(Courtesy of Chenita B. Johnson)*

Above left to right: African American CaucusFCDP-Jacquelyne Barber Branch "Barber Shop Talk" at Hollywood Cuts Barber Shop on Green Street *(The Winston-Salem Chronicle. Courtesy of Winston-Salem African American Archive-vertical file)* Candidates Forum at FCDP Headquarters (*Courtesy of African American CaucusFCDP-Jacquelyne Barber Branch*

First African American Global Social Activist

Madie Hall Xuma
(WSSU Archives-University Photograph Collection. Winston-Salem State University Archives-C.G. O'Kelly Library)

Madie Beatrice Hall Xuma (b. 1894-d.1982), known as the "Mother of a Nation," was born in Winston-Salem, North Carolina to Dr. Humphrey H. Hall and successful real-estate tycoon, Ginny Cowan Hall.

SOCIAL AND COMMUNITY ACTIVISM

When she became the first President of the African National Congress(ANC) Women's League in the 1940's, Madie Xuma became the first global activist from Winston-Salem.

Originally, Madie wanted to follow in her father's footsteps like her brother Leroy and become a physician. Although she was accepted to Howard University Medical College, her father disapproved of this career choice, fearing for her safety due to the sexual assaults that frequently occurred to female doctors who traveled alone during house calls.

Groomed by both of her parents to be of service to others, but unable to serve as a physician, she chose teaching as her avenue of service to the African American community and advocated empowerment through education. She received a BA Degree in Education from Winston-Salem Teachers College in 1937, and in 1938 received her master's Degree in Education from Columbia University. It was at Columbia University, she met her future husband Alfred Bitini Xuma, the first black medical doctor in apartheid South Africa. He later became the first president of the African National Congress (ANC). One of their first recruits to this organization was a young activist named Nelson Mandela.

She eventually went to live in South Africa. Upon her arrival, she immediately began work to empower black South African women by forming the ANC Women's League in the 1940's.

In 1951, Madie created the ZenZen clubs for women that became a part of the YWCA. This was greatly contested and objected to by the South African Government as well as the South African YWCA, which did not allow membership of the Young Woman's Christian Association to black women. As an executive committee member of the international YWCA, Madie used every chance available to speak of the evils of apartheid during her visits to various countries.

A year after the death of her husband in 1963, she moved back to Winston-Salem and resided at 1016 Cameron Avenue, the home of her nephew, Attorney Harold Kennedy, Jr.

First African American Executive Director of a Federally Funded Non-Profit

Mrs. Louise Wilson
(Courtesy of the Bradshaw Estate)

The first Executive Director of Experiment in Self Reliance (ESR) was Mrs. Louise Wilson. She became the first African American in the county to hold the position as Executive Director of a federally funded non-profit. The Experiment in Self Reliance (ESR) was chartered in 1964. Part of President Lyndon Johnson's War On Poverty, its purpose is to eliminate poverty and homelessness and to allow residents to speak freely about their problems and needs.

In June 2014 ESR moved from its home at the "Old City Hospital," building off East Fifth Street into a new facility on 3480 Dominion St NE, in Winston-Salem.

Ribbon cutting of new ESR building (left to right) Larry Herzberg, Fred Bazemore, Vivian Burke (NE Ward City Council member), DeeDee Adams (N Ward City Council member), Twanna Wellman-Roebuck (ESR Executive Director), Dell James, Dr. Frank James, Tommy Hickman, Mayor Allen Joines and William Womble.*(Courtesy of Experiment in Self Reliance)*

First African American President of the Forsyth County Homemakers Extension

Mrs. Louise Hawkins
(Courtesy of Chenita B. Johnson)

Licensed minister and mentor locally and nationwide, Mrs. Louise B. Friday Hawkins, affectionately known throughout Winston-Salem as "Mother Hawkins," became the first African American elected President of the Forsyth County Extension Homemakers Council in 1972. The Forsyth County Extension Homemakers Council existed for 50 years before Mrs. Hawkins was elected president.

The County Council was composed of 42 extension clubs and 900 members. It promoted education through programs that encourage and assist members in achieving higher standards of family living, homemaking, community service, leadership and citizenship. It also involved community programs such as 4-H.

Through her position as president of the county council, "Mrs. Hawkins has represented Forsyth County in Seattle Washington and Columbia Missouri." [58] She led many self-help community forums at the county extension office, creating an environment of empowerment for those who for the first time realized they could do or be anything.

Mrs. Hawkins later became a member of the Mayor's Women of Winston Committee. "She won the state award for giving 1,300 hours of her time to volunteer work; she won the top award for County Leader of the Year presented to her at Bermuda Run Country Club and the State Leader of the Year Award." (59) The State Leader of the Year Award was presented to her by then Senator Steve Neal.

Mrs. Hawkins believed that service to family and the community was of greatest importance, and she was never afraid to take steps considered beyond her place as an African American and a woman. Her motto was, "You can if you think you can."

Notable Moments

The first in her family to attend high school, she graduated from Atkins High School in 1937. She became a stenographer as a part of the W.P.A. Program. W.P.A. was a part of the New Deal, begun in 1933 by President Franklin Roosevelt, which helped millions of unemployed in the United States during the Great Depression.

She worked at R.J. Reynolds Tobacco Company and became a Union Shop Steward at the tobacco company. Later, to support her family, she worked in a private home as a cook for the Clifford Perry, Sr. family.

Mrs. Hawkins supported public education and parental involvement. She was elected PTA president in two different decades, first at Kimberley Park Elementary School and then at North Elementary school.

She served as past Worthy Chief of the Order of St. Luke and later became one of the first women licensed as minister in the Holiness Church of God. Although later confined to a wheelchair by a stroke, she began a prison ministry in Yadkinville, North Carolina, continuing to inspire others to always strive for the best.

Article from Winston-Salem Journal *(Courtesy of Chenita B. Johnson)*

African American of Community Service Firsts

Mr. Clark S. Brown, Sr.
(Courtesy of Clark S. Brown and Sons Funeral Home)

Mr. Clark S. Brown, Sr., is the founder and owner of Clark S. Brown and Son's Funeral Home in Winston-Salem. He came to Winston-Salem in 1930 from Roanoke Virginia and immediately became active in the growth of the community. According to the April 24, 1938 article in the Winston-Salem Journal and Sentinel, Mr. Brown was a leader among people. He strongly believed that a man should be involved in the community in which he lived, and that service is the price you pay for the space you occupy.

He became the first African American member of the Greater Winston-Salem Chamber of Commerce, the first to serve on the board of the local Red Cross, the Civil Defense Council, City Recreation Commission and the state ABC Board.

In 1964, Mr. Brown and Mr. John Wheeler of Durham became the first two African Americans in the 20th Century to serve as delegates to the Democratic National Convention.

Clark Brown and Sons Funeral Home is located at 727 N. Patterson Avenue in Winston-Salem.

Current funeral home on Patterson Ave

First Brown Funeral Home at 201 E. 7th Street

2nd Brown Funeral Home at 125 E. 7th and Chestnut Streets.
It was the former home of Dr. H. H. Hall
Photos (Courtesy of Clark S. Brown and Sons Funeral Home)

Mr. Brown (Standing back right) with boys' work crew
(Courtesy of Winston-Salem African American Archive)

First to Take on State Eugenics Program

Representative Larry Womble
(Courtesy of the Bradshaw Estate)

Representative Larry Womble was born in Winston-Salem, North Carolina, June 6, 1941. As an elected official for more than 30 years, he worked tirelessly on behalf of the people of Forsyth County and North Carolina focusing on those affected by the injustices within our state.

One program he worked to put in the spotlight was the state-sponsored eugenics program which allowed for the violation of citizens by their state government. Through his focus and efforts, North Carolina became the first state in the country to apologize and work toward compensating victims of the 20th Century eugenics program.

The state's sterilization program was part of a nationwide eugenics movement to stop people considered unfit, from having children. Those targeted by this mass sterilization were the poor, those considered promiscuous, the physically impaired and were also primarily African American. The state of North Carolina forcibly sterilized over 7,000 of its own citizens through this program.

It was also due to Larry Womble's efforts that for the first time in state history, bipartisan leadership in state government was at the forefront of such an issue.

Historical Marker on US 401 (McDowell Street) in Raleigh commemorating North Carolina Eugenics Board.
(Public Domain)

In 2003, Representative Womble was able to persuade then Governor Mike Easley to officially end and apologize for the eugenics program. He sponsored a bill to get the eugenics law off the books in North Carolina and assisted a task force that led to a monument, a display for the victims, and compensation for the 7,600 surviving victims. To protect them from exploitation, his House Bill 374 seals the records of these citizens who were forcibly sterilized by the state of North Carolina, and to allow access for only them, their families, or their representatives.

Notable Moments

Larry Womble served nine terms as representative from the 71st District in Winston Salem Forsyth County, North Carolina.

He graduated from Atkins High School in Winston-Salem, and obtained degrees from Winston Salem State University, the University of North Carolina at Greensboro (UNC-G) and Appalachian State University.

He began his career of public service in 1981 while working as assistant principal at Old Town Elementary School. He ran for and won a seat on the Board of Aldermen (City Council), representing the Southeast Ward. Thirteen years later, he was elected to the N.C. House of Representatives where he served until his retirement in 2012.

Youngest Director of the Urban League

Talmadge Willard Fair
(Courtesy of Talmadge W. Fair)

Talmadge Willard Fair (T. Willard Fair), was born in 1939 to John and Mary Lou Fair in Winston-Salem. After high school graduation he attended Johnson C. Smith University in Charlotte, NC, graduating in 1961 cum laude in Sociology. He received a master's Degree from Atlanta University School of Social Work two years later.

Considered a revolutionary and civil rights activist, Fair is CEO of the Urban League of greater Miami in Florida. He is the first African American from Winston-Salem and is the youngest CEO and President in the history of the Urban League, taking the position at age 24 in 1963 with a staff of three.

Under his leadership and enthusiasm, within a decade, he grew the agency to the largest Urban League affiliate in its history with more than 400 fulltime employees, 24 part-time employees and four consultants in the organization.

Notable Moments

T. Willard Fair was given his unusual name by an insurance broker when he came home as an infant from the hospital. He had yet to be named so the broker suggested they name him Talmadge. The name is said to be ironic in that it is also the name of Georgia segregationist and Senator, Herman Eugene Talmadge, Sr. That Talmadge was one of the Senators who boycotted the Democratic National Convention after Johnson signed the Civil Rights Act of 1964 into law.

Talmadge Fair has championed civil rights throughout south Florida despite receiving death threats. He successfully lobbied for African Americans to hold jobs in businesses such as Eastern Airlines, Florida Highway Patrol and the Fontainebleau Hotel. He served as an adjunct professor at the Atlanta University School of Social Work, Bethune-Cookman College, Florida International University, and the National Urban League's Whitney M. Young, Jr. Center for Urban Leadership. He co-founded with former Governor Jeb Bush, the Liberty City Charter School, the first charter school in the state of Florida.

In 2010, he was appointed by President Barack Obama to the President's Commission on White House Fellowships Miami Regional Selection Panel. He was reappointed to this position in 2011. In 2013, T W Fair was honored for his service of 50 years as CEO of the Miami Urban League, and in 2015, he was honored by the Black Alliance for Educational Options for addressing the needs of African American Children.

Talmadge W. Fair
(Courtesy of T. W. Fair)

Chapter Four

Municipal Officials and Elected Representatives

"If an African American is a man, he is entitled to All the rights and privileges of any other man. There can be no grades of citizenship under the American Flag."

John Adams Hyman, United States Representative from
North Carolina, 1875-1877

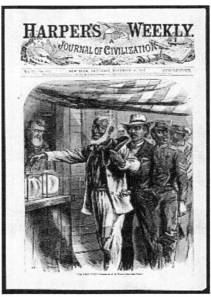

Engraving of First black voter drawn by A.R. Waud- An 1867 Harper's Weekly
cover commemorates the first vote cast by African American men
The passage and ratification of the Reconstruction.
(Public Domain Wikimedia. www.loc.gov/pictures/)

The power of the ballot box has been the consistent driving force and equalizer behind our democratic process, allowing all citizens to shape their world through the vote. This was never more pronounced than after the Civil War with the passage of the 13th, 14th, and 15th Amendments by the United States Congress, allowing blacks to become full participants in the process especially with the ratification of the of the 15th Amendment in 1870 establishing voting rights.

This made blacks in North Carolina an electoral force at the ballot box.

There were, however, challenges against their voting rights such as the passage of a series of election laws by the state legislature that gave judges and registrars almost unlimited power in determining not only the qualifications but also the eligibility of voters.

These laws were specifically "designed to redistrict black political power, especially in areas where they outnumbered whites. One such law was the county law enacted February 27, 1877 which nullified the strength of the Negroes at the ballot box."[60]

There was also the "heavily fought constitutional amendment of 1900, a propaganda campaign for white supremacy, led by Charles B. Aycock, then democratic candidate for governor."[61] This amendment stripped more than 80,000 black voters of their right to vote.

Called the Suffrage Amendment, it was meant to restrict the vote to only those who could pay a poll tax or read parts of the constitution. Basically, the voters of North Carolina were voting on a proposal to restrict the black vote. While the state constitution did not allow taking away the vote by race, because most black voters were poor and illiterate, they would be the ones affected by this law. However, the grandfather clause was included in this amendment to allow for those voters who could vote in 1867 and their descendants. This clause allowed poor and illiterate whites to vote. Winston and Forsyth County were not immune to this form of voter suppression and intimidation. J. T. Thompson and Hunter Wall, two white registrars, were charged by four blacks for their refusal to register black voters.

The four black voters were themselves charged with creating false charges against these two men and they were fined. The charges against Thompson and Wall were eventually dropped.

According to *History of African Americans in North Carolina*, Charles Aycock considered whites who were against the amendment, public enemies who deserved the contempt of all mankind.

Another political contemporary named Alfred M. Waddell of Wilmington implored whites to tell blacks who came to vote to leave, and if they refused, they should kill them ,shoot them down.

In a meeting in Forsyth County, white speakers insisted they would pledge life and honor that white men shall rule this country.

African Americans in these North Carolina Counties, including Forsyth County, were undaunted. They persevered and forever changed their representation throughout all levels of government and municipalities.

Kimberley Park Elementary School polling place 1964
(Winston-Salem Journal. Courtesy of Winston -Salem African American Archive- vertical file)

Elected Officials

First African American Alderman

In "May 5, 1881, Israel Clement became the first black elected to the Winston Town Commissioners" (Alderman). [62] A tobacco roller for Hamilton Scales Tobacco Company, Clement was well respected in the community by whites and blacks. He had earlier been "offered the position of police chief but preferred to continue work in the tobacco factory where he could make more money." [63]

Before the city was divided into wards, Israel Clement ran at-large, and was elected commissioner by a large vote. He died of typhoid fever, at age 35 on April 2, 1882, about one month before his term expired. Clement left a legacy. When he died, the Board of Commissioners presented a resolution to honor his memory.

Nine years after the election of Israel Clement, other African Americans, including Clement's son Rufus Clement, won seats on the Board of Town Commissioners. These elected black officials were: J.B. Gwyn, a grocer serving February 1890 - February 1892 for the 3rd ward; Aaron Moore, tobacco worker, serving February 1890 - February 1892, for the 3rd ward; Rufus Clement February 1891-February 1892 3rd ward and February 1894-May 1896 3rd ward; J.G. Lattie, a funeral director and embalmer, February 1894-May 1896 3rd ward; Henry Pendleton, tobacco worker May 1896-May 1900 4th ward; S.H. Hargrave, tobacco worker at Brittny and Whitaker, May 1898 - May 1900 5th ward and J.F. Hughes, post office custodian.

Possibly, due in part to the Amendment of 1900 which stripped blacks of the vote in North Carolina, there were no other African Americans elected to office in Forsyth County until 1947 with the election of Rev. Kenneth R. Williams.

WINSTON

Never in the history of the town has there been such a division among the voters. There were 14 printed tickets, we learn (we did not count them), at the polls. More than usual interest was manifested, and a somewhat larger vote polled than is generally the case with us in Town elections. The question of taxation for the erection of buildings for the graded school failed by 19 votes. As a matter of interest, we publish the names of the gentlemen voted for, with the number of votes each received, as follows:—

FOR MAYOR:
A. B. Gorrell,...169 | J. C. Buxton,..129
S. D. Franklin, 92

FOR COMMISSIONERS:
P A Wilson, Sr. 256 | T J Wilson,.. 73
J A Gray,......222 | C J Brown,... 57
R D Brown....180 | S A Ogburn,.. 67
P H Hanes,...162 | S H Smith,... 116
I L Clement,..137 | D H Starbuck, 66
J A White,....134 | J E Gilmer,.. 55
S Byerly,.....131 | John Griffith,. 48
G W Hinshaw,.127 | M W Norfleet, 49
J W Alspaugh,.123 | R D Johnson,. 42
James Martin, 121 | J H Martin,.. 36
P W Dalton,...120 | S H Hodgin,.. 30
C Hamlen,....104 | W B Glenn,.. 17
G L Miller,.... 89 | Scattering,.. 21
Jacob Tise,... 75

FOR GRADED SCHOOL COMMISSIONER:
Jas. A. Gray,...............232
FOR GRADED SCHOOL BUILDINGS,.. 231

From this exhibit it will be seen that P. A. Wilson received the largest vote, 256, and W. B. Glenn the smallest, 17.

The ticket, as elected, stands:—
For Mayor—A. B. Gorrell.
Commissioners—P. A. Wilson, J. A. Gray, R. D. Brown, P. H. Hanes, I. L. Clement, col., J. A. White, S Byerly.

The Board may be regarded as a representative one, all interests and both races having one or more members.

We are not prepared to endorse the

DEATH OF A WORTHY COLORED CITIZEN.—At his residence in this city on Sunday last, April 2, of typhoid fever, ISRAEL L. CLEMENT, aged 35 years. The deceased, a colored man, was a member of the Board of Town Commissioners, a Master Mason in the colored lodge of that order here, a leader among his race, and respected by all as an upright, honest, conscientious man. The funeral exercise took place on Monday 8 o'clock p.m., at the Methodist E. Church, col., Rev. R. Smith the pastor, officiating.

An immense concourse of colored people, the Mayor and City Council in a body, together with quite a number of white citizens, attended. The Order of Good Samaritans and Masons were out in a body, the latter order performing the burial service. Rev. R. Smith delivered a very well considered and entirely appropriate funeral discourse. At its close, by invitation, Rev. C. C. Dodson, pastor of the M. E. Church, South, paid a touching tribute to the deceased, basing his remarks upon the quotation "An honest man is the noblest work of God." His remains were taken for interment to the Colored Cemetery, Sa'em, followed by as large a procession as ever attended a burial in the place.

On the left- 1881 Election results showing Israel Clement *(Winston-Salem Peoples Press May 5, 1881. North Carolina Room Forsyth County Central Library)* On the right- Obituary for Israel Clement *(Union Republic April 6, 1882. North Carolina Room, Forsyth County Central Library)*

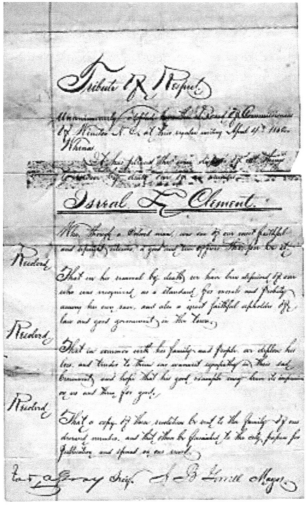

Resolution for Israel Clement
(North Carolina Room, Forsyth County Central Library)

The First All African American Political Ticket

After the strike of 1889, the legislative response to the organizing of African Americans and their consistent strength at the ballot box was to increase and implement election laws across North Carolina to suppress the black vote.

Forsyth County used a North Carolina election law to deny votes by denying the right to register, and by challenging voters at the polls on Election Day.

Gerrymandering of the wards in Forsyth County was also used. The Board of Commissioners redrew the three wards having the First and Second Wards predominantly white. These two wards would represent one third of the population and would be represented by 6 commissioners. The Third Ward, which was the factory and warehouse district, Urban and predominantly black, was represented by 3 commissioners.

To combat this voter suppression, the black community organized and ran their *Colored Men's Ticket* against the incumbents in the 1890 municipal elections. This ticket, which included John B. Gwyn, a grocer, John F. Hughs, a post office custodian and Rufus Clement, a janitor, swept all three seats and removed the white incumbents including R. J. Reynolds. Although there was still a white representative majority on the Board of Commissioners, and the African American elected representatives could still be out voted, the Commissioners would now have to deal with the representatives of the African American community concerning policy in the town.

First African American Alderman in the 20th Century

Rev. Kenneth R. Williams
(WSSU Archives-University Photograph Collection. Winston-Salem State University Archives-C.G. O'Kelly Library)

When Rev. Kenneth Raynor Williams, was elected Alderman for the 3rd Ward in Winston-Salem in 1947, he became the first black elected to the Board of Alderman in Winston-Salem in 47 years, and he was "the first black elected to political office in the south since reconstruction."[64] He was also the first African American to defeat a white opponent. He led the ticket in the primary, "receiving 2106 votes. He was elected with 2369 votes."[65]

Williams was followed in this office by Reverend Crawford and Funeral Home owner and director, Carl Russell.

Notable Moments

Kenneth R. Williams was a 1928 graduate of Columbian Heights High School, he served two terms as Alderman. In 1961, he became Chancellor of Winston-Salem State College (Winston-Salem State University) serving for 10 years. In 1963 Wake Forest College honored him with honorary Doctor of Laws degree, the first by the college to an African American.

Kenneth R. Williams (standing- 2nd from right), Mayor Kurfees (seated center) and Board of Aldermen, 1949. *(Courtesy of the Bradshaw Estate)*

First African American Mayor Pro Tempore

Carl H. Russell, Jr
(Courtesy of Russell Funeral Home)

Carl H. Russell, Jr. was "the prominent black politician in the city in the 1960's and 1970's." [66] He was also a successful businessman, establishing Russell Funeral Home in 1939. Russell was elected to the board of Aldermen in 1961 and served 10 years In 1966, he became the city's first African American Mayor Pro Tempore, a position he held for eight years. Although successful and well respected he ran an unsuccessful write-in campaign for mayor in 1977.

The Russell Funeral Home is located on 822 Carl Russell Avenue in Winston-Salem.

Notable Moments

The Carl Russell, Jr. Recreation Center on Carver School Road in Winston-Salem was named in his honor.

First African American Mayor of Evanston, Illinois

Lorraine Hairston Morton
(Courtesy of the City of Evanston, Illinois-Photo by Dave Rodeilus, Evanston Photographic Studios. Public photo)

Lorraine H. Morton was born December 8, 1918 in Winston-Salem, North Carolina. She was the youngest child of Keziah Hairston, a schoolteacher, and William Patrick Hairston, a businessman who was a cofounder of Winston Mutual Insurance Company.

This Winston-Salem native became the first African American Mayor, first Democratic Mayor, and longest-serving Mayor of Evanston, Illinois.

She graduated from Winston-Salem Teacher's College in 1938 with a Bachelor of Science in Education and continued her post graduate studies at Northwestern University in Evanston where she received her Master's in Curriculum (education) in in 1942. There she met her husband Dr. James Thomas Morton and permanently moved to Evanston in 1953 where she became an educator.

Morton, taught at Foster Elementary School, a school for African American children, but later she crossed the color line and became the first African American to teach outside of the black schools of Evanston. She was also part of the first group of teachers to be given merit pay in District 65. Retiring in 1989. she entered public service and agreed to serve as Alderman of the Fifth Ward of Evanston, a position she held from 1982-1991.

In 1993, Lorraine Morton ran for Mayor of Evanston. After a run-off election against Ann Rainey, Alderman of Evanston's Eighth Ward, Morton was elected Evanston's first African American and first Democratic Mayor. She was the second woman to hold that position and would eventually become Evanston's longest-serving Mayor by holding that office for sixteen years (1993-2009).

Notable Moments

During her tenure, she worked to create a relationship between the Northwestern University and the community of Evanston.

Due to her community service, Lorrain Morton was bestowed many honors from various institutions including Saint Francis Hospital of Evanston and the Evanston Arts Council. She was presented the Alumni Merit Award in 1996, was bestowed an honorary Doctorate of Law in 2008 at Northwestern University, and the University created a scholarship in her honor called the Lorraine H. Morton Scholarship for the Master of Science in Education Program in the School of Education and Social Policy.

She also received an Honorary Doctorate for public service from Kendall College in Chicago, and The Civic Center in Evanston was renamed for her when she retired in 2009. It is now the Lorraine H. Morton Civic Center.

In 2010, Winston-Salem State University created the Lorraine Hairston Morton Endowed Scholarship for students majoring in education who are committed to community service. At 99 years of age, she was honored once again when the Council of Evanston unveiled a portrait of her by the artist Richard Halstead at a special reception in April 2013 in the council chambers.

First African American Deputy Mayor of Boston, Massachusetts

Dr. Clarence "Jeep" Jones *WSSU* Yearbook Public photo
(WSSU C.E. "Big House" Gaines Athletic Hall of Fame - WSSU Department of Athletics. winstonsalem.prestosports.com)

Dr. Clarence "Jeep" Jones became the first African American Deputy Mayor of Boston, Massachusetts.

Jones was born in Roxbury, Massachusetts on April 17, 1933, and attended and graduated from the Boston public schools. He was later recruited to come to Winston-Salem and attend Winston-Salem Teacher's College. There, under Coach Big House Gains, he was a member of the 1953 CIAA Champion basketball team, the very first championship team in any sport at the school. After graduating in 1955 with a bachelor's Degree in Education, he served two years in the Army and later earned a master's degree from Goddard College in Plainfield, Vermont.

After returning to Boston, he became involved in the community as a teacher and worked as a city employee. In this capacity, he created many firsts in Boston, such as being the first minority youth worker, the first African American juvenile probation officer, and the first African American chairman of the Boston Redevelopment Authority (BRA).

Clarence Jones had such a great rapport with the children of Roxbury and the community in Boston that Boston's Mayor asked him to work as Deputy Mayor. Becoming the first African American to serve in that position, he served as Deputy Mayor from 1968 to 1981. Jones later became the chairman of the Boston Redevelopment Authority (B.R.A.), a position he held for three decades. He was on the board of the B.R.A. since 1981 and has been the chairman since 1989. In his position as chairman, Jones was a central figure in the transformation of the Boston Skyline and neighborhoods.

Dr. Clarence Jeep Jones retired after 32 years of service to his community.

Notable Moments

Dr. Jones has been honored with a park named after him (Clarence "Jeep" Jones Park-Roxbury, MA); a room named after him at Boston's first black-owned hotel; he received an honorary Doctorate in Public Service from Northeastern University in 2005 and a Living Legend award from the Renaissance School in 2012. He was also inducted into the WSSU C.E. "Big House" Gaines Athletic Hall of Fame for his outstanding accomplishments as a basketball student athlete.

First African American Women Elected to the Winston-Salem Board of Aldermen

Mrs. Virginia Newell (left) and Mrs. Vivian Burke(right).
(Winston-Salem Chronicle. Courtesy of Winston-Salem African American Archive-vertical file)

In 1977, Mrs. Vivian Burke and Mrs. Virginia Newell were the first African American women elected to the Board of Aldermen.

Vivian H. Burke a representative of the Northeast Ward, was a counselor at Lowrance Intermediate School, (later Hanes-Lowrance Middle School), on Indiana Avenue. She became the first woman Mayor pro tempore in Winston-Salem and has the longest tenure of anyone to have served on the Board of Alderman/City Council. She is also a founding member of the North Carolina Black Elected Municipal Officials, and an integral part of the Citizens Review Board.

Virginia Newell, a representative of the East Ward, was an Associate Professor of mathematics at Winston-Salem State University and continues to be a community activist championing equity in public education.

First Time Half the Board of Alderman is of African American Representation

In 1981, for the first time in Winston-Salem history, half of the Board of Alderman was represented by African American elected board members. These board members were Mr. Larry D. Little, Mrs. Vivian Burke, Mrs. Virginia Newell and Mr. Larry Womble.

Left to right: Larry Little, and Virginia Newell
(Winston-Salem Chronicle. Courtesy of Winston-Salem African American Archive-vertical file)

Left to right: Larry Womble *(Courtesy of Winston-Salem African American Archive)* and *Vivian Burke* *(Winston-Salem Chronicle. Courtesy of Winston-Salem African American Archive-vertical file)*

First Student to Serve in City Council

Derwin Montgomery
(WSSU newsletter. Courtesy of Winston-Salem State University)

When Derwin Montgomery was sworn in as council member on December 7, 2009, he became the "first Winston-Salem State University student to serve on city council."[67] As a senior at Winston-Salem State University, he won the 2009 East Ward primary by 57 percent of the vote. Montgomery also became the youngest elected representative on the Winston-Salem City Council in the city's recorded history as well as the youngest elected official at that time, in the state of North Carolina.

Derwin Montgomery
(City of Winston-Salem. Public photo)

First African American Sheriff

Bobby Kimbrough "Lord High Sheriff"
(Winston-Salem Journal-Photo by Andrew Dye/Journal. Courtesy of Winston-Salem African American Archive-vertical file)

Bobby F. Kimbrough, Jr. is the first African American in the history of Winston-Salem/ Forsyth County to hold the position of Sheriff. He was elected November 6, 2018.
Kimbrough received 71,301 votes or 53 percent of the ballots cast, besting three-time incumbent sheriff and former FBI agent, Bill Shatzman who received 62,093 votes or 47 percent of the ballots cast.

The Winston-Salem native graduated from North Forsyth High School and earned his undergraduate degree from High Point University. He began his career in law enforcement with the Winston-Salem Police Department in 1984 as a public safety officer which combined the duties of a police officer and firefighter. He continued to serve with the Winston-Salem Fire Department as an arson investigator and assistant Fire Marshall in 1989, and later served with the North Carolina Department of Probation and Parole working with high-risk offenders.

Kimbrough went on to serve in the United States Department of Justice as a special agent in the Drug Enforcement Administration (DEA) from 1995 until his retirement in 2016.

On December 3, 2018, in the biggest courtroom in the Forsyth County Hall of Justice, Bobby F. Kimbrough, Jr., surrounded by over 400 people including his parents and his sons, was officially sworn in as the "Lord High Sheriff" of Forsyth County. Todd Burke, Senior Resident Forsyth Superior Court Judge, administrated the oath of office. After he took the oath of office his parents pinned his badge.

Various remarks during the ceremony were given by Mayor Pro Tempore Vivian Burke, District Judge Denise Hartsfield, former Winston-Salem Mayor Martha Wood, Attorney Michael Grace, Bishop Sir Walter Mack, Bishop Todd Fulton, Cedric Russell, Olin Shuler, County Commissioner Chair Dave Plyler and two of Kimbrough's seven sons, Jordan and Jamesen.

Notable Moments

Bobby Kimbrough was a part of the historic election of seven African American men as Sheriffs in seven of the largest NC counties; Forsyth, Durham, Cumberland, Buncombe, Guilford, Wake, Mecklenburg and an African American woman in the smaller county of Pitt. Five counties; Durham, Guilford, Forsyth, Cumberland and Buncombe elected African American sheriffs for the first time in their county histories. Buncombe county elected its African American sheriff with a 90 percent white population.

The elected NC sheriffs were: Bobby Kimbrough- Forsyth County, Danny Rogers – Guilford, Gerald Baker – Wake, Ennis Wright – Cumberland, Quentin Miller – Buncombe, Clarence Birkhead – Durham, Gary McFadden – Mecklenburg, and Paula Dance - Pitt.

First African American Elected to the County School Board

Dr. Lillian Lewis
(Courtesy of the Bradshaw Estate)

On November 8, 1960, Dr. Lillian B. Lewis became the first African American to be elected county-wide to serve on the county school board. Unlike the city board which at that time was appointed, the county board was an elected position.

The school systems were black and white schools in the city, and black and white schools in the county.

Dr. Lewis ran again and won her seat in 1962. She was a part of the board when voters approved the consolidation of the city and county school systems in Forsyth County, North Carolina.

In 1968, voters approved making the entire consolidated school board elected positions.

Dr. Lewis decided not to run for her seat in 1970.

Dr. Lillian Lewis (seated end right) and County School Board
(Courtesy of the Bradshaw Estate)

First African American Elected to the Winston-Salem/Forsyth County School Board

Beaufort Bailey
(Winston-Salem Chronicle. Courtesy of Winston-Salem African American Archive-vertical file)

In 1974, Beaufort Bailey became the first African American to be elected to the Winston-Salem Forsyth County Board of Education. Prior to that time, city board members were appointed.

Bailey lost his seat in 1978 but won it again in 1982. "His loss in 1990 prompted the state legislature to adopt a district plan that ensured black representation on the school board" [68] in Winston-Salem Forsyth County. School Board members are now elected in Districts and At-Large: District 1 elects two representatives, District 2 elects four, and an additional three are elected At-Large.

First African American School Board Member Elected At-Large

Robert Barr
(Winston-Salem Chronicle. Courtesy of Winston-Salem African American Archive-vertical file)

Pastor Robert Barr of Agape Faith Church in Forsyth County was elected to the Winston-Salem Forsyth County School Board in November 2014.
Barr is the first African American to be elected to the At-Large Seat and the first African American Republican elected to the Board. John Davenport, an African American Republican who served on the board, was appointed after the retirement of Democrat member, Geneva Brown.

Notable Moments
Robert Barr graduated from Winston-Salem State University in 1998 with a bachelor's degree in Education. He also has a master's Degree from Wake Forest University and a Doctorate in Education from Appalachian State University.

First School Board with Three Elected African American Members

In November 2014, Victor Johnson, Jr. and Deanna Taylor of District 1 and Robert Barr, an At-Large representative, were elected to the Winston-Salem Forsyth County School board. It was the first time three African Americans were elected to serve on the board at the same time.

2014 New School Board members including Robert Barr (far Left), Deanna Taylor (third from left)
(WS/Forsyth County Board of Education- Public photo).

Victor Johnson (right) with former WSFCS Superintendent Beverly Emory (left) *(Winston-Salem Chronicle. Courtesy of Winston-Salem African American Archive-vertical file)*

First African American Woman to Chair the Winston-Salem / Forsyth County Board of Education

Malishai "Shai" Woodbury
(*Winston-Salem Forsyth County Schools. Public photo*)

Malishai "Shai" Woodbury was elected as Chairwoman of the Winston-Salem Forsyth County schoolboard by its members and became the first African American woman in Winston-Salem history to hold that position. She was elected to the schoolboard as a District 1 representative on November 6, 2018.

Notable Moments

This 2018 board made history twice. It was the first time the board of education was made up entirely of women. Barbara Hanes Burke another representative elected from District 1 and an African American woman was elected vice-chairwoman of the board.

Woodbury, a graduate from Carver High School, in 1992, and from Carolina in 1996 began working for Guilford County Schools and began teaching at night in the history department at NC A&T State University.

First African American County Commissioner

Mazie Woodruff
(Courtesy of the Bradshaw Estate)

In 1978, Mazie Woodruff "became the first black and only the second woman to serve on the Forsyth Board of County Commissioners." [69] This was prior to the county having district elections. She lost her seat in 1986 but regained it four years later.

Mazie Woodruff with Board of commissioners
(Courtesy of the Bradshaw Estate)

First African American Man to serve as County Commissioner

Walter Marshall
(Forsyth County, NC.-Public photo)

In 1997 Walter Marshall became the first African American man to serve as County Commissioner, in District A, when he was selected to fill the unexpired term of Mazie Woodruff, the first African American to serve on the Forsyth County Board of Commissioners. He later ran for and won the seat, serving 20 years as commissioner until he unexpectedly passed away February 22, 2017.

Notable Moments

Marshall was a community activist, and an advocate for education and civil equality. In 1988 as President of the NAACP of Winston-Salem, he led the organization to file a suit against the Forsyth County Board of Commissioners and the Winston-Salem Forsyth County Board of Education. This resulted in the formation of the current district elections for both Boards.

First African American Elected to the Oklahoma State House

Hannah Diggs Atkins
(Courtesy of Mrs. Gloria Diggs Banks)

Hannah Diggs Atkins, a native of Winston-Salem, was born November 1, 1923 to the late James T. Diggs, Sr. and Mabel Kennedy Diggs. She is also the sister of James T. Diggs, Jr. and Dr. Edward O. Diggs (see chapter 8), the first black medical student at the University of North Carolina at Chapel Hill. She made history in 1968 when she was elected to the Oklahoma House of Representatives District 97, becoming the first African American woman elected to the Oklahoma House of Representatives.

Diggs and her family moved to Oklahoma in 1951 when her husband Dr. Charles N. Atkins became a resident physician at the former Edwards Hospital.

While working as a librarian for the Oklahoma County Library System and as a reference and law librarian for the State of Oklahoma, Hannah Atkins became active in civic affairs. Immediately after the death of Martin Luther King, Jr., she entered politics. Her campaign featured the help of young supporters known as Hannah's Helpers. She was elected to the Oklahoma State House and was re-elected five times, serving twelve years in the Oklahoma State House. She was the highest-ranking woman executive in Oklahoma State government due to her simultaneous appointments to the positions of Secretary of State of Oklahoma and Secretary of Social Services until her retirement in January 1991.

Notable Moments
Hannah Diggs Atkins graduated as valedictorian from Atkins High School at age 15. In 1943, she earned her undergraduate degree in Biology and French as an honors student from Saint Augustine's College, in Raleigh, N.C., where she was advised and mentored by John Hope Franklin. Furthering her education, she obtained a graduate degree in Library Science in 1949 from the University of Chicago.

Her husband Dr. Charles Atkins was also the first African American to serve on the Oklahoma City Council.

First African American Senator Elected from Forsyth County

Earline Parmon
(Public domain)

On November 6, 2012, Earline Parmon became the first African American Senator man or woman, elected from Forsyth County in the 166 years of the county's existence. She served in the NC Senate from 2013 until 2015.

Parmon previously served 10 years as a State Representative in the NC General Assembly, 12 years as a Forsyth County Commissioner and was the first African American and woman elected as Chair the Forsyth County Democratic Party.

Municipal Representatives

First African American Fire Company

The first African American Fire Company in Winston was formed at the insistence of African American citizens of the town. On July 2, 1888, "Robert Searcy and other colored citizens appeared before the Winston Board of Alderman with a petition signed by numerous citizens asking that a Hook and Ladder Truck be purchased for the Town. The fire committee was instructed to purchase the truck properly equipped at a cost of no more than $400." [70]

Seven years later 20 black men became the first firemen of The Black Hook and Ladder Company #2. Included in this first group of firemen was Thomas M. Hairston the foreman, former Aldermen Justice G. (J.G.) Lattie, Aaron Moore, Henry Neal, and H. S. Seward. Their uniforms were furnished by the Board of Aldermen.

This company, located on Seventh and Depot Streets, was identified with the North Carolina Volunteers Association, and the men attended all fires in the city. "The original name was the North Carolina Colored Volunteer Fireman's Association. The organization was a counterpart of the North Carolina State Association, which had been chartered prior to this." [71]

The Winston Company was interactive with other companies across the state. An example is their hosting of the State Firemen's Convention in 1897 and August 1906 in Winston.

Following these fire companies were Hose Reel Companies No.1 and 2. The Captain was John Smith and Henry Elam was Lieutenant. The firemen were Irving Scales, Harvey Clanton, Odell Clanton, Archie Scales and Charles Rorie. They were in Salem and Columbian Heights, with the latter stationed in Columbian Heights. It endured for 27 years, becoming the Colored Hook and Ladder and Hose Company, and later The Colored Fire Company. However, on August 27, 1915, Mr. J.L. Graham, who represented a local committee, appeared before the board as had Mr. Searcy and others 27 years earlier. This meeting was to protest the disbanding of the Colored Fire Company. The Board of Aldermen was acting on a recommendation of Fire Chief Nissan who recommended the disbandment because they had provided for a paid department, and unless the Board took other action, this would move forward. The Board took no action, and on August 27, 1915, the Colored Hook and Ladder and Hose Company was disbanded. "The Board gave permission to Social Services to occupy the Vine Street building formally occupied by the Colored Fire Company." (72)

Belt won by firemen for competition. The belt was given by the Winston Fire Department. The inscription reads Championship 1897. *(Photo by North Carolina Museum of History. Courtesy of the Bradshaw Estate)*

TOURNAMENT ADJOURNS

All Business Transacted and Races Run—Report from National Association.

The colored Volunteer Firemen's Association of North Carolina closed its annual tournament here yesterday. All the business had been done the previous two days and the races yesterday morning ended the tournament.

Prof. L. R. Randolph returned from the National Firemen's Association yesterday and submitted his report. He stated that President J. D. McNeill, of the State and National Association of Firemen, was thoroughly in sympathy with the colored firemen of the State.

There were only three entries in the hand reel contest yesterday morning.

State Tournament *(City of Winston-Salem. Public photo)*

First Hired African American Firemen

The First Hired Black Firemen:
Front left to right-: John F. Meredith, George W. Penn, Lt. L. C. Williams (training officer), Willie J. Carter, Lester E. Ervin, Jr., back left to right-: Raphael O. Black, Robert L. Grier, Johns H. Ford and John R. Thomas
(Winston-Salem Chronicle. Courtesy of Winston-Salem African American Archive-vertical file)

On October 9, 1950, 35 years after the Board of Aldermen abolished The Colored Hook and Ladder and Hose Co on August 27, 1915, the Mayor and the Board of Aldermen, which included Rev. Kenneth R. Williams, "adopted a resolution authorizing the employment of Negro firemen." [73] The first black fire company had been a volunteer effort and served the city from 1892 to 1914.

On March 1, 1952, eight black firemen were hired to begin a five-year training program at fire station #4 on North Dunleith Street (Third and Dunleith Streets) where the Seventh Day Adventist Church is now located. This also created the first integrated Fire Department in the state of North Carolina. These hired firemen were John F. Meredith, George W. Penn, Willie J. Carter, Lester E. Ervin, Jr., Raphael O. Black, Robert L. Grier, Johns H. Ford and John R. Thomas.

Unlike the black volunteer fire company that answered all fires, Station #4 would only serve the neighborhood where it was located.

Station number Four *(Courtesy of the Bradshaw Estate). Above* Sgt. Raphael O. Black and Sgt. Lester Ervin *(Winston-Salem Chronicle. Courtesy of Winston-Salem African American Archive-vertical file)*

First African American Fire Chief in North Carolina

In 1957, six years after he was hired as a fireman, Lester Ervin, Jr. became the first African American Lieutenant of the city of Winston-Salem Fire Department. He later becomes the first African American in the state to be Duty Fire Chief, and then named Captain in charge of Company #4.

On July 21, 1980, Lester Ervin, Jr. became the "first black fire chief in the city and in state history." [74] He retired in 1989 after 38 years of service.

Lester Ervin, Jr.
*(City of Winston-Salem Fire Department-WSFD.
City of Winston-Salem. Public photo)*

First African American Woman Battalion Chief of the Winston-Salem Forsyth County Fire Department

Shirese Moore
*(City of Winston-Salem Fire Department-WSFD-
City of Winston-Salem. Public photo)*

In November 2015 Shirese Moore became the first African American woman and only the second woman to hold the position with the department. As Battalion Chief she visits each of the nine stations in the district, coordinates response on the scene of structure fires or other emergencies.

The Winston-Salem native applied in 1999 and passed the agility test and the requirements to become a firefighter. Climbing through the ranks, she became a fire engineer and then a Captain, a position she held for more than nine years.

Notable Moments

Shirese Moore was originally assigned to Central Fire Station #1, located on Marshall Street in Winston-Salem. At the time she was one of only seven women in the (WSFD) Winston-Salem Fire Department, but the women had to carry their own weight because there were no physical accommodations for them. Also due to lack of women firefighters Moore had to live and sleep under the same roof with nine white males at Central Fire Station #1, during the 24-hour shifts. To allow her privacy, the Fire Captain gave up his quarters. Out of 25 applicants, months of assessments and tests she was one four chosen for the position of Battalion Chief.

First Community Petition for African American Police Officer

The first consideration for an African American police officer in Winston began August 7, 1880 with an altercation between two African American women in the town. When the white police officer called to the scene could not break up this altercation, he called for assistance of other officers. One of the women arrested was roughly treated by these officers, greatly disturbing and enraging the crowd of African Americans at the scene, who threatened to intervene with the arrest. The police panicked, the militia was called and according to Forsyth County North Carolina Room librarian and historian Fam Brownlee, three black men, Horace Jeffers, James Henly, and Spencer Tunstall, were arrested. Charges against Jeffers were later dropped and the other two were released on $500 peace bonds.

After this incident, leading white citizens, including Superior Court

Judge Darius H. Starbuck, petitioned the town commissioners to appoint a black police officer as an additional policeman in the Town of Winston to avoid these incidents in the future. They named Israel Clement as the new officer. The commissioners responded that they had requested this of Mr. Israel Clement one year prior and he refused, saying he could not afford to take the job because he made more money as a tobacco roller at Hamilton Scales Tobacco Company than he would as a police officer.

The petition for an African American police officer was dismissed. However, nine months later in May 1881, Israel Clement did become the first African American elected to the Winston Town Commissioners.

First Hired African American Police Officer

John Joyce
(City of Winston-Salem Police Department. Courtesy of Winston-Salem African American Archive-vertical file)

John Joyce was the first hired African American officer. He was operating the Detention Center for African American boys from 1933 - 1940. Afterward, he worked as a watchman at the armory. In 1941, he joined the new plain clothes division of the police department, serving as a police informant.

The announcement of his appointment as special police officer occurred September 29, 1941 as part of a citywide festival held at Bowman Gray

Stadium. The announcement was made by then Police Chief Walter F. Anderson in the presence of 7,000 attendees (5,000 black and 2,000 white) at the festival.

Joyce became a part of the police department's uniform division in 1944. The 1945 Winston-Salem City Directory has him listed as a special officer of the City Police Department. He was joined in the uniform division by George Dillahunt, a former jitney owner and watchman for the Safe Bus Company.

First African American Police Officers

John Joyce and George Dillahunt
(Winston-Salem Police Department. Courtesy of Winston-Salem African American Archive-vertical file)

According to the City of Winston-Salem Government Meeting Notes, on March 7, 1919, a group led by prominent African American leader, F. M. Fitch, approached the Mayor and Board of Aldermen and suggested "if it was possible to secure one or two-colored men of the right type, and give them authority of an officer to work among the colored people only. He felt they might be able to ferret out crime that it would be impossible for a white officer to do.

The Mayor referred the request to the Police Committee and assured the colored people that it would be given serious consideration of the committee."[75] No African Americans were hired in Winston-Salem until October 1, 1941 when the department began the plain clothes division.

It was December 12, 1944, 25 years after F. M. Fitch approached the Mayor and Board, that the discussion of hiring uniformed African American police officers was revisited. The result was the hiring of John Joyce and George Dillahunt as the first African American hired police officers in the city. Both men were graduates of North Carolina A&T. John Joyce was the first hired black officer.

While Mayor Gold supported the use of black police officers, he allowed these officers to only serve in the black section of the city with restricted authority to that section. This meant these black officers were not allowed to arrest a white person without requesting the presence of a white officer whenever practical even for a capital offence or felony.

Separate facilities were provided for the new black officers at City Hall.

First African American Policewoman

Lillian Bonner
Left to right: Lillian Bonner, Hazel Venable, Ruth McClenny, and Catherine Holland *(Courtesy of the Bradshaw Estate and Winston-Salem African American Archive-vertical file)*

On October 1, 1952, the city of Winston-Salem hired its first four policewomen which included an African American woman named Lillian Bonner. She was the first hired African American policewoman in the city.

These women were hired in the only position afforded to women at the time who were sworn officers but did not carry weapons, they became meter maids.

In 1976, 26 years later, Lillian Bonner was promoted to Corporal and transferred to the Community Services Unit. This unit served as a liaison between the police department and the department of social services. She retired from the police department in 1982.

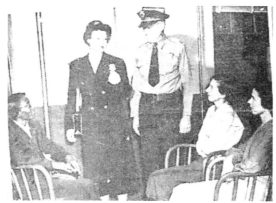

Lillian Bonner (seated left) with other policewomen in training
(Winston-Salem Journal. Courtesy of Winston-Salem African American Archive-vertical file)

First African American Police Captains

The first African American policemen to be promoted to the rank of Captain in Winston-Salem were Oliver D. Redd and J. A. Landon. They became the city's first African American Captains in 1978.

Oliver Redd had 10 years on the force and oversaw the motorcycle policemen, traffic women, and the school guards. "He was appointed assistant Chief of Police in Winston-Salem in June 1980." [76]

Despite earlier obstacles of city officials "who didn't feel blacks were competent enough to be officers," [77] in 1962, Landon and Redd became the department's first African American Sergeants after an Alderman exerted pressure on the police department. More than 10 years after joining the force. J.A. Landon received his first promotion to Detective Sergeant.

and with 26 years on the force, commanded District II, which covered the North East area of the city.

Oliver D. Redd(l) and J. A. Landon(r)
(Winston-Salem Chronicle. Courtesy of Winston-Salem African American Archive-vertical file)

O.D. Redd Assistant Chief of Police
(Winston-Salem Chronicle. Courtesy of Winston-Salem African American Archive-vertical File).

First African American Chief of Police

Chief Pat Norris
*(City of Winston-Salem Police Department.
City of Winston-Salem. Public photo)*

In 2004, 52 years after Lillian Bonner was sworn in as the first African American woman police officer, Patricia Norris, a native of Winston-Salem, became the first African American Chief of Police in the city and the second woman in that position. She was hired by the city in 1976, working as an aid in traffic engineering. She entered rookie school in 1977. As a patrol officer, she rose through the ranks in each geographical region of the city: "Crime Prevention unit, Criminal Investigation Division and Professional standards. She was sworn in as Police Chief in 2004."[78] She retired from the police force after serving four years as Police Chief.

In 2008, she became Chief of Police and Director of Public Safety at Winston-Salem State University. In 2011, Chief Norris became the first African American and first woman to serve as President of the North Carolina Association of Chiefs of Police (NCACP).

First African American Man to be Chief of Police

Chief Barry Roundtree
*(City of Winston-Salem Police Department.
City of Winston-Salem. Public photo)*

Barry Roundtree was sworn in as Winston-Salem Chief of Police on Sunday July 4, 2013 at City Hall. The oath was administered by Superior Court Judge Todd Burke.
A 25-year veteran of the Winston-Salem Police Department, he is the First African American man and only the second African American to hold this position.

Roundtree is an alumnus of Winston-Salem State University and University of North Carolina at Greensboro. He had been promoted to Assistant Police Chief by former Police Chief Pat Norris.

Roundtree and family *(Winston-Salem Chronicle. Courtesy of Winston-Salem African American Archive-vertical File)*

First Time Six African American Women are Chiefs of Police in Major North Carolina Cities

Catrina A. Thompson
*(City of Winston-Salem Police Department.
City of Winston-Salem. Public photo)*

Catrina A. Thompson became the 15th Chief of Police of Winston-Salem, North Carolina on September 1, 2017. When she assumed her position as Chief, she became part of North Carolina History. For the first time in the state of North Carolina there were six sitting African American women who were Chief of Police in major city police departments.

Thompson joined Cassandra Deck-Brown of Raleigh, C.J. Davis of Durham, Patrice Andrews of Morrisville, Gina Hawkins of Fayetteville and Bernette Morris of Morehead City in this position.
It should also be acknowledged that Winifred Bowen who became Chief of Police in the Town of Littleton, N.C. (in Halifax County) in 2014 and Sharon Hovis, who became Chief of Police in the Town of East Spencer in 2015, are also African American trailblazers, in this position.

First African American Sheriff's Deputy

Eldridge Austin
(Winston-Salem Journal. Courtesy of Winston-Salem African American Archive-vertical file)

The first African American to hold the office of Sheriff's Deputy was Eldridge Austin. Austin graduated from Atkins High School in 1951 and continued his education at Winston-Salem Teachers College (Winston-Salem State University) from 1951- 1954. He served four years in the United States Navy and received an honorable discharge.

When Austin began his career at the Sheriff's Department in Forsyth County on October 13, 1961, it was not integrated as was the city of Winston-Salem Police Department.

He worked in the department for 30 years rising through the ranks and was promoted to the rank of Captain in 1976 and in 1985 promoted to Major, a rank he held until his retirement in 1991. He was later followed by African American Deputies, Arcenure Griffin, and Garland Wallace Sr.

First African American Detective

Detective Walter Lee Long
(Winston-Salem Chronicle. Courtesy of Winston-Salem African American Archive-vertical file)

The first known African American Police Detective in Winston-Salem was Walter Lee Long. He moved to Winston in 1887 with his brother and became a Pullman porter, but he always wanted to be a policeman.

When he applied to the Winston police force in 1912, times in the town had changed since Israel Clement was offered Police Chief and Walter Long was told it was impossible for him to become part of the police force. Since he could not study law enforcement in North Carolina, he studied detective work with a West Virginia agency, came back to Winston four years later in 1916 and opened his own Private Detective Agency, devoting 25 years to crime detection.

Walter Long not only worked with law enforcement in Winston-Salem, he used his skills in other North Carolina cities and eastern seaboard states as far away as New York.

He was so revered as a law enforcement officer, that when he died in 1941, the Winston-Salem Journal recognized him in a full obituary article.

(Courtesy of Winston-Salem African American Archive-vertical file)

Walter Long Obituary Photo
(Winston-Salem Journal 1941. Courtesy of Winston-Salem African American Archive-vertical file)

First African American On Grand Jury

Throughout the southern states, African Americans were not always listed on local voter rolls which caused them to be excluded from serving on juries in local courts.
In Winston-Salem, "January 1938, a county grand jury contained a black for the first time since Reconstruction."[79]

First African American Postal Workers

Prior to 1910, Winston-Salem had three black postal carriers: John Hughes, Monroe Cuthrell, and Pete Easley. Other blacks with the postal service worked as custodians or in the maintenance department."[80]

In 1953, the Winston-Salem post office had two mail carriers and three mail handlers. One of the carriers was R. W. Hickerson.[81]

R. W. Hickerson
(Winston-Salem Chronicle. Courtesy of Winston-Salem African American Archive-vertical File)

First African American Civil Service Worker in North Carolina

Charles McLean
(Courtesy of the Bradshaw Estate)

When Charles McLean became Deputy Collector of Revenue in Greensboro, he became the first African American in the state of North Carolina to hold a civil service position.
Mr. McLean, a Winston-Salem resident, was a graduate of Winston-Salem State Teacher's College (WSSU). He worked in Winston - Salem as a teacher and a principal. He also served as State President of the National Association for the Advancement of Colored People (NAACP).

First African American City Employment Office Operator

Mollie A. Poag was the first African American operator of an employment office in the city. Her office was in the Bruce Building at the corner of Sixth Street and Patterson Avenue in Winston-Salem. The building was named for Dr. William H. Bruce, an African American physician who built the building in 1927.
There had been prior employment agencies in Winston that were run as businesses and were privately owned, such as the William Oates Employment Agency. William Oates was a tobacco worker who opened the employment agency in 1915. It was located on 108 1/2 E. Fourth Street Three years later in 1918, Davis C. Barnes managed the Labor Bureau and Real-Estate Company on 408 Church Street and William K. Penn was the proprietor of the Forsyth Employment Office at 925 N. Linden Street. Mollie Poag, "was the first such person in the city" [81] employed for such a position. She is listed in the 1933 city directory as a Clerk of the Colored Branch City Employment. One year later, she was listed as Manager of a city employment office in the 1934 City of Winston-Salem Directory. In the 1945 directory, she is listed as Interviewer in the U.S Employment Office (colored division).

Mollie Poag
(Courtesy of Society for the Study of Afro American History SSAH Calendar).

First African American Meter Reader

According to The Winston-Salem Chronicle, James Banks an employee of Duke Power was the first African American employed meter reader in the south.

First African American Census Takers

In 1950, "22 blacks served as census takers for the 1950 census. It was the first-time black census takers had ever been employed in Winston-Salem." [82]

First African American Municipal Hall Worker

In 1963, Bryska Peoples was the first African American elevator operator at Winston-Salem's City Hall. She also became the first African American to assume the task as clerk in the municipal building in the finance department on the second floor. Her replacement was another African American woman named Annie Bell (Jackie) Philson.

First African American Recreation Center Director

Rupert Bell became the first African American to serve as Recreation Center Director in Winston-Salem. Employed by the City of Winston-Salem's Recreation Department in 1945, he became the director at Happy Hill, Fourteenth Street and Skyland Recreation centers. As center director he organized and was the first director of the Golden Age Senior Citizens Club.

Bell retired from Parks and Recreation December 1976. February 1979. In recognition of his years of service and contribution to the city's recreation program, the Board of Alderman resolved to rename the East Winston Park, the Rupert W. Bell Park. The resolution was adopted on March 7, 1979.

The Rupert Bell Park and Neighborhood Center is located at 1501 Mt. Zion Place in Winston-Salem.

Notable Moments

Rupert Bell graduated from Columbian Heights High School where he was an all-around athlete. He excelled in basketball, baseball, and was an all-State running back. After graduation, he attended Winston-Salem Teachers College (Winston-Salem State University), North Carolina A&T State University and Clark University.

Rupert Bell Neighborhood Center
(City of Winston-Salem North Carolina Parks and Recreation Department. City of Winston-Salem. Public photo)

First African American Drafts Person

Albert Porter

Albert Porter (right) with Bryan (last name unknown) (left) and Conrad Whittington (center) Department of Public Works Department-Utilities and Engineering. (*Courtesy of Mr. Albert Porter*)

The first African American hired as a draftsperson for the city of Winston-Salem, North Carolina was Mr. Albert Porter, Jr. He was hired in April 1966.

First African American Assistant City Manager

John P. "Jack" Bond, III
(*Winston-Salem Chronicle. Courtesy of Winston-Salem African American Archive-vertical File*)

In 1972, John P. "Jack" Bond, III became "the city's first black assistant (deputy) city manager." [83] With his promotion, he became the highest ranking African American in Winston-Salem City Government. He had earlier served as Deputy Director of the Community Action Agency and the Executive Director of the Concentrated Employment Program under the Experiment in Self Reliance.

First African American City Personnel Director

Alexander Beaty
(Winston-Salem Chronicle. Courtesy of Winston-Salem African American Archive-vertical File)

On October 25, 1977, Alexander Beaty was named Winston-Salem's first African American Personnel Director. He assumed this position on November 1, 1977.
Six months after assuming the position of Personnel Director, Alexander Beaty was appointed Assistant City Manager in May 1978.
In "2009, the City of Winston-Salem opened the Alexander R. Beaty Public Safety Training and Support Center.
The $10.8 million, 146,000 square foot facility was built in the shell of the Thomasville Furniture Plant on Patterson Avenue, and consolidates police and fire training facilities for both rookie and in-service (continuing education) training. Beaty worked closely with the police and fire departments during his tenure."[84]

Beaty Building presentation
(Courtesy of Winston-Salem African American Archive-vertical file)

First African American Director of Winston-Salem/Forsyth County Library System

Sylvia Sprinkle-Hamlin
(Forsyth County. Public photo)

Sylvia Sprinkle-Hamlin is the first African American and woman to serve as Library Director of the Forsyth County Public Library System. She began her career as Department Head of the Children's Outreach in 1979 and held many positions in the library system prior to her position as Director in 2000.

Sprinkle–Hamlin is a native of Winston-Salem. She received a B.S. degree in Education from Winston-Salem State University and a master's degree in Library Science from Clark Atlanta University.

Notable Moments

Sprinkle–Hamlin is on various boards and associations in North Carolina, including the North Carolina American Library Association, the board of directors for the North Carolina Black Repertory Theatre Company and the Women's Leadership Council of United Way. She is also the executive producer of the National Black Theatre Festival, the biannual entertainment event that was founded by her late husband, Larry Leon Hamlin.

In 2014 she was appointed to the North Carolina Public Librarian Certification Commission by Governor Pat McCrory. This commission adopts rules and regulations to be followed in the certification of public librarians. In 2016 Sylvia Sprinkle-Hamlin was selected along with other notable North Carolinians by Governor McCrory, to be featured in the 2016 Heritage Calendar celebrating the African American Experience in North Carolina.

First Woman Appointed to the Board of Elections

Joan Cardwell
(Obituary. Public photo)

Joan Cardwell was the first woman and the first African American woman to be appointed to the Forsyth County Board of Elections in 1979. She later became Chairperson of this same board serving 27 years on the Forsyth County Board of Elections.

First African American City Attorney

In 2008, Angela I. Carmon became Winston-Salem's "first black female and first African American city Attorney. At the time of her appointment, she had been city assistant attorney since 1988." [85]

Angela I. Carmon
(Winston-Salem Chronicle. Courtesy of Winston-Salem African American Archive-vertical File)

First African American County Attorney

Davida Martin
(Winston-Salem Chronicle. Courtesy of Winston-Salem African American Archive-vertical file)

Davida Martin became the first African American county attorney for Forsyth County. She was appointed January 1, 1998.

First African American County Budget Director

Ronda Tatum
(Forsyth County. Public photo)

In 2009 Ronda Tatum was the first woman and first African American to become Forsyth County budget director. She later became the first woman to become assistant county manager in 2014.

First African American District Judges

Roland H. Hayes

(Journalnow file photo. Courtesy of Winston-Salem African American Archive-vertical file)

Roland H. Hayes, a graduate of Atkins High School and later Winston-Salem Teachers College became "Forsyth County's first black District Court judge. He was appointed by Governor James B. Hunt, Jr." [86] in 1984. December 3, 1996, 12 years after he was sworn in as District Court judge in Forsyth County, "he was appointed as chief district court judge in district 21 which serves Forsyth County, by the chief justice of the North Carolina Supreme Court Burley Mitchell, Jr." [87]

According to Layla Garms in the Winston-Salem Chronicle, February 14, 2013, Judge Hayes was re-elected several times by the people of the county until a state law that prohibits judges from serving after age 71 forced him to retire in 2002.

Loretta Biggs

Judge Loretta Biggs as district court judge
(Winston-Salem Chronicle. Courtesy of Winston-Salem African American Archive-vertical File)

Winston-Salem resident, Loretta Copeland Biggs is "the first black woman district court judge in the county and only the second woman. She was appointed to the judgeship February 2, 1987 by Governor James G. Martin. She was sworn in Friday, February 13, 1987 by Abner Alexander, the chief judge of Forsyth district court."[88] Biggs served in this position from 1987 to 1994. Prior to this she had served as an Assistant District Attorney in Forsyth County from 1984 to 1987. From 1994 to 2001, she worked in the United States Attorney's Office for the Middle District of North Carolina and served as Executive Assistant

United States Attorney She was later appointed to the North Carolina Court of Appeals in 2001 by then Governor, Jim Hunt. On September 18, 2014, President Barack Obama nominated Loretta Biggs to the vacant seat of James A. Beaty, Jr., to serve as a United States District Judge for the United States District Court for the Middle District of North Carolina.

She was sworn in on March 6, 2015 at the United States District Court, in Greensboro, NC and became the first African American woman to serve on a federal court in North Carolina.

Notable Moments

Loretta Biggs hearing before the Senate Judiciary Committee began on November 13, 2014 and she was reported to the full Senate for a vote on December 11, 2014. She was confirmed five days later, with her federal judicial commission coming on December 19, 2014.

Onto a New Bench

Loretta Biggs of Lewisville (left) smiles with Joan Cardwell, the chairwoman of the Forsyth County Board of Elections, as they celebrate Bigg's swearing-in as one of three new judges on the N.C. Court of Appeals.

Judge Loretta(left) Biggs and Mrs. Joan Cardwell Chairwoman of the Forsyth County Board of Elections, (right) after swearing in as a judge on the Court of Appeals *(Photo by Charles English- Winston-Salem Journal. Courtesy of Winston-Salem African American Archive-vertical file)*

Judge Loretta Copeland Biggs, left, Judge Loretta Biggs was sworn in on March 6, 2015 at the United States District Court, in Greensboro, NC as United States District Judge for the United States District Court for the Middle District of North Carolina. *(Photo by Erin Mizelle- Winston-Salem Chronicle. Courtesy of Winston-Salem African American Archive-vertical file)*

First African American State Legislative Nominee

William Crawford
(*Discover, Winston-Salem September 27, 1990. Courtesy of Winston-Salem African American Archive-vertical file*)

In 1964, William R. Crawford, was "the first black in North Carolina since reconstruction to be nominated to the state legislature." [89] He is also the second African American to serve as city Alderman after reconstruction.

Notable Moments
Crawford was a 1928 graduate of Columbian Heights High School in Winston-Salem. Crawford Park, at 4226 Oak Ridge Drive in Winston-Salem, is named in his honor.

Chapter Five

Businesses and Entrepreneurs

"Having gained their freedom but receiving no means by which to earn a living, not even the promised forty acres and a mule, many Negroes migrated from rural areas to the nearly industrializing cities of the New South in the late nineteenth century"[90] to become economically successful.

The industrial economy in Winston was exploding with labor-driven jobs in tobacco factories and the various textile mills. African Americans were a part of this growth. As they rose on this exploding economic tide, they were inspired to begin their own businesses and professions, which later included black owned restaurants, grocery stores, barber shops, teachers, ministers, physicians and lawyers, all of which helped to create the Black Business District in downtown Winston-Salem.

While it is not presently known when the first black business opened in Winston-Salem Forsyth County, it is known that most were "established because many white establishments refused to serve African Americans."[91] "This came about due to the social relationship created legally between blacks and whites primarily dealing with public associations such as hotels, restaurants, parks, neighborhoods and libraries. Therefore, out of necessity, African American entrepreneurs fulfilled a need."[92]

The First African American Businessman

According to the Winston-Salem Chronicle, the first black businessman may have been George Fries, keeper of the Ealing Saloon.

The First African American Blacksmith

According to the Twin City Sentinel, dated May 4, 1935, the first African American blacksmith was Mr. Hill.

African American Pioneer Gravediggers

Ben Ellis, Mr. Reynolds, and Mr. Davenport were early grave diggers in the city.

First African American Truck Driver for Local Company

Arthur Lee Holmes, is said to be the first African American in Winston-Salem to drive an 18-wheeler delivery truck for a company. Holmes was a driver for the local 7-Up bottling Company in Winston-Salem.

Early African American Hotel

Mrs. Nannie Bethell/Bethel operated the black hotel at 135 E. 7th Street," [93] in the 1880's. Hotel Bethel was the first modern and sanitary hotel. It was located near Pythian Hall. Nannie Bethell/Bethel was the wife of Lloyd Presbyterian Pastor William (W.L.) Bethell/Bethel. Their daughter was Mrs. Carrie Lanier, wife of Attorney J. S. Lanier.

First African American Merchants Association

The African American Chapter of the National Retail Merchants Association was established in January 1918 in Winston-Salem. One of its local initiatives was to raise funds for the support of World War I effort.

First African American Business District

Church and E. Third Streets
(Courtesy of Lester S. Davis. Winston-Salem African American Archive)

After the explosion of the African American population into the town of Winston in the late nineteenth century, services and businesses opened to serve this community. By the 1920's, there was a distinct African American business district in the town. Everything from medical offices, grocery stores, churches, community buildings and businesses were available in this area for African Americans in Winston.
The heart of this African American business district were the areas of Chestnut Street, East Seventh Street; Patterson (Depot Street) Avenue and South Liberty Street; Church and Third streets; and Third, Fourth, and Fifth Streets East of Main Street. It flourished in the 1920's through the 1960's until the heart was cut out and the area destroyed. This was due to urban renewal and gentrification, displacing most African American businesses as many of them moved or closed.

BUSINESSES AND ENTREPRENEURS

This downtown area was transmogrified, as it was overtaken by R.J. Reynolds Tobacco Company for parking lots and later by Wake Forest/Baptist Medical Center and other non-black owned businesses. This adversely changed the population and the look of this downtown area of Winston-Salem, thus closing an important historic chapter in Winston-Salem

First African American Barbers and Beauticians

Early Barbers

Rev. MacDonald

Rev. Douglas MacDonald operated a barbershop in 1877."[94] He died June 30, 1880.

Alex Gates

The proprietor of Gates' Hair Renewer Alex Gates, an early barber pioneer, "operated a barbershop in 1880 at the location where Zinzendorf Hotel was built."[95] He operated the shop with James Smith under the Merchants Hotel.

Ad for Gates Barbershop *(People's Press Dec. 1881. North Carolina Room Forsyth County Central Library)*

The First Sanitary or Tonsorial Barber

According to the Twin City Sentinel, May 4, 1935, John Austin operated the first sanitary (or tonsorial) barbershop in the city.

First African American Barbershop with Diverse Clientele

Crawford B. Cash (C.B. Cash), was the proprietor of the largest African American barbershop in the city "that also served white clientele. The shop was located on the corner of Fourth and Liberty Streets where the Pepper Building now stands. He and his son Artie moved to Third Street in the block where Wachovia now stands." [96] They ran advertising for the barbershop in the local paper and city directories.

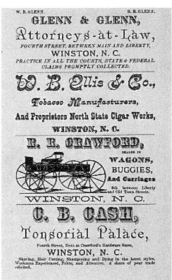

Ad for C.B. Cash Barbershop.
(turnercoswinston1889yonk_0018directory-cb cash. North Carolina Room Forsyth County Central Library)

BUSINESSES AND ENTREPRENEURS

First African American Beauty School and Licensed Beauty Care Operations

Annie R. Upperman began and managed the Upperman School of Hair Dressing and Beauty Parlors in Winston-Salem. "The school graduated licensed beauticians" [97] and enabled its graduates to become licensed beauty care operators.

The Upperman School was located on 408 Church Street in Winston-Salem. The first listing of the school was in the 1915 City Directory. Sally A. U. Yarbrough was proprietor of the facilities.

Irene Murray Douglas and Mozelle File graduated from the Upperman Beauty School and were among the first licensed beauty care operators in Winston-Salem. According to the 1930 City of Winston-Salem Directory, Mozelle E. File later became president of Electro-Magic Hair Grow Company and Elite Beauty Shoppe.

Pioneering African American Cosmetologist

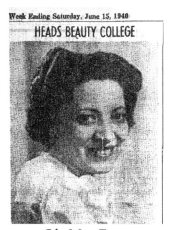

Ola Mae Forte
(Courtesy of Winston-Salem African American Archive)

La-Mae Beauty College opened in 1937 by Ola Mae Forte." [98] She was a graduate of Madame C. J. Walker's Beauty College in Chicago. La-Mae Beauty College was located at 602 North Patterson Avenue and paved the way for the graduates to obtain employment in beauty salons across the country.

The graduating class of the La-Mae Beauty School held at Hanes Memorial Church 1939-40. Left to right front row:Miss Margaret Glover,Mrs. Ester Carlson,Mrs. Ola M. Forte the founder and director of the school,Miss Isabelle Jackson,Miss Nettie Mae Lewis;second row left to right:Mrs. Sallie McCallum,Mrs. Estelle Wright,Mrs. Virginia S. Bouldini,Mrs. Zepplyn Averett,and Miss Hazel Pearson;Third row left to right:Mrs. Mertha Powell, Miss Anna Pearl Speas,Miss Tereatha Beaty,Miss Blanche Ragans and Miss Ethel Warren. *(Courtesy of the Bradshaw Estate)*

First African American Food Services

The First Grocery Store in East Winston

Albert "Pomp" Penry was reputed to be the owner of the first grocery store in East Winston." [99] He is listed as a grocer in the 1889-1890 Winston-Salem City Directory. He and his wife Maggie lived on Seventh Street where they also grew their grocery business.

The First African American Supermarket

Operated by O.S. Brown, The League Grocery Store was a black community project that could be called the "first supermarket for blacks in Winston-Salem in the 1920's." [100] The League Grocery Store had been a part of and served the African American community for a long time. It is listed in the 1904/05 City Directory on 515 E. Eighth Street.

African American Owned and Operated Super Market

Five Star Supermarket
(Courtesy of the Bradshaw Estate)

In 1997, the Five Star Supermarket opened in Winston-Salem as the only full service African American owned and operated supermarket in North Carolina. It was begun by Noble McGregor, Harry Hankins, Laverne DeJournette, Benjamin Penn, and Chris Wallace.

African American Ice Cream Manufacturer

Charles B. Wilson was owner and operator of the Adelphia Ice Cream Company located at 207 E. 7th Street.

He is listed in the 1918 City Directory as ice cream manufacturer and is the first African American owner and manufacturer of ice cream in the city.

First African American Cafe'

Robert Shoaf
(Courtesy of the Bradshaw Estate)

In 1928 Robert Shoaf was an entrepreneur who owned and operated the first café in the downtown garage. "He also owned and operated a bail bonding business and real estate agency." [101]

First African American Owned Soul Food Restaurant in Downtown Winston-Salem

Meta's Restaurant
(Facebook. Public photo)

The first African American owned restaurant in downtown Winston-Salem is Meta's Restaurant. Following in the footsteps of entrepreneurs Robert Shoaf and William Scales, Almeta Poole, owner and operator opened the restaurant in 1994.
The restaurant located on 102 w. 3rd street in downtown Winston-Salem gained popularity for serving authentic African American soul food.

First African American Entrepreneurs

General Barringer

General Barringer was an early entrepreneur in Winston. In the 1879 City Directory, he is listed as operating a lunch house. In 1884, he was proprietor of the American Hotel and Barbershop. It was located on Liberty between Fourth and Fifth streets. And in 1889, he owned a vegetable stand.
Barringer was a member of First Baptist Church, which was an integral part of the development of education for African Americans in Winston-Salem.

William Scales

William Samuel Scales was an uneducated tobacco worker who became one of Winston's most successful businessmen. "His wealth was estimated to be over $200,000."[102] In 1895, he owned a café and pool hall downtown. He established the first African American owned bonding agency, opened a night club, three theaters, (the Rex, the Lincoln and Lafayette), and was partner in the Howard-Robinson-Scales Funeral Home. In 1913, Mr. Scales became President of the Forsyth Savings and Trust Bank.

February 1923, William Scales, along with Aladine Robinson and R. W. Scales, purchased the Reynolds Plant to furnish building cement blocks. Made of crushed stone dust, the cement blocks were guaranteed not to hold dampness and would later return to solid rock. Named the Scales Cement Block Manufacturing Company, it was located at 4 Suggs Building.

The plant made fifteen types of cement from two to twenty-four inches. These building materials were important in aiding the building demand of Winston-Salem.

William Scales
(Courtesy of Linda Dark - Winston-Salem African American Archive)

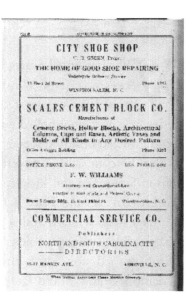

Ad for Rex and Lincoln Theaters *(Winston-Salem Journal. North Carolina Room Forsyth County Central Library)*
Scales Cement Block Company
(City Directory. North Carolina Room Forsyth County Central Library)

William Oates

William Oates operated the first of three early employment agencies in Winston before 1920.

In 1916, William Oates Employment Agency was located at 108 ½ East Fourth Street. This agency lasted until 1918. It was later replaced by The Labor Bureau managed by David C. Barnes, which was located on 408 N. Church Street where he also managed a Real Estate agency. And William K. Penn was the proprietor of Forsyth Employment office on 925 N. Linden Street.

Dr. William Bruce, Sr.

Dr. William (W.H) Bruce, Sr.
(Courtesy of the Bradshaw Estate)

Dr. William (W.H) Bruce, Sr. was a prominent local African American physician who originated and manufactured a drink in the 1930's known as Carbogin. The drink was very popular and to keep up with demand he had a large force of employees working through the day and sometimes through the night.

Carbogin was manufactured in the W. H. Bruce Building which was located at 560-562 Patterson Avenue. Built by Dr. Bruce in 1927, this office building housed a barbershop, and a pharmacy. In the 1930's it included the office of Doctors Humphry H. Hall, and Leroy Hall, as well as the Horton Branch of the Public Library.

The building was also the location of the office of Dr. W. H. Bruce, Jr. until the 1950's when he built the Women's Clinic on Highway 311. The Women's clinic later became the Turner Rest Home.

Carbogin advertisement
(*Courtesy of Winston-Salem African American Archive*)

K. Howard

Funeral Home Director *K. Howard*
(*Courtesy of the Bradshaw Estate*)

Mr. K. Howard "was one of the earliest African American undertakers in Forsyth County."[103] He started his business in the late 1890's. Years later he was joined by Mr. Aladine Robinson and Mr. William Scales, and created the Howard-Scales-

Robinson Funeral Home. The funeral home was located at the corner of Patterson Avenue and Seventh Street. It later became the Pyramid Barbershop. The building is now designated as a historical building.

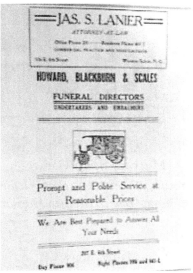

Ad for Howard, Blackburn, Scales Funeral Home
(City Directory. North Carolina Room, Forsyth County Central Library)

Ralph and Harvey Morgan

In 1918, Morgan and Scales Garage was owned and operated by African American entrepreneurs. "The Morgan Brothers, Ralph and Harvey later became the first Jitney owners and helped established the Safe Bus Company." [104]

Morgan/ Scales Garage
(Courtesy of Winston-Salem African American Archive and The Bradshaw collection/ Blanch Morgan Hopson)

James Shaw

(Courtesy of Mr. James Shaw)

Mr. James Shaw owned and operated the largest Gulf Dealership in the southeastern United States 1967-1970. In 1970 Mr. Shaw became the first African American major franchise tire dealer in the country and worldwide with a B. F. Goodrich franchise.

Mr. Shaw was not always a businessman. He was employed at R. J. Reynolds Tobacco Company sweeping floors. He was inspired to begin his own business after a conversation with a supervisor. The supervisor asked him how far he wanted to go in Reynolds. His reply was he'd like to be President. When he was laughed at and told he would never be President because he was black, Mr. Shaw decided to write his letter of resignation, and later told his wife, he would find something to do.

After tendering his resignation to R. J. Reynolds Tobacco Company, Mr. Shaw never looked back. An opportunity to buy a gas station (Gulf station) was presented to him and later the same occurred with B. F. Goodrich Tire Company. When he opened Shaw Tire, his franchise tire company, on Liberty Street, Reynolds Tobacco Company became his biggest customer.

Committed to the thriving of and creating better business for his community, Mr. Shaw joined the Better Business Bureau, and later became the first black person in the country to chair a Better Business Bureau.

Notable Moments

Mr. Shaw was appointed by the Governor, to the N.C. Aeronautics Council and founded the Tom Davis A.C.E Academy (Aviation Career Education) in Winston-Salem. It is part of a state wide program that trains middle and high school students in aviation.

Mr. Shaw was formally in charge of the Liberty CDC and became known as the Dean of Liberty Street. He worked to revitalize the area where he created so many firsts.

Mr. James Shaw and R.J. Reynolds Co. Vice-President
(Courtesy of Mr. James Shaw)

Jerry D. Watkins

Jerry D. Watkins was the first African American in Winston-Salem to own a new car dealership. He opened Jerry Watkins Cadillac-GMC on 7726 North Point Boulevard July 28, 1983.
In 1990 he is listed number 2 out of 100 black businesses across the United States in Black Business Magazine. His dealership was later replaced by North Point Chrysler Jeep Dodge Ram Dealership located on the same lot.

Watkins paved the way for Lloyd Leonard, an African American car dealer to open the Twin City Chrysler Plymouth dealership on Miller Street one year later.

Thomas P. Chestnut

The first African American owned printing company in the city was the People's Printing Company. In 1911 Thomas P. Chestnut is listed as proprietor of the People's Printing Company located on 106 E. Fourth Street in Winston.

John N. Brown later became manager of the People's Printing Company. John and his wife Grace lived on 803 Ida Belle Avenue in Columbia Heights. Ida Belle Avenue is now Stadium Drive.

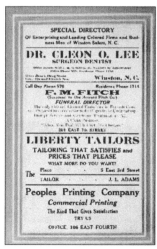

Ad for Peoples Printing Company, listed with other Black businesses.
(Winston-Salem 1912 directory. North Carolina Room, Forsyth County Central Library)

Largest African American Bookstore in the Southeast

The largest collection of African American books in the southeastern United States was located at Special Occasions bookstore. The bookstore was the operation of Ed and Miriam McCarter.
The business was located on Martin Luther King, Jr. Blvd from 1984 until 2011.

Special Occasions Book store
(Courtesy of the Bradshaw Estate)

First African American Owned Contract Office Furnishings

Tom Trollinger
(Courtesy of the Bradshaw Estate).

Thomas Trollinger, real estate broker, developer and a former Assistant Vice-President in purchasing with Wachovia Bank of North Carolina opened Contract Office Furnishings, Inc. in 1977.

This multimillion-dollar business was a full-service office furnishings dealership. It was the first African American owned and operated company of its kind in Winston-Salem.

Contract Office Furnishings represented over 200 manufacturers of office furniture and equipment. Some of its client references included, BB&T Financial, Philip Morris, Syngenta Crop Protection, Progress Energy, Glaxo Smith Kline, NCCU, and Winston - Salem State University.

Contract Office Furnishings building
(Courtesy of the Bradshaw Estate)

First African American Owned Shopping Center

William Brandon began the EastWay Plaza Shopping Center in 1992. Located off New Walkertown Road in Winston-Salem, it included 16 stores. It is the first and largest African American owned shopping center in Forsyth County.

EastWay Plaza
(Courtesy of the Bradshaw Estate)

African American Owned Early Educational Supply Company

The first early education supply company operated and owned by an African American in Winston-Salem was Peace Paper and School Supply. The company carried a full line of early childhood educational equipment from paper to playground equipment.

Owned by Jim Peace, it opened in 1987 and within one year, the company quickly gained customers from the Carolinas, Virginia, New York, New Jersey and Pennsylvania.

Jim Peace
Life as an entrepreneur *(Afro American newspaper July 26, 1988 googlenews)*

First African American Owned Marketing Company

(Courtesy of Lafayette Jones and Sandra Miller Jones)

In 1990 Segmented Marketing Services, Inc. (SMSI), opened its doors. It is the first African American owned marketing company in Winston-Salem. The company is owned by Lafayette Jones, a former executive with Proctor & Gamble, Johnson Publishing, ConAgra Foods and Kraft Foods and Sandra Miller Jones, a former marketing manager for Quaker Oats.

Sandra Miller Jones is the first African American Manager at the Quaker Oats Company and managed several of the company's franchises as well as the multi-million-dollar Quaker Oatmeal account.

The marketing firm has expertise in multicultural marketing and retailing and includes marketing managers and bilingual merchandising representatives in the top 20 African American and Hispanic markets nationwide. It is one of the most successful African American marketing firms in the country.

Notable Moments

Urban Call Marking and Publishing Inc is the Parent Company of SMSI Healthy Living Solutions Inc and Urban Call

Sandra M. Jones was the first African American woman to graduate Kellogg School of Business /North Western University. Kellogg is the number one school in marketing.

Lafayette Jones created the advertising for products such as mand-wich and marketing for Orval Redden Barker, and created the proud lady logo on black haircare products.

First African American Shipping and Packing Company

Eli Bradley
(Winston-Salem Chronicle. Courtesy of Winston-Salem African American Archive-vertical file)

The first African American owned and operated packing and shipping company in Winston-Salem is Eli's Pack and Ship.

Entrepreneur Eli Bradley a former expeditor with B/E Aerospace (formerly Fairchild Industries) and Sara Lee Corporation opened the company in 1990 and created a market in Winston-Salem, where one did not previously exist. The company gift-wraps , and, packs and ships items across the country and internationally.

Eli Bradley, a Winston-Salem State University Business degree graduate, got the idea for an independent packing and shipping company after a visit to Miami Florida where he saw an independent store that did this process. Returning to Winston-Salem, he opened his pack and ship company at 302-A South Stratford Road in the Thruway Shopping Center where it was known as Thruway's Packaging Store. He was the first African American tenant in the shopping center. Bradley later became the first African American tenant at Hanes Mall when he opened the first full packing and shipping services at the mall. This gave him a pack and shipping company in two locations, and acquired a vast clientele which included Dr. Maya Angelou.

Eli's Pack and Ship is the oldest authorized shipping facility for UPS, FedEx, the U.S. Postal Service, DHL, and ABF Freight in the city of Winston-Salem.

Youngest Member of the Winston-Salem Chamber of Commerce

Elasya Jessup
(Black Business Ink. Courtesy of Winston-Salem African American Archive-vertical file)

The youngest member in the history of the Winston-Salem, North Carolina Chamber of Commerce is young entrepreneur Elasya Jessup. She is the owner of Elasya B's Candy Tree, a candy store which opened May 3, 2013 at 500 W. Fourth Street in the Lowey Building in downtown Winston-Salem.

Jessup made local history when at the age of 9 years she became an honorary member of the Winston-Salem Chamber of Commerce in May of 2013, making her the youngest member in the history of this organization and first African American of her age.

Due to her age Elasya is helped in her business by her parents, both named Shannon; her older sister, Aria Johnson and brother, Austen.

Notable Moments

The variety of treats sold at the store includes candy apples, cotton candy and candy creations in the shapes of trees and sundaes, gift baskets, beverages and dipped pretzels.

She began her business by selling candy apples door to door in her neighborhood in High Point, North Carolina, and later at the Fall Bazaar at Whitaker Elementary school in Winston-Salem. Requests continued after the event and the family opened a holiday kiosk at Hanes Mall. It became so profitable they needed to expand to a larger space which led them to the Lowey Building in downtown Winston-Salem.

Elasya B's Candy Tree Fourth Street view
(Facebook. Public photo)

First African American Owned Drug Store

In 1900, pharmacist William A. (W. A.) Jones, operated "the first drug store," [105] for African Americans in Winston. The W.A. Jones drugstore contained modern conveniences such as a soda fountain and electric fans. He operated his business in conjunction with his brother, Dr. J.W. Jones' Medical office on Main Street.

Dr. John Wise Jones grew up on the plantation of Dr. Beverly Jones, a white physician in Bethania. He developed his interest in medicine by helping the physician on the farm.

William Jones later moved his business to 110 1/2 E. Fourth Street across from the municipal building. He was later joined by drugstores operated by Doctors H. H. Hall and William Henry Bruce located on Patterson Ave. and Sixth Street, Rufus Hairston and Cicero Neely on Church Street and Dr. J. C. Williamson on Eighth Street and Ridge Ave.

W.A. Jones drugstore
(Courtesy of Forsyth County Public Library Photograph Collection, Winston-Salem, NC)

First Insurance Company for African Americans

Winston Mutual Life Insurance Company began as the Winston Industrial Association. The vision for the Winston Industrial Association began in 1897 in the thoughts of schoolteacher, Robert W. Brown. His plan was to have an economic plan of security for black people, as well as providing "health and accident insurance to black tobacco workers."[106] After Mr. Brown secured the help of physician J. W. Jones, Atty. J. S. Fitts and grocer, Jim Ellington, a charter was granted to the Winston Industrial Association on "August 6, 1906, for the purpose of paying benefits in case of death, sickness, and disability. The first policy was issued August 21, 1906"[107] to Susan Ann Snyder.

The founders of the Winston Industrial Association were: Dr. J. W. Jones, John A. Blume, R. W. Brown, J. W. Lewis, J. C. McKnight, C. H. Jones, George W. Hill, L. L. Johnson, Dr. W. A. Jones, Atty. J. S. Fitts, J. A. Ellington, Wentz Rucker and Atty. J.S. Lanier.

Winston Mutual Life Insurance Company on 5th Street
(Photo taken by Chenita B. Johnson)

The company continued to grow and in 1915 it merged with the Mountain City Mutual Company of Asheville and became the Winston Mutual Life Insurance Company.

The Winston Mutual Life Insurance Company moved to East Fifth Street in 1969. In 1985 it merged with Golden State Mutual Life Insurance Company of Los Angeles.

Winston-Mutual *first location, main office 1957.* Winston-Mutual 5th Street.
(Courtesy of Lester S. Davis. Winston-Salem African American Archive)

First Licensed Stenographic Office

Naomi McLean was founder, owner and director of McLean's Stenographic and Tutoring service located on Patterson and Sixth Street, in the Bruce Building in Winston-Salem. When the school opened in July 26, 1939 it was the "first and only licensed stenographic office." [108]

McLean's Stenographic and Tutoring service
(Courtesy of the Bradshaw Estate)

Mrs. McLean received her business certification from the Phyllis Wheatly Institute in the city and her bachelor's degree in business administration from Central Christian College in Huntington West Virginia. She continued her educational training at Winston-Salem Teachers College.

Mrs. McLean opened the Star Stenographic School of Business on September 17, 1941. The Star Stenographic School was an integrated school even in the 1940's. White students were attracted to the school due to Mrs. McLean's professional reputation. Thirty-Five years later, on April 1976, Mrs. McLean hosted a recognition program at Rising Ebenezer Baptist Church "honoring graduates of the school from 1943 through the 1970's for outstanding service maintaining good records, doing efficient work and being promoted to higher positions." [109]

When the school closed its doors in 1987 it had operated for forty-eight years with an "A" rating.

McLean's Stenographic and Tutoring service
(AC Phoenix Newspaper)

August 31, 1963 graduating class Star Stenographic School of Business
(Courtesy of Jacquelyne B. Barber)

African American Electronics Institute

Delwatts Radio and Electronics Institute was started by African American ex-soldiers during the late 1940's. This institute also had summer sessions for persons interested in preparing for jobs in radio electronics." [110] Curtis Todd was President, Robert Brown Vice-President and Winston Moore was Secretary-Treasurer.

The institute was located at 1437 39 ½ E. Fourteenth Street in Winston-Salem.

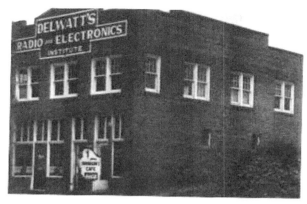

Delwatts Radio and Electronics Institute
(Courtesy of the Bradshaw Estate)

First African American Clothiers

African American Hat Manufacturer

The Brown Derby Hat Works was the only black owned hat manufacturer in the state in 1935." [111] The company was located on 314 Patterson Avenue in the W. L. Robinson building and was under the management of Tom Neely, Willie "Chic" Motley, and B.O. Sanford. The building currently is still part of the 300 block of Patterson Avenue and between 4th and 3rd streets.

First African American Modern Dry Cleaners

DeWitt Livingston Morgan (b. 1893-d.1964), established the Morgan-Hoffman Cleaners which was "one of the first black cleaners to use modern equipment." [112] Initially the business opened in 1909 on Third Street as Morgan Cleaning and Dye Company. In 1914, he opened as Morgan Cleaning and in 1923 it became Morgan-Hoffman. Morgan did not have a partner he was always listed at the register of deeds as the sole proprietor of his businesses. According to his son David Morgan, VI, the name Hoffman came from the name on the new equipment used in his establishment. Morgan was given a discount on the purchase of equipment by advertising the company's name.

BUSINESSES AND ENTREPRENEURS

D.L. Morgan
(Winston-Salem Chronicle. Courtesy of Winston-Salem African American Archive-vertical file)

Morgan opened plants in various parts of the city including 234 N. Cherry Street, 509 Glenn Avenue as well as downtown in the 1930's and employed many black workers. Although the cleaners had a reputation for fine cleaning throughout the city, because he was African American, Morgan could not do business on the West side of town. To alleviate this problem, Morgan opened "Victory Dry Cleaners staffed by whites," [113] but all actual cleaning work was still done at the Morgan Dry Cleaning branch.

 Victory Cleaners ad *(Winston-Salem Journal Sentinel. North Carolina Room Forsyth County Central Library)*

First African American Men's Furnishings Business

The Camel City Clothing Company, managed by Ernest Johnson, was established "by Negroes for Negroes."[114] This retail business for men's furnishings, was located at 17 E. Third Street, in 1935. In 1945 it was located at 102 E. Third Street.
The May 24th, 1935 issue of the Twin City Sentinel stated it was the only business of its kind established exclusively for Negroes. The April 24th, 1938 Winston-Salem Journal and Sentinel stated it as the largest business of its kind in North Carolina. It also is noted that Ernest B. Johnson was the first black drafted to leave Winston for foreign fields.

The First African American Shoemaker and Bootmaker

The first African American listed as owner of a shoemaking business in Winston is James S. Edwell. He is listed in the 1879 Winston Business Directory as a shoemaker. His Boot and shoemaker shop was located on Main and 4th Street.

First African American Pilot at Piedmont Airlines and Owner of an Airline

The first African American pilot for Piedmont Airlines in Winston-Salem and the first African American to own and operate an air service in the United States is Warren H. Wheeler. He began his aviation career with Piedmont Airlines in 1966 and was later followed by William Wilkerson, Jr. (Bill Wilkerson) in 1989. Wilkerson was the second black person to earn the rank of Captain with the company. He flew 15 years for Piedmont Airlines, which became a part of US Airways.

Warren Wheeler was born in Durham, North Carolina on October 1, 1943 to John H. Wheeler, and Selena Warren Wheeler.

BUSINESSES AND ENTREPRENEURS

Warren H. Wheeler
(Courtesy of Winston-Salem African American Archive-vertical file)

His love of flying came very early in life when his sister, who had taken flying lessons before him, took him on a plane ride. He began taking flying lessons with the dream of becoming a pilot. He received his private pilot's license at age 15. After he graduated High School, Wheeler attended North Carolina A&T State College in Greensboro, North Carolina, (N.C. A&T State University) to study electrical engineering. He left after his first year at the University, to continue his aviation training and pursue his goal to receive a commercial pilot's license.

Due to racial segregation in North Carolina as well as the rest of the South, Warren Wheeler had to continue his aviation education at the American Flyers School in Ardmore, Oklahoma. There he was the school's first African American student and graduate.

In 1962 at the age of 19, he was fully accredited from the American Flyers School with his commercial license and licensed with his multiengine rating to fly multi- engine planes.

Although he had his credentials from a topflight training school, Wheeler found that jobs for African Americans were few and that he lacked adequate hours of flying experience to obtain a position with a major airline. To obtain the flight hours to meet the requirements for employment by the major commercial airlines, Wheeler opened his own flying school in 1962 at the Horace Williams Airport in Chapel Hill.

With the financial backing of his parents Wheeler purchased his first small aircraft and began instructing white students from the University of North Carolina at Chapel Hill. In addition to the school, he began a charter service.

Warren Wheeler successfully operated the school and charter service for three years to acquire enough flight hours to qualify for employment from a major airline however, no one would hire him because of his race. He was not considered for an application from a major company until Governor Terry Sanford recommended him to Tom Davis, President of Piedmont Airlines. Sanford had flown on charter flights with Warren Wheeler as a pilot while he was governor. Davis allowed Wheeler to take the pilots exam for the airline. He passed and became qualified as a pilot.

In March 1966, at the age of twenty-two, he became the first African American and one of the youngest pilots that Piedmont Airlines hired. In 1989 Warren Wheeler became a pilot for US Air, the successor to Piedmont Airlines. Two years later he became chair of Virginia's aviation board. He retired with US Air in 1995, but he continues to operate Caribbean Wings, servicing clients in the Virgin Islands.

Notable Moments

In 1969 Warren H. Wheeler, established Wheeler Flying Service, the first African American owned and operated air service in the United States. At its peak, the airline flew more than 40,000 passengers annually in chartered flights, with approximately 80% of his business being white businessmen. His business grossed $380,000 in 1975 due to the contracts from companies throughout the Raleigh-Durham and Research Triangle Park area.

The company grew from 208 passengers a month to more than 1,000 passengers each month. With the increased revenue, Wheeler was able to purchase a building, computerized facility, and an aircraft maintenance hangar allowing for the addition of several planes to the fleet. He then changed the company's name to Wheeler Airlines.

Wheeler Airlines provided nationwide service for his clientele. His flights competed directly with Piedmont Airlines and won.

He scheduled regular flights from Raleigh-Durham to Greenville and Charlotte, North Carolina; Newport News, Virginia; Richmond, Virginia; and New York's LaGuardia Airport. The airline also served smaller eastern North Carolina towns such as Kinston, New Bern, Nag's Head, and Wilson.

In 1983-Wheeler created Caribbean Wings as a subsidiary of Wheeler Airlines. It was the only minority-owned airline in the United States for 22 years until it closed in 1991. In that time from 1969 to 1991-Wheeler trained numerous African American pilots, copilots, and aircraft mechanics with the goal of encouraging more minorities to seek employment in the field of aviation. One such person was Jill E. Brown-Hiltz, who became the first black woman pilot of a major airline. She joined Wheeler Airlines starting at the ticket counter, she worked her way up to flying as a copilot with the airline logging more than 800 flight hours, to qualify for a commercial airline. In 1978, Brown made history when she was hired by Texas International Airport and became the first African American woman to fly with a major U.S. commercial airline.

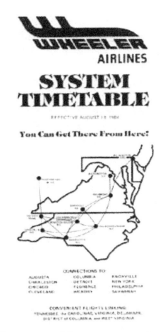

Wheeler Airline timetable cover, 1984.(*Public Domain*)

First African American in Management at R. J. Reynolds Industries

Marshall B. Bass became the first African American hired in management at R J Reynolds industries, formally R, J. Reynolds Tobacco Company. A native of Goldsboro, NC, Bass was hired at Reynolds in 1968 after a long and illustrious military career. He rose through the management ranks as Manager personnel development 1968-1970, Corporation manager personnel development 1970-1976, Corporation director personnel development, 1976-1982, and the first African American elected Sr. Vice President, in 1982.

After a 23-year career Bass retired in 1991 as an elected senior vice president for global public relations for the company, RJR Nabisco Inc. In that capacity he was responsible for managing worldwide public and governmental affairs issues for the corporation. At that time RJR Nabisco had operational facilities and marketed its products in over 123 countries around the globe.

Notable Moments

Marshall B. Bass was a community and civic minded individual belonging to various organizations and boards, including being president of Marshall B. Bass & Associates, Trustee at N C A & T State University, Treasurer, Winston-Salem State University enhancement campaign and licensed lay leader at St. Stephen's Episcopalian Church.

Chapter Six

Banks and Financial Institutions

Two decades after the Civil War, African Americans were no longer just sharecroppers or farmers; they were factory workers, domestic workers, business owners, and homeowners. They were highly successful individuals and a large working class, who were building a community and creating wealth. Despite this wealth creation, discrimination in white established financial institutions continued to deny loans and made it difficult to obtain startup funds.

Due to this discrimination of white owned banks and lending institutions financial institutions were created by African Americans to aid the growing community.

BANKS AND FINANCIAL INSTITUTIONS

The First African American Building and Loan

The first organization to help encourage and increase black homeownership was the Twin City Building and Loan Association, later The People's Building and Loan Association. Begun in 1903 it is said to be the reason for the segregation ordinance passed in 1912, as many whites felt black citizens were achieving too much too fast.

In 1904 the city directory listed S.G. Atkins as President, R.W. Brown as Secretary and J. H. Brim as Treasurer. It was located on 315 ½ Main Street. In 1911 it moved to Sixth Street on the corner of Depot Street and S. G. Atkins was again President, A. J. Brown was Secretary and T. H. Hooper was Treasurer. Realtor Charles H. Jones also served as Treasurer of the Building and Loan. By 1923 the Twin City Building and Loan had $50,000 in capital. In 1924, it was listed as The People's Building and Loan Association and it was listed with a phone number, 877. J. S. Hill was listed as President and A.J. Brown as Secretary-Treasurer.

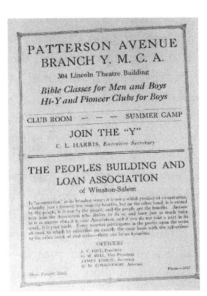

Ad for The Peoples Building and Loan in 1928 Yearbook
Columbian Heights High School
(*Courtesy of Winston-Salem African American Archive-vertical file*)

The First Full Service African American Bank

Forsyth Savings and Trust Company
(Courtesy of the Bradshaw Estate)

The first full service African American bank in Winston-Salem was The Forsyth Savings and Trust Company. Organized by a group of professional African American men, the bank was located at 408 N. Church Street and opened May 11, 1907 as a full-service institution with $1 million in capital.

James S. Hill was the bank's first President, Charles H. Jones, the 1st African American real estate broker, was Vice-President, and Francis (Frank) M. Kennedy, lawyer and notary public, was Cashier. The Board of Directors consisted of Simon Green Atkins, George Reynolds, and J. H. Turner. By 1908 John A. Blume became Vice-President.

The company later bought the assets of the Citizens Bank and Trust which was operated by local physician Dr. J. W. Jones, and Mr. J. S. Hughson The Forsyth Savings and Trust Company prospered and by 1928 had a business volume of over $12 million. The bank "served the negro community until it became one of the casualties of the Great depression."[115] However, the Board of Directors was able to save the depositors funds "when the bank was consolidated with Wachovia Bank and Trust." [116] While this saved the depositors funds it caused personal loss of property and assets of the directors.

First African American Credit Union

W. M. Nesby
(Courtesy of Winston-Salem African American Archive)

The Victory Credit Union was "chartered on April 18, 1946" [117] as the first black Credit Union in Winston-Salem. It was organized and founded by W. M. Nesby.

He and other credit unions organized in North Carolina were started under a program in 1937 by the North Carolina Agricultural Department in the belief that blacks needed such services more than any other group.[118] The Credit Union Began with five members and $52.25 in assets, and within 10 years the credit union grew to over $590,000.

The Victory Credit Union in Winston-Salem later became a part of Truliant Credit Union.

First African American Chamber of Commerce

The first Black Chamber of Commerce was created in the 1940's. It included doctors, lawyers, bankers, principals, plumbers, funeral directors and insurance agents.

Officers were Aladine Robinson, Dr. Joseph Walker, Attorney W. Avery Jones, Albert H. Anderson, and Dr. J. D. Quick.

AFRICAN AMERICAN FIRSTS

The Chamber Officers Front left to right: *Aladine Robinson, Dr. Joseph Walker, Standing Left to Right: Attorney W. Avery Jones, Albert H. Anderson, and Dr. J. D. Quick (Courtesy of the Bradshaw Estate)*

First African American Bank Manager

J.J. Sansom, Jr.
(Public photo)

In 1952 James Joseph Sansom, Jr. (sometimes misspelled as Sampson) accepted a position with Wachovia Bank and Trust Company in Winston-Salem, at its Third Street Branch, becoming the first African American manager for a neighborhood bank branch of a major financial institution. This was the first time in Winston-Salem as well as in the country, where African Americans operated in management of a major banking company outside of the black community.

J. J. Sansom was an experienced Durham bank official and a law instructor at North Carolina College (North Carolina Central) in Durham. He began his banking career in 1939 at Mechanics and Farmers Bank. "He returned to Mechanics and Farmers in 1958 as Vice President of the Raleigh Branch. Later he became Senior Vice President and succeeded John Wheeler as President and Chairman of the Board in 1978. He officially retired in 1987 but continued to serve as a consultant for the bank." [119]

Post card of the interior of the Third Street Bank office
(Courtesy of Winston-Salem African American Archive)

First African American Woman Bank Manager

Georgia Smith became the first African American woman to become branch manager of a bank in Winston-Salem. In 1975 she became manager at the Wachovia Bank and Trust Company north office on the corner of North Patterson Avenue and Glenn Avenue.

A Winston-Salem native, Smith graduated from the Star Stenographic School of Business in 1944 and later the American Institute of Banking. She began her career at Wachovia Bank in 1958 as a teller at the branch on Church Street.

The Church Street Branch moved to the corner of Third and Church Street and became widely used by African Americans in the city due to its proximity to the bus stop. The walk from the stop was shorter than walking up the hill to the old bank.

Mrs. Georgia Smith
(Winston-Salem Chronicle January 24, 1976. Courtesy of Winston-Salem African American Archive-vertical file)

Smith became Secretary to the Time Payment officer and named Assistant Manager in 1971. In 1973 she became a Personal Banker.
On March 19, 1990, the Wachovia Bank building on the corner of North Patterson and Glenn Avenues was renamed the Black-Phillips-Smith Government Center in honor of Mr. George Black, the renowned brickmaker and mason, Mr. Garret E. "Roy" Phillips and Mrs. Georgia M. Smith, both of whom are retirees of Wachovia Bank and Trust Company.

Plaque of George Black, Garret Phillips and Georgia Smith Located on front entry wall at Black-Phillips-Smith Government Center 2301 N. Patterson Avenue. *(Photo taken Chenita B. Johnson)*

Chapter Seven

Attorneys

Black lawyers were not permitted to practice law in North Carolina until after the Civil War, and these early lawyers acquired their legal education by being apprentices in the offices of white lawyers. Howard University (Washington D.C.), opened its law school January 6, 1869, and began to train African American lawyers. Shaw University (Raleigh North Carolina) opened its law school in 1888 being the first school in North Carolina to offer legal training to African Americans. [120]

J. S. Lanier
(Courtesy of the Bradshaw Estate)

First Africans American Admitted to the Forsyth County Bar Association

(Winston-Salem Journal July 18, 1963. Courtesy of Winston-Salem African American Archive-vertical file)

According to the July 18th, 1963 Winston-Salem Journal, the Forsyth County Bar Association made state history when for the first time it admitted nine African American Attorneys to an unqualified membership. The requirement was payment of annual dues.

All attorneys in the state of North Carolina had to be members of the North Carolina State Bar, Inc. but not necessarily county associations. The decision of the executive board was almost unanimous having two decenters George W. Brady who spoke against it and Harold R. Wilson who submitted his resignation from the organization.

The nine African American attorneys admitted into the Forsyth County Bar Association July 17th, 1963 were: Richard C. Erwin, Jr., the first attorney admitted; Harold Kennedy and Annie Brown Kennedy the only husband and wife attorneys in the area; Curtiss Todd; H.O. Bright; Oliver T. Denning; W. Avery Jones; Hosea V. Price; and H. Glenn Davis the youngest black attorney in the area at the time.

While these attorneys were members of the Southeastern Lawyers' Association, which was a professional group of black lawyers from North Carolina, South Carolina and Virginia, prior to this action, African American Attorneys in Winston-Salem Forsyth County had no state or county organization.

R. Erwin
H. Price
A. Kennedy
C. Todd
H. Kennedy
H. Bright
O. T. Denning
W. Jones

H. Glenn Davis (photo not available)
(Courtesy of the Bradshaw Estate and Winston-Salem
African American Archive)

The First African American Attorney

John Shepherd Fitts
(Winston-Salem Journal Oct. 7, 1923. Courtesy of Winston-Salem African American Archive-vertical file)

John Shepherd Fitts was the first Africa American attorney in this city. He was a member of the First Baptist Church in Winston. Originally from Georgia, Fitts attended and graduated from Shaw University in Raleigh, NC April 20, 1891 and began his law practice in Winston between 1892 - 1893.

According to the Winston-Salem Journal October 7th, 1925, J.S. Fitts applied for his license, to the North Carolina Supreme Court, along with white and black candidates and while all but 16 whites failed, he was the only black candidate to pass.

Fitts recruited Shaw alumni, James Lanier to come to Winston to practice law. Both attorneys were well trained and competent; however, "they were not allowed to try cases in the Superior Court without seeking the assistance of white attorneys." [121] This did not impede their progress as both became financially successful and well respected. When James Lanier died in 1960, he was the oldest African American attorney in North Carolina. The Winston-Salem Journal wrote an editorial in his honor.

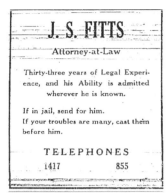

Left to right: J. S. Fitts advertisement *(Winston-Salem Journal Oct. 7, 1923. Courtesy of Winston-Salem African American Archive-vertical file)*
J.S. Lanier *(Winston-Salem Journal. Courtesy of Winston-Salem African American Archive-vertical file)*

First African American Editor of the Yale Law Journal

Jasper Alton Atkins
(WSSU Archives-University Photograph Collection. Winston-Salem State University Archives-C.G. O'Kelly Library).

The son of educators, Dr. Simon Green Atkins and Oleona Glenn Pegram, Jasper Atkins was probably the first African American person from Winston-Salem to finish law school, graduating from Yale University law school in 1922. After graduating from Slater Academy (later WSSU) in 1915., he attended Fisk University in Nashville, TN, where he graduated magna cum laude in 1919.

As a student at Yale, Atkins was a member of the debating team and a law library monitor, where he directed the indexing of 31 volumes of the Law Journal. He was also the first African American elected to serve on the board of editors of The Yale Law Journal and the first African-American elected to the Order of Coif, the national honor society. In 1922, Atkins graduated cum laude and was the first African American to graduate with honors from Yale Law School.

Jasper Atkins practiced law in Muskogee, OK, and later in Texas. There, he was editor of the Houston Informer and Texas Freeman, but in 1936 due to the serious nature of his brother's illness, he returned to Winston-Salem to take the position of Executive Secretary of Winston-Salem Teachers College.

First African American Woman Attorney

Ann B. Kennedy with sons Harvey and Harold-1954 article
(Courtesy of Winston-Salem African American Archive-vertical file)

Annie Brown Kennedy became a woman of firsts after passing the bar in 1954 and beginning her law practice. While she was the second African American woman to practice law in the state of

North Carolina, she became the first African American woman to practice law in Forsyth County, the first and only woman to serve as President of the Forsyth County Bar Association, and the first African American woman elected to the NC General Assembly in 1982.
Ann Brown Kennedy has also become the first woman to be inducted into the Bar Associations General Practice Hall of Justice.

First African American Admitted to the Forsyth County Bar Association and the First African American Representative in the N.C. General Assembly

Judge Richard Erwin
(Courtesy Bradshaw Estate)

Attorney Richard Erwin was the "first Black lawyer admitted to the Forsyth County Bar Association and became the first Black to serve as president of that association." (122)
In 1977 Richard C. Erwin became the first black Legislator to represent Forsyth County in the North Carolina General Assembly, the first to win a state-wide election in North Carolina, and he also became the first African American judge on the North Carolina Court of Appeals. He was appointed by President Jimmy Carter to serve as judge of the US District Court for the middle district of North Carolina.

Chapter Eight

Physicians and Medical Institutions

Prior to 1900 there were very few doctors available in Winston or Salem, and any medical facilities or services that were available were not accessible to African American residents.
The Twin City Hospital, at its beginning, barred African Americans from receiving services until July 29, 1912 when African Americans were admitted but in small numbers. In 1914, one year after the consolidation of Winston and Salem, the New City Hospital reserved only 66 of its 225 beds for African American patients, and African American physicians were not given admitting privileges in the hospital, barring them from servicing these patients. Even in 1921, when a north ward was added to the hospital to accommodate more African American patients, African American doctors could admit their patients but were not able to service them and any surgery performed on these patients was by white surgeons.

African American doctors in Winston-Salem were relegated to practicing in their offices or their patients' homes. Yet, this oppressive environment did not deter these medical professionals. They found ways to use their skills to serve their community.

There were physicians such as Dr. Alexander Hamilton Ray, who opened a private hospital in the 1920's named Ray's Hospital, located at Thirteenth and Ridge Avenue. After it was destroyed by fire it was rebuilt and renamed Young Memorial Hospital and Dr. J. C. Williamson had a hospital on the South West corner of Vargrave and Stadium Dr. in Winston-Salem.

Dr. Alexander Hamilton Ray
(Courtesy of Winston-Salem African American Archive-vertical file)

PHYCISIANS AND MEDICAL INSTITUTIONS

Alexander Hamilton Ray Hospital site at the intersection of what once was Thirteenth Street and Ridge Avenue. It was listed in Winston-Salem's city directories from 1920 to 1925 and was a 15-20 bed hospital run by Dr. Alexander Hamilton Ray. The hospital wasn't too far from the current Highland Avenue. Across the street is Kennedy School and the open lot next to it is the future site of The Career Center of Winston-Salem Forsyth County Schools. *(Courtesy of Special Collections & University Archives/Wake Forest University)*

Alexander H. Ray Health Center during construction, c. 1952. Named in honor of Dr. Alexander H. Ray, this facility was completed in 1952 on the campus of Winston-Salem State University.
(WSSU Archives-University Photograph Collection. Winston-Salem State University Archives-C.G. O'Kelly Library)

First African American Physician In North Carolina

Dr. James Shober
A photograph of James Francis Shober published ca. 1900
(Image Ownership: Public Domain BlackPast.org)

Dr. James Shober (b. Aug. 23, 1853 - d. Jan. 1, 1889) is known as the first official African American physician with a medical degree in the state of North Carolina. He was born in or near Salem, the Moravian town just outside of Winston, North Carolina (later Winston-Salem). His mother was an enslaved eighteen-year-old mulatto named Betsy Ann Waugh (1835-59). According to William S. Powell of NCPedia, there is circumstantial evidence suggesting Betsy Ann was the daughter of John H. Schulz, a white resident of the town, and that although she was enslaved, "Shober's father was a white man named Francis Edwin Shober," [123] a twenty-two year old resident of the Salem Moravian community who had recently graduated from the law school at the University of North Carolina. He became a businessman, who later was elected to the legislature .and was also co-founder of the first Sunday school in North Carolina.

Betsy Ann married an enslaved man named Davis Shober (1822-67) who was thirteen years her senior and owned by a relative of Francis Shober. When James Shober was about six years old, his mother Betsy Ann died, and he was sent to the Waugh Plantation (which became Waughtown

N.C., and now Winston-Salem, N.C.) to live with his grandmother.
Dr. James Shober, "graduated 2nd in his class from Lincoln University in Oxford, Pennsylvania in 1875, with an A.B. Degree. He then went to Howard University's School of Medicine and was of 48 graduates, the only one from N.C."[124] After receiving his M.D. from Howard University in 1878, Shober returned to North Carolina. He married Anna Maria Taylor in 1881, and practiced in Wilmington, N.C. until his death at the age of thirty-six, in 1889.

First African American Physician in Forsyth County

Henry Humphrey Hall

Born in Salisbury, North Carolina Dr. Henry Humphrey Hall became the first African American physician in Forsyth County in the 1890's.
An 1889 graduate of Leonard Medical School at Shaw University in Raleigh, North Carolina, Dr. Hall moved his practice from Salisbury to Winston in 1891, with his wife Ginny Cowan Hall who was also educated at Shaw University. His office was located at 216 E. 2nd Street in Winston. In 1902/1903 he was located at 432 Main Street and even had a bell phone number of 252 in the office.
When Dr. Hall first arrived in Winston, there was a flu epidemic and doctors were losing people every night. According to his daughter Madie Xuma, the white doctors would not help him until they heard of the success of this black doctor in combating the flu from the black domestic workers in the White homes. While people were dying every night, he had not lost a patient and his patients were getting well. Whites began to flock to him, and the white doctors asked what he was using. His response to them was what he used, he learned it in school and if they wanted to learn it, they better go back to school.
For a while Dr. Hall was the only physician for the entire African American community. He was instrumental in obtaining the services of and bringing black doctors such as Dr. John W. Jones to Winston. Dr. J. W. Jones grew up near Bethania on the plantation of White Physician, Dr.

Beverly Jones. Helping the doctor on his farm began his interest in medicine.

Dr. Hall was active in the community. He built the Hall Building in 1913. It was an office building on Patterson Avenue near Goler Memorial Church. He was the treasurer of Goler Memorial A.M.E. Zion Church and "helped to organize and staff the city's 1st black hospital, aiding the organization of the Twin City Medical Society, the black counterpart of the then White Forsyth County Medical Society." [125]

Dr. Hall also "established the medical department at R. J. Reynolds Tobacco Company." [126]

Shaw University Leonard Medical School graduating class 1889. Leonard was the first medical in the nation to offer a four-year program.
(Public domain. Wikimedia Commons)

The First African American Eye, Ears, Nose, and Throat Doctor

Doctor William E. Young was the first specialist of this type to reside in the City in the 1920's. He shared a physicians and surgeons practice in 1921, with Dr. Isaac S. Cunningham at 408 N. Church Street. Their practice was listed as Cunningham and Young in the 1921 City Directory.

First African American Woman Doctor

According to the Society for the Study of Afro American History in Winston-Salem / Forsyth County, the first African American woman doctor in Winston-Salem was Mary Langson, who was a Chiropodist. In 1935 her office was in the basement of the Robert E. Lee Hotel.

First African American Surgeon

Dr. H. Rembert Malloy
(WSSU Archives-University Photograph Collection. Winston-Salem State University Archives-C.G. O'Kelly Library)

Dr. H. Rembert Malloy, born July 19, 1913, was the first African American Physician in the south whose practice was limited to surgery. He attended Howard University in Washington, D.C. where he trained as a student under Dr. Charles Drew the inventor of storing blood plasma.

"Dr. H. Rembert Malloy made medical history on December 1948. He performed a rare and delicate operation on an infant girl at Kate Bitting Reynolds Hospital. He reinserted the baby's intestines. The surgery took 2 hours and 30 minutes. It was the first time the operation had been performed and it was a success."[127]

A Lesson in the Rare Operation Here

...matic Episode Points Up Distinguished Medical ...rk Accomplished Among Negroes by Negroes Here—

It requires an unusual incident for the press of the nation to take more than passing notice of the fine work that is being done in Winston-Salem at the Kate Bitting Reynolds Hospital. Last week a Negro baby was born there with its intestines outside its body and Dr. R. Rembert Malloy performed a two and a half hour's operation to save the child's life. The case will be submitted to medical journals. There have been only 96 such cases on record and about half that number died after operations.

It should be stressed to the public outside Winston-Salem and outside the South that Kate Bitting Reynolds Hospital is an institution exclusively for Negroes. It has high standards and is superior in equipment and staff to many white hospitals of the nation. Such instances as reported above are rare from the news point of view but serve to illustrate the progress made in medical practice and education by the Negro race in this section of the South.

Twin City Sentinel article
(Courtesy of Winston-Salem African American Archive-vertical file)

First African American Dentist

"Dr. Cleon Oscar Lee led the way for the practice of dentistry in the city. He graduated from the University of Pennsylvania in 1901"[128] and held certificates in North Carolina and Pennsylvania.

In 1906 his office was located at 311 ½ Church Street in Winston-Salem, but in 1910 he moved to the Jones Building. By 1913 Dr. Lee had a phone line in his office and his home. He moved again in 1918 to 408 Church St.

Dr. Lee was active in social, religious and education issues of the city and was a member of state and local medical bodies.

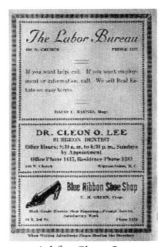

Ad for Cleon Lee
(City Directory. North Carolina Room Forsyth, County Central Library)

First African American Chiropractor

Dr. Christopher McConney was the first Chiropractor in Winston-Salem. In 1928 his office was in the Lincoln Theater building in the city. He later moved to 311 N. Church Street.

Notable Moments
Dr. McConney was also a minister with the New Bethel Baptist Church.

First African American Woman Chiropractor

Dr. Cynthia Durham, DC, is said to be the first African American woman licensed in the Chiropractic profession in Winston-Salem. Dr. Durham began her private practice in 1999 after the retirement of Chiropractor, Dr. Phillip Ingram, keeping the practice on 5201 North Silas Creek Parkway where he and his wife established it in 1963.
She graduated from Life Chiropractic College, Marietta, GA. with a BS in nutrition degree and Doctor of Chiropractic degree. She has also completed post-graduate training in Acupuncture and Exercise Rehabilitation.

First African American Physician to Use X-Ray Machine

Dr. John C. Williamson opened a Health Retreat at his home on Vargrave and Stadium Drive. He was the first African American Physician in Winston-Salem to utilize the x-ray machine in his practice. However, it was expensive and only a few were able to afford this technology.

Williamson Hospital. Williamson's Hospital was a house located at 830 Stadium Drive. It was bought for $2,000 in 1913 by Dr. J. C. Williamson and used as his home, office and hospital. *(Courtesy of Special Collections & University Archives/Wake Forest University)*

First African American Member of the City Hospital Commission

Dr. Edward Davis was the first African American member of the City Hospital Commission.

First African American Named as a Fellow of the American College of Surgeons

Joseph Monroe Walker, Jr.
(Courtesy the Bradshaw Estate)

Joseph Walker was the first African American practicing surgeon in North Carolina named as a fellow of the American College of Surgeons in 1951. He was also the first African American Physician named to the courtesy staff of the Old City Hospital.

He later became President of the Kate Bitting Reynolds Memorial Hospital professional staff.

Walker was born in Augusta, Georgia. He graduated from Morehouse College in Atlanta, and he received his medical degree from the University of Illinois School of Medicine.

First African American Medical Student at the University of North Carolina

Edward O. Diggs
(WSSU Archives-University Photograph Collection. By permission Winston-Salem State University Archives-C.G. O'Kelly Library)

Edward O. Diggs, a graduate of Winston-Salem State Teachers College, was working as a mail clerk in Greensboro in 1951 when he applied to the Medical School at the University of North Carolina at Chapel Hill. He was accepted on April 24, 1951 by a vote of 6 to 1 and became the first African American to attend UNC Medical School.

According to an article in the *Baltimore Afro-American*, his acceptance was the first time a black student was admitted to a southern state supported institution of higher learning without a court order. After receiving his acceptance Diggs simply responded he was glad he was accepted.

First African American Full-Time Faculty Member at Bowman Gray School of Medicine

Dr. Joseph Gordon
(Courtesy of Wake Forest University)

Joseph Gordon became the first African American faculty member at the Bowman Gray School of Medicine in 1965 when he joined the faculty as Assistant Professor of Radiology.
Originally born in Jamaica and raised in New York City. Gordon attended St. Augustine's College in Raleigh and later graduated from the University of Chicago, receiving his Medical degree in 1948 from Meharry Medical College in Nashville, TN After serving in the medical core during the Korean War, he came to Winston-Salem in 1956 as Director of Radiology at Kate Bitting Reynolds Hospital. There he began the School of Radiologic Technology and he began unofficial relationships with two Bowman Gray Radiologists.

Notable Moments
Gordon was a member of several professional associations. And after his retirement in 1988, Dr. Gordon became a civic leader. He was the first African American to be elected as a trustee of the Z. Smith Reynolds Foundation in 1970.
A scholarship program for minority undergraduate students at Wake Forest was a created and named in his honor.

First African American Graduate from Bowman Gray School of Medicine

Dr. William T. Grimes Jr
(Courtesy of Wake Forest University)

In in 1972 William Grimes became the first African American to graduate from the Bowman Gray School of Medicine. As a student, he was President of the student government and of the student chapters of the American Medical Association and National Medical Association.

First African American Woman Graduate from Bowman Gray School of Medicine

In 1975, Yvonne J. Weaver became the first African American woman to graduate from the Bowman Gray School of Medicine. She was followed in 1977 by B. Parthenia Richardson, Marilyn L. Bell, Claudette A. Hardy, and Lerla G. Joseph.

Dr. Yvonne J. Weaver
(Courtesy of Wake Forest University)

Top Left to right : B. Parthenia Richardson and Marilyn L. Bell. Bottom Left to right: Claudette A. Hardy and Lerla G. Joseph
(Courtesy of Wake Forest University)

First African American Physicians Admitted to The North Carolina Medical Society (NCMS)

Dr. Joseph Gordon (Left) *(Courtesy of Wake Forest University)*
Dr. Joseph Monroe Walker, Jr.(Right)
(Courtesy of Winston-Salem African American Archive)

In 1955 Doctors Joseph Gordon, MD and Joseph Walker, Jr. MD were the first African American physicians admitted to the NC Medical Society as Scientific Members.

The foundation for this admittance began in April of 1951, when the Old North State Medical Society, a society for African American Physicians in North Carolina, requested that they be admitted as a Constituent to the American Medical Association separate from the NCMS (North Carolina Medical Society) or that the NCMS lift its racial barriers and admit African American Physicians to the Society. The AMA refused the request.

The issue was raised again in 1954 when the Guilford County Medical Society passed a resolution urging the NCMS to delete the word "white" from its Bylaws.

The House of Delegates refused that request, but The House did vote to allow each County Society to admit black physicians as "scientific members" of the NCMS.

A Scientific member can attend all scientific and business sessions, and they could vote and hold office, but scientific members could not attend any social functions. Therefore, at the annual meeting in January of 1955 the NC Medical Society brought forward a resolution recommending that the society admit black physicians as scientific members with the same rights and stipulations as the county societies had placed on them. After much discussion a vote on the amendment passed 104 to 37.

Two years later the first African American physicians were admitted to the society.

In 1961, The Old North State Medical Society again requested full unrestricted membership to the NCMS for African American physicians. In 1964, the President of the NCMS, George Paschal, MD, broke the tradition of medical segregation during his Presidency and in the face of much criticism of his peers he asked the House to approve a Constitution and Bylaws change that would remove the words "white" and "scientific members." One year later, May 2, 1965, the House voted 117 to 28 to allow all physicians equal membership.

Early African American Nurses

Early practicing nurses in the city in the 1920's were Mrs. Girlie Jones Strickland, Miss Daisy Teer and Mrs. Annie K. Brown.

In the fall of 1920 these nurses along with a group of graduate nurses of the city began The Edith Cavell Nurses Club. It was named for Edith Cavell a nurse who was martyred in WW I.

The club taught service, promoting better health among the citizens and creating a better spirit and desire for more members of the profession among Negroes.

Mrs. Girlie Jones Strickland was the first President; Miss Daisy Teer was Vice President and Mrs. Annie K. Brown Secretary.

Out of this organization was born the North Carolina State Association of Colored Graduates Nurses, Incorporated.

First Professionally Trained African American Nurses

Emma Barrett was among the first professionally trained nurse in the city.

First African American County Health Nurse

Lula Morrison
(Courtesy of Society for the Study of Afro American History SSAH Calendar Salute to women 1995)

Lula Morrison was the first African American Forsyth County Public Health Nurse as well as the first to drive a county car.

She also worked in the Forsyth County Home for the Elderly and Indigent; the Tampa Negro Hospital in Tampa Florida; Forsyth County Sanitarium; Kate Bitting Reynolds Memorial Hospital and Forsyth County Health Department, from where she retired.

First Bachelor of Nursing Degree Program for African Americans

In 1957, Winston-Salem Teachers College, now Winston-Salem State University, graduated its first 12 students in their Bachelor of Nursing degree program.

The Nursing Degree program at Winston-Salem Teachers College opened in 1953 with 33 students. Prior to this, due to segregation in North Carolina, students would have to travel as far as New York for training.

The Nursing Program was established by an act of the North Carolina General Assembly.

First nursing graduates
(Courtesy of Winston-Salem African American Archive)

The first director was Mrs. Beverly W. Knight and Mrs. Gwendolyn Andrews was the first instructor in the Nursing Program. She later retired as Vice-President for Nursing at Wake Forest University Baptist Medical Center.

In 2003 the Nursing Program at Winston-Salem State University, became the Division of Nursing in the School of Health Sciences. In 2007, the Winston-Salem State University School of Health Sciences had 1,500 students, with 80 percent of its students in the nursing program. The Division of Nursing has graduated over 3,000 healthcare professionals and its undergraduate program is the largest producer of registered baccalaureate nurses in the region.

First African American Hospital

On May 14th, 1902 the Slater Hospital, the first hospital for Blacks in Winston, opened. It was "adjoining Slater Normal and Industrial School."[129] The hospital was a frame building on the site of the current Bickett Hall on WSSU's campus. It was built with equal sums of $3650 raised by Dr. S. G. Atkins and contributions by R. J. Reynolds.

Slater Hospital
(WSSU Archives-University Photograph Collection. By Winston-Salem State University Archives-C.G. O'Kelly Library)

"An advisory board was appointed, consisting of three black (Dr. H.H. Hall, Dr. J.W. Jones and Hargraves), and three white (Drs. Bahnson, Dalton and Pfohl) physicians.
A Ladies Auxiliary was also appointed, and the 6 original members being authorized to add another 9 people. Miss Lula Hairston was named the head nurse at a salary of $300 per year and a home in the building."[130]
The hospital lasted for 8 years, however, even with the support of Booker T. Washington and others, due to lack of finances and other problems, the Slater Hospital closed about 1912.
On August 9, 1937, twenty-five years later, there was a new hospital for blacks in town named Kate Bitting Reynolds Memorial Hospital. Affectionately called Katie B, it was built with a donation of "$200,000 from Mr. and Mrs. W. N. Reynolds and $125,000 from the Duke Foundation."[131] Land was provided by the city of Winston-Salem and the new hospital opened in 1938 as part of the hospital system with a capacity of 125 beds. Considered to have been one of the finest hospitals for African Americans in the South and the country, Katie B. had a school for training Black doctors and nurses as a part of the hospital.
The hospital fulfilled the need and demand from the black community. It was so successful that "Mr. Reynolds donated an additional $90,000 for another wing to the hospital."[132]

Doctors at KBR
(Courtesy of Lester S. Davis. Winston-Salem African American Archive)

Some nurses and doctors on the steps of KBR
(Courtesy of Lester S. Davis. Winston-Salem African American Archive)

PHYCISIANS AND MEDICAL INSTITUTIONS

New Residents at Kate B. Reynolds Hospital, 1947. Left to Right J. D. Davis, Cornelius Mathews, D. R. Wilson, T. R. McAlphin, C. W. Williams, R. L. McCree, A. B. Blount, G. A. Johnson, Norman Jones.
(Courtesy of Lester S. Davis. Winston-Salem African American Archive)

Some KBR nurses
(Courtesy of Lester S. Davis. Winston-Salem African American Archive)

Inventor of the First Organ Preserving Machine

Dr. John Feemster of Winston-Salem developed the first machine capable of storing any body organ for long distance transport. The machine he developed kept any organ for transplant, in near perfect condition for up to 24 hours. This organ preserving machine was about the size of a dish washer and could be rolled onto a plane for quick transportation. It was the first such device designed to preserve any body

DR. JOHN FEEMSTER
... former Winston man ...

Dr. John Feemster
(Courtesy Winston-Salem African American Archive-vertical file)

organ and the first portable machine capable of pumping bottled blood using a natural pulse instead of a steady flow.

The organ itself was kept cool and saturated with oxygen under high pressure. This machine was announced at the American Medical Association in San Francisco July 1968.

The son of Mr. and Mrs. John D. Feemster, of 2039 Lincoln Avenue in Winston-Salem, he was a Surgical Fellow at the University of Minnesota in Minneapolis.

Dr. John Feemster graduated from Atkins High School in Winston-Salem. He received his Bachelor of Science degree with honors in 1959 from Knox College at Galesburg, Illinois, and his Doctor of Medicine Degree with Honors in 1963 from Meharry Medical College in Nashville, Tennessee where he graduated top of his class. He was a Fellow at Oak Ridge Institute of Nuclear Studies and N. Y. Memorial Hospital for Cancer and Allied Diseases. He interned in surgery at the University of Minnesota in 1964 and went to Albert Einstein Medical College.

Machine Preserves Organs

(Courtesy Winston-Salem African American Archive-vertical file)

Chapter Nine

Real Estate

After 1865, Emancipated African Americans began to work and earn money of their own. Soon they desired to own their own land and property and homes." (133)
In 1880, property ownership of African Americans in Winston was less than $10,000 but within twenty years it increased to about $200,000. By 1935 personal and real estate property of African Americans in Winston-Salem had a value of $2,692,120. This did not include church property which was $382,000 and these assets helped to progress the African American community.

Happy Hills Settlement.
Houses on top of Pitts Street. Doris and Richard Byers and Edith and "Pike" Page houses. *(Courtesy of the Bradshaw Estate)*

First Retirement Farm for the Formally Enslaved

One of the most valued properties in the city of Winston-Salem was a part of the 700 acres farm owned by Francis Fries and used by him as a place to send his enslaved workforce that became too old to work in his woolen factory mill in Salem. Fries gave these retired enslaved persons a pig, a cow and a place to live for the rest of their lives.

According to his great-grandson W. F. Shaffner, Jr. in a 1966 article of the Winston-Salem Journal, it was his great-grandfather's version of Social Security more than 100 years ago.

Called Fries Quarters, the farm was unwanted by family heirs but Shaffner's grandmother accepted the land, and the African American residents lived there as her executor's fee.

Before being divided in 1949, the farm attached from Pine Valley Road to Peace Haven Road and along Robinhood Road. It included the site of the home built by R. J. Reynolds, Jr., which when it was subdivided, the central core containing the house was given to Wake Forest.

First Freedman Settlement and First Resident

In 1870 "Elias A. Voglar, a longtime supporter of the African American community proposed building an African American settlement southeast of Salem, cross Salem Creek."[134] The area was originally called the Negro Quarter due to slave quarters built on a part of what used to be farmland of Dr. Frederich Schumann. He later renamed it Liberia. The name came from slaves of the Schumann's who were emancipated and "sent to Liberia West Africa in 1836"[135] after a love feast in the African Moravian church in Salem.

In 1872, a freedman named Richard Siewers asked the Moravian church for permission to purchase a lot on this property. This created a settlement for African Americans in Salem. This settlement became "one of the first settlements in the south where freedmen could purchase land. The lots sold for $10.00 each. Today the neighborhood is called Happy Hill Gardens."[136] It is the oldest African American neighborhood in Winston-Salem.

The first Happy Hill resident was Mr. Lemely.

Edward Lemly at his house on Liberia Street

Left to right: Mr. Lemely, the first Happy Hill resident in front of his house on Liberia St and Other early residents, Columbus and Alice Pitts
(Courtesy of the Bradshaw Estate)

The First Planned African American Community

In 1891 Dr. Simon Green Atkins, born enslaved in Chatham County, founded the settlement that became known as Columbian Heights. He received an invitation by representatives of the Land and Improvement Company to see their property. When he saw it, he suggested to them that "it be opened to Negroes to buy homes and in 1891 he and his family became the first settlers. In 1892 the area was named Columbian Heights after the National Columbian 1892 Expedition, which commemorated the four hundredth anniversary of the settling of the New World October 12, 1492." [137] This event commonly known as the World's Fair, was held in Chicago.

This area soon became THE place to live for African American professionals, ministers and skilled craftsmen. It was in this community Dr. Simon Green Atkins began Slater Industrial Academy on September 28, 1892, later to become Winston-Salem State University.

Columbian Heights was one of three early prominent neighborhoods in Winston for African American professionals. The other two were East Fourteenth Street (called Mickey Mill Road until 1915) and Patterson Avenue near Liberty Street.

The First Homes for the African American Working Class

The first neighborhood community established for working class African Americans was the Boston Cottages, a development by the Boston Cottage Company. This was an investment company incorporated in 1895 with the purpose of erecting cottages and not large houses. This neighborhood catered to a different clientele than that of Columbian Heights. It is a community of one story small to medium size single family homes to house those who had once lived in sharecropper shacks and worked on farms.

Now working for wages, these workers can have homes for their families that they could rent or own.

Long before the development by the Boston Cottage Company, the area already had African Americans living there. The community had a school on the corner of what is now Grant and Taft Avenues. The first church established in the community, the Boston Cottage Methodist Episcopal was founded in 1893. It grew out of the need to have a church in the community due to the distance of St. Paul's Methodist Episcopal Church. This church later became St. Home Methodist Episcopal Church.

According to the 1993 Architectural and Planning Report: Winston-Salem's African American Resources, the boundaries of the community were: at the southernmost border, First Avenue (now 14th Street); the streets running north and south were named for Presidents; Grant, Washington, Harrison, Cleveland, Lincoln, Garfield; Old Town is on the east border and the western boarder is the location of the Methodist Children's Home where Roosevelt, Taft and Gillette dead end into the fields that separate the neighborhood and The Children's Home.

The 1904-05 city directory listed the neighborhood as a suburb of Winston west of Old Town Road, and it is later identified as the colored section west of North Cherry Extension. The main street became Thurmond (formally Washington).

The neighborhood community is now recognized as the Boston-Thurmond area. It is one of the few surviving African American neighborhood communities in Winston-Salem left primarily intact.

The First African American Subdivisions

Morwell

The first subdivision in the city that attracted a mix of African American professionals, working class and renters, had been privately owned property that became known as Morwell. It predated the Alta Vista subdivision which was specifically created for African American professionals. Morwell began with the purchase of seven acres of property on the east side of what is now Pittsburg Avenue, in 1911 by James Webster Wellman at an estate sale, from African American entrepreneur William Samuel Scales. Harvey Franklin Morgan (later a jitney driver, and of the Safe Bus Company) bought a 50% interest in the property.

By 1920 James Wellman, and his wife Emma, built and were residing in their two-story home on the property. With them were their children, a farm laborer named Edward Dickson, and Harvey Morgan. After gaining two more lots from the Kimberley Park subdivision from the south, James Wellman and Harvey Morgan entered into partnership with Henry Brown to run a general store which served the neighboring residents of Old Town Road, who were Black and White farmers, tobacco, tire factory and textile workers.

As development came north from Kimberley Park, Wellman and Morgan commissioned engineer J.A. Walker to plat a thirty-six-lot subdivision on their property and called it Morwell, which is an amalgamation of their surnames. The property was east of North Cherry Street and West Twenty-Fifth Street. They sold parcels of land to residents and to investors.

Mr. Wellman, an entrepreneur, later erected a gas station on Cherry and West Twenty-Fifth Streets.

According to the book, *Winston-Salem Architectural Heritage*, in 1930, occupants in homes on what is now the 400 block of West Twenty-fifth Street north side were: Frederick and Maria Fitch of Fitch Funeral Home; a tailor Harris Ferrell and his wife Nora; physician Henry Hall and his wife Mildred; janitor Robert Lewis and his wife Adalaide; gardener Walter Turner and his wife Sallie; Attorney Franklin Williams and his wife Susan Most of the homes on this street are still standing.

Alta Vista

Alta Vista is said to be the first African American subdivision in the South planned and developed specifically for African American professionals. Just as Buena Vista, the subdivision for white residents in Winston-Salem, was named for its beautiful scenic view, Alta Vista meant high view or view from above.

The neighborhood was planned in 1927 and located north of the Boston Cottages (Thurmond) area. It was bounded by Twenty-Sixth Street, Twenty-Fourth and a Half Street, Cherry Street and Kirkwood. Other streets were Hempstead St., Ocono Street, and Amhurst.
The homes in this subdivision were of modern design with garages and reflected the success of the African American professionals who built and purchased homes in this area.
According to the book *Winston-Salem's Architectural Heritage*, white developers sold the lots with restrictive covenants such as, the properties could not be subdivided for 25 years without the developer's consent.
The first homes were built on Twenty-Fifth and Twenty-Fourth and a Half Streets West of Cherry Street, by 1930.
The first residents were John and Emma Anderson proprietors of Anderson's kitchen; a porter, William Roscoe Anderson and his wife Olivia; a laborer, Clay Carter; William and Effie Drake. William Drake worked at Royal Dry Cleaning and Tailoring and at Flack's Sandwich Service; chauffer Brack A. Dulin and his wife Connie. Other notables were Mr. John M. Clyburn and his wife Vernie who built a home and resided at 2518 N. Cherry Street in 1938. Dewitt Livingston Morgan of Morgan-Hoffman Dry Cleaners, and his wife Mary resided at 2500 N. Cherry Street. The house was later purchased by Elmore W. Harding a merchant, and his wife Lillian. Robert Lee and Katherine Miller Young built a home at 711 West Twenty-Sixth Street and John M. Adams a cofounder of Safe Bus Company and his wife Ada resided at 818 Twenty-Fifth Street. The house is still on the corner of West Twenty-Fifth Street bordered by

Twenty-Fourth and a half, and Amhurst Streets. In 1959 Charles and Irma Gadson, (the daughter of Mr. James Wellman), built their home, considered to be the home of the future, at 2511 N. Cherry Street.

It is one of the earliest homes in Winston-Salem designed by Greensboro architect W. Edward Jenkins, one of the first registered African American architects in North Carolina. Jenkins and Gadson both attended North Carolina A & T University. In 1949 Charles Gadson established Twin City Electrical Contracting.

Although it was platted in 1927, the full development of the Alta Vista neighborhood did not occur until after the depression, in the 1940's.

In 1945 J. E. Elliot a civil engineer platted the Alta Vista addition which consisted of three blocks on West Twenty-Sixth Street's north side.

The subdivision was later separated by University Parkway, but Alta Vista is still one of the most intact African American neighborhoods in the city of Winston-Salem with many of the early homes still standing.

Various developments for African American professionals such as Monticello Park, Northwood Estates, Castleshire, Ebony Hills, Winston-Lake Estates and the upscale Lake Park soon followed Alta Vista.

First Public and Federally Funded Housing Project

The first public housing project in Winston-Salem was Happy Hill Gardens. It was developed to decrease poor housing conditions in the Happy Hill area of Winston-Salem, by building economically affordable housing with modern conveniences. Subsidies for the construction of the development were secured by then Mayor Richard J. Reynolds, Jr., making Happy Hill Gardens the first federally funded housing project in North Carolina.

Located near Rising Ebenezer Baptist Church, the public housing development contained 338 brick structures and was completed in 1952. This development was almost identical to the College Village apartments erected four years earlier in the prominent white community of Buena Vista, located on the west side of town.

Happy Hill Apts. *(City of Winston-Salem. Public photo)*

College Village Apts. *(photo taken by Chenita B. Johnson)*

First Official Racial Division of Neighborhoods

In 1912, the town of Winston passed ordinances prohibiting blacks and whites to live on the same streets. The first of these Jim Crow ordinances was adopted June 13, 1912 in regard to the African Americans moving to East Winston. The next ordinance adopted July 5, 1912, by the Board of Aldermen, called the *Segregation Ordinance,* allowed the city government to legally mandate segregation and ordain the creation of ghettos in the city.
According to Langdon Opperman author of Winston-Salem's African American Neighborhoods, 1870-1950; this followed the method invented

in Richmond Virginia, of designating blocks throughout the city, black or white according to most of the residents.

The ordinances were said to "secure for whites and colored people respectively the separate location of residence for each race." [138]

This ordinance did not prohibit the residence of citizens prior to it, nor would it prevent servants from residence in the homes of employers.

Violation of one or more of these ordinances would be a $50 fine and or 30 days in jail for each offence and each day of the violation.

After the enacting of these ordinances, Winston merges with Salem the following year in 1913. A Supreme Court challenge of these segregation laws of Richmond, Virginia and Winston-Salem North Carolina in 1914 ruled the laws unconstitutional. However, these ordinances of the Jim Crow era, has left a lasting impact throughout the city concerning housing patterns of Winston-Salem residents to this day.

First African American Home Owners

First Homeowners in Winston were Mrs. Annie Brooks, Abraham Grater and Mrs. Hickerson.

Louis Heggie

The home built by grocer Louis Heggie was the first brick house owned by an African American in Winston. Built in the 1880's it was a two-room brick home located on Linden (now Research Parkway) and E. Seventh Streets. The house was torn down in 1934.

Another home built in the 1880's near Linden on E. Seventh Street, was the old Penry house which was also considered to prominently stand out among the palatial residences of blacks on that street.

Corner of Linden and 7th Street now 7th Street and Research Parkway
(Photo taken by Chenita B. Johnson)

Corner of 7th Street and Research Parkway formally
Linden and 7th Street *(Photo taken by Chenita B Johnson)*

Jasper Carpenter

In 1908, an African American woman rented and moved into a house on the corner of Woodland and English streets in Winston. This area was a white area and she was burned out. It was not until 1941 that this began to change. In that year, Jasper Carpenter became the first African American to purchase a house in the community around the former Winston-Salem City Memorial Hospital, which was located on the corner of East Fourth Street.

Jasper and his wife Mamie originally lived on 1604 E. Eleven ½ Street. After the move to Fifth Street he was not burned out, but whites began a mass exodus known as *white flight* and in less than 12 months most had moved from the area.

John A. Carter

In 1929, John A. Carter, an instructor at Winston-Salem Teachers College (WSSU), Principal at Columbian Heights High School and future Principal of Atkins High School, purchased a lot at 1100 Rich Avenue and forever changed a neighborhood.

John A. Carter
*(Atkins Yearbook /Maroon and Gold, 1958.
Courtesy of Jacquelyne B. Barber,)*

Carter and his wife lived on Wallace Street in Columbian Heights, when they moved to their new home in 1931 in Reynolds Town, then considered a white neighborhood. They became the first African Americans to live in Reynolds Town (Cameron Park).

First Neighborhood Catastrophe

In 1881 the Winston Water Company built a triangular looking reservoir of brick and cement to supply drinking water for the growing town of Winston. The reservoir was located at the top of the hill where Trade and Eighth Streets intersect.

In 1904, twenty-three years later a second water works project was begun to keep up with the demands of the population of the town. Two new pumps were added to bring water from Frazier Creek to the old reservoir and the new metal holding tank.

Residents living near the reservoir often complained that water leaked from under the walls, but their complaints went unheeded by town officials, including the mayor, who assured them that the structure was safe. It was not safe, and the pressure became too great for the old reservoir. On Wednesday morning November 2, 1904 at 5:20 am, the north wall collapsed sending millions of gallons of water down Trade Street over the train tracks towards the sleeping black neighborhood below.

The water swept away eight houses, injuring the same number of residents and killing nine residents. This number included the entire William Poe family whose bodies were found washed over a mile away to the bottom of Trade Street and emptied into Belo's Pond. One couple rode the wave of water on their bed and came to rest unharmed at Peters Creek where North West Boulevard winds.

To stave off any lawsuits, the town officials offered to rebuild the homes and paid for medical bills and burials of the affected residents. Upon inspection of the events, one town official commented that the flooded area looked like a pond. It was this observation of the tragedy that created the nickname, *the pond*, for the area around the old reservoir.

The Union Republic Newspaper reported the event as the saddest chapter in our history.

Broken reservoir, 1904
(Courtesy of Forsyth County Public Library Photograph Collection, Winston-Salem, N.C.)

Flooded houses, 1904
(Courtesy of Forsyth County Public Library Photograph Collection, Winston-Salem, N.C.)

First Mail Service for the First African American Settlement

Happy Hill, the first African American settlement in Winston, did not have door-to-door mail service until after WWII. Resident and community advocate Wade Bitting petitioned the Aldermen and received approval to have street names put up and numbers put on houses. Prior to his efforts, residents had to get their mail at the Salem post office.

Mr. Bitting, his family, and other men of the area personally placed the numbers on the houses. It took a few years, but Happy Hill residents became as other city residents and began receiving mail delivery to their neighborhood homes.

Early African American Realtors

W.H. Goler
(*Courtesy of Winston-Salem African American Archive*)

Among early African American Realtors in Winston, Dr. W.H. Goler leads the list. Beginning in 1900 he owned many rental houses on Patterson Avenue, and several business buildings.

Dr. Goler was also considered a pioneer in the establishment of Goler AME Zion Church of Winston-Salem. He was followed in real-estate ownership by Mr. Charles H. Jones, a bail bondsman and real-estate broker in the 1930's.
It was said at this time Mr. Jones was worth about half a million dollars.

Mr. Charles H. Jones
(Society for the Study of Afro American History SSAH- calendar)

First African American Carpenters

The first African American carpenters in the city were Rev. Pearson and Mr. Bowman.

First African American Contractor

John H. Smith
(Courtesy of the Bradshaw Estate)

Mr. John H. Smith was one of the earliest contractors in Winston. He attended and graduated Slater Normal and Industrial School (WSSU). After graduation, Dr. Atkins hired him to teach industrial arts at the school.

Smith eventually formed his own construction company establishing one of the first African American constructing companies in Winston-Salem. Partnering with William Henry Hauser, he created the Smith-Hauser Construction Company. They had an ad in the 1915 Winston-Salem City Directory.

Mr. Smith constructed not only buildings on the WSSU campus but also throughout Winston-Salem.

First African American Plasterers

Among the first African American plasterers were Herbert Searcy, and Wash Joyce. Mr. Joyce was the father of John Joyce, the first African American policeman in Winston-Salem.

Herbert Searcy was listed in the 1894/95 Winston-Salem City Directory as a plasterer.

First African American Brick Mason

Eli Clayton was one of the first bricklayers in the city. In 1889-1890 he lived on Macktown Road.

First Goodwill Ambassador from Winston-Salem

Mr. Black and President Richard Nixon
(Courtesy of Winston-Salem African American Archive-vertical file)

In 1971, renowned brick maker Mr. George Black became a "celebrity and good will ambassador," [139] when he was sent by President Richard Nixon, as a representative of the United States to Guyana, South America to teach the Guyanese the art of Brick making.
He is the first resident bestowed this honor

Mr. Black was born in Liberty, North Carolina, but came to Winston with his father and brother at the end of the 19th century. He learned the art of brick making though years of working at the Old Hedgecock Brickyard [140] and refined his skill by using old cast away brick moldings.

In the 1920's he built his own brickyard behind his home and working with another brick maker, named Alex Walker, he made bricks for various public and private building projects such as Colonial Williamsburg, NC Baptist Hospital, and Salem College.

His bricks were also used for the Old Salem Fire House reconstruction in Old Salem and the old Wachovia Bank buildings on Waughtown Street and on the corner of Patterson and Glenn Avenues.

His work can also be seen on Arber Road, in the curvy boarder walls of the former home of Tom Davis, the founder of Piedmont Airlines.

On March 19, 1990, the former Wachovia North Branch on the corner of Patterson and Glenn Avenues was renamed, the Black-Phillips-Smith Government Center in honor of Mr. George Henry Black, Mr. Garret E. "Roy" Phillips and Mrs. Georgia M. Smith.

This building is now a neighborhood satellite office for City services.

Mr. Black's home in Winston-Salem, at 111 Dellabrook Road is now in the National Register of Historic Places.

There is a statue of Mr. George Black that stands at the Forsyth County Government Building on Chestnut Street.

Mr. Black is standing in front of and holding a brick from the North Carolina Baptist Hospital Main building in 1978. Affectionately called Old Main, the building was being demolished. Mr. Black was the original mason for the building in 1923. *(Courtesy of Winston-Salem African American Archive).*

Public Statue of Mr. Black statue at the government building at 201 Chestnut Street in Winston-Salem. *The statue was created by Sculptor Grace Napper. (Photo taken by Chenita B. Johnson)*

Chapter Ten

Communications

AFRICAN AMERICAN FIRSTS

Communication is the life of any community.

The African American community in Winston-Salem/Forsyth County created various forms of communication institutions to relay information about issues of concern that affected the community, as well as ways to help in community mobilization.

Top: Camp Meeting Choir *(Courtesy* of Winston-Salem African American Archive) Above: WAAA Radio staff *(Winston-Salem Chronicle. Courtesy* of Winston-Salem African American Archive-vertical file)

First Newspaper for African Americans

Jefferson Davis Diggs
(Courtesy of the Bradshaw Estate)

The First newspaper for blacks in Winston-Salem was the Holiness Review, by Rev. Jefferson Diggs a monthly sponsored by St. Paul Methodist Ep. Church. He also started the United Holy Church of America in the 1900's and was an advocate of better facilities and job opportunities for blacks. He also founded the Ministers Union." [141]

The Holiness Review was located at 124 East Seventh Street in Winston according to the 1902 City Directory.

Other newspapers were to follow this civic minded trailblazer: The Carolina Times (1930-1935) Editor Clarence Irvin, who also published a weekly, The Post newspaper (1932-1940), Editor William Alexander with Carl Russell as circulation manager; Winston-Salem Enterprise, under editor Rev. Elijah Johnson Pastor of St. John CME and business manager William R. Saxon; and Carl H. Russell had a weekly, the People's Spokesman (1946-1948). Rev. W. LeRoy Davis, who had been a reporter for Piedmont Publishing, left and published his own Journal and Sentinel, (1945-1946). Later community publishers following in these footsteps are: The Winston-Salem Chronicle (1975-present), Editor and founder Ernie Pitt; The A.C. Phoenix (1985-2016), Editor and founder Rodney J. Sumler;

The W Times (2003-present), Editor and founder Joe Watson, Jr. and the East Winston Press (2010), Editor and founder Harold Lee Hairston.

Notable Moments
In the early 1900's Rev. Jefferson Davis Diggs helped to layout the school district to help keep down racial friction.

First African American Columnist

Hoyt Wiseman, Sr.

One of the first black columnists was Hoyt Wiseman, Sr. During the 1920's he began reporting news from the black community in the Winston-Salem Journal and Sentinel." [142]
Hoyt Wiseman wrote the column, "News of Colored People."
According to Journalnow online, June 3, 2013, he was described in the 1932 directory as reporter for the Journal and Sentinel.
While he may have been the first African American writer for the paper to be labeled reporter, Hoyt Wiseman was not allowed to work at the news office. He worked out of a satellite office in the old YMCA building on Patterson Avenue.

First African American Reporter

A. Alexander Morisey

According to "Ask Sam" journalnow online, the first black reporter to work in the Winston-Salem Journal and Sentinel newsroom was A. Alexander Morisey. Unlike previous black columnists for the paper, such as R. O'Hara Lanier, Lillian Ragsdale, Hoyt Wiseman, A. A. Mayfield and Rev. LeRoy Davis, who worked in satellite offices, Morisey was the first black reporter in the south to work in a previously all white newsroom.

Morisey joined the Journal and Sentinel in 1949 and left in 1955. He later became a public relations manager with the New York Times from 1969-1973. He was replaced at the Journal and the Sentinel by African American reporter Luix V. Overbea who became a founding member of the National Association of Black Journalists.

Another reporter, Robert Miller began his career at the paper as a janitor and became a reporter in 1962.

Internationally Published Spokesperson for Native People

Chief Buffalo Child Long Lance

Sylvester Clark Long in Denver, Colorado, 1923
(Wikimedia Commons, the free media repository en.wikipedia.org)

Flamboyant, articulate, creative, Native American advocate, Chief Buffalo Child Long Lance, was born Sylvester Clark Long in Winston, North Carolina (Winston-Salem), on December 1, 1890.

He was the first journalist, writer and actor from Winston, who became internationally prominent as a spokesperson for the causes of Native people. He was one of the most well-known of North American Natives of the 1920's, however Sylvester Long was one of five children of Joseph

Sylvester Long, a janitor at the former West End High School in Winston, North Carolina, and Sallie Matilda Lindsey Long.

Joseph Long was a former enslaved African American born in Yadkin County, but he and his wife were said to be of mixed Native American ancestry.

Sylvester Long lived in Winston with his parents, and siblings Abe Miles Long, (the manager of the all *Negro* balcony at the Carolina Theater on West Fourth Street); Walter Lee Long, (the first black detective in Winston-Salem); Newman Grimes Long, and Katie Mae Long Hines.

He attended the Depot Street School, until age thirteen when he joined the Robinson's Traveling Circus.

Due to his bronze complexion, high cheek bones and straight black hair, the owner thought he was a Native American boy and placed him with the Native Americans in the Wild West show. Long never corrected the owner and he began his life as a Native American, leaving behind the segregation and restrictions of an African American under Jim Crow laws in Winston and the South.

As part of the Wild West Show, Long learned basic Cherokee words, phrases as well as sign language. He also learned archery and became skilled at trick horse riding. He had a magnetic personality and was a great showman.

After six years with the Wild West Show, he applied and attended the Carlisle Indian Industrial School in Pennsylvania. To give him acceptance among his peers, at the school, Long was allowed to change his name to Sylvester Chahuska Long Lance. He later attended St. John's Military School and in 1915 received a special appointment to West Point but did not attend. It was at St. John's Military School that he received the nickname "Chief" as being the only Native American in the class.

When World War I began in 1914 Long went to Montreal to enlist in the Canadian Expeditionary Force. He was trained in France.

After serving four months of fighting on the front lines he was injured. While recovering Long Lance was assigned to clerical duty at the London intelligence service. When the war ended in 1918, he had been promoted to the rank of acting Sergeant, and requested to be discharged to Calgary, Alberta. There he worked for three years as a journalist with the Calgary Herald. The Herald sent him on an assignment to the Siksika Blackfoot

Reservation. From this assignment he began a decade of advocacy, experiencing and reporting on the harsh living conditions of the Plains Indians with the restrictions of life on the reservation due to the policies of the Department of Indian Affairs and wrote articles advocating Native Rights.

Due to his advocacy of Native Rights, in 1922, Long Lance was given the ceremonial name Buffalo Child by a Blackfoot Chief, named Mountain Horse and was adopted by the Kainai Nation of the Blackfoot Confederacy. After this name change, he moved to Vancouver as a freelance writer for the Vancouver Sun writing about Native American life on the reservation.

In 1924, as press representative for the Canadian Pacific Highway, Long Lance reached a diverse audience through his published articles on the Indians of Western Canada, in National magazines such as Cosmopolitan, and Good Housekeeping.

In 1927 Long Lance moved to New York City and a year later due to his national notoriety, the Cosmopolitan Book Company published Long Lance's autobiography as a boy's adventure book on Indians, in 1928. Titled *"Long Lance: The Autobiography of a Blackfoot Indian Chief"*, it detailed his fabricated life growing up as the son of a Blackfoot Chief with the Blackfoot Indians of the Western Plains of Montana. The international success of this book made him an international celebrity and it received the praises of literary critics and anthropologists.

Long Lance had always been an advocate for Native Rights, but now his notoriety allowed him to speak before groups and historical societies for $100 per speech.

In 1929, Long Lance starred in the silent film, *The Silent Enemy: An Epic of the American Indian*, which showed the traditional ways of Ojibwa people. Released in 1930, this movie was praised and touted by critics as the most realistic depiction of Native American life in the movies. Long Lance was also praised by the critics for his interpretation of the starring role of Baluk, the Ojibwa brave.

Because of Long Lance's success with his book and the movie, he was requested by B. F. Goodrich Rubber Company to design a running shoe for them based on his moccasins. The shoes had rubber soles, which he endorsed through advertising.

During the height of his success, Long Lance became the toast of the New York Social scene and had many friends of the social elite.

It was during this time that he met with his brother Walter Long, after twenty-two years. It was a bittersweet reunion, because their father was ill, and the family needed help to pay his medical bills. Long Lance began to continuously send money home, but he could not return to see his father.

Long Lance's fame began to wane due to a question of his ethnicity by a Native American adviser to the film, The Silent Enemy, who alerted the legal advisor of the studio.

The investigation found his true identity and rumors spread that Long Lance was *black*. His endorsements left and so did his friends on the social ladder. Even Irvin S. Cobb, a writer in New York who listed him as a friend and whose home he visited, commented when the truth was revealed, that they were so ashamed that they had entertained a Nigger in their home.

In 1932, Long Lance suspiciously died in the Los Angeles, California home of a wealthy socialite and friend, actress Anita Baldwin. Walter Long, came to California to see what had happened to his younger brother, but was unable to get any information. He returned home with only Long Lance's scrapbook which was found among his personal effects.

Long Lance was not sent home to Winston-Salem as had been requested by his family. He was buried at Inglewood Park Cemetery in Inglewood California in the Canadian War Veteran Section.

He left assets to St. Paul's Indian Residential School in Southern Alberta. He bequeathed his papers to his friend Canon S.H. Middleton. They were given to J. Zeiffle, a dealer who later sold them to the Glenbow Museum in Calgary, Alberta Canada in 1968.

COMMUNICATIONS

Chief Buffalo Child B.F. Goodrich Ads
(Courtesy of Winston-Salem African American Archive-vertical file)

First African American Radio and Television Broadcasting

WAAA Radio

Standing left to right first WAAA staff: Larry Williams, Bernard Baker, Togo West, and Bruce Miller. Seated left to right, Lucile Douthit, Leroy Johnson, Velma Friende *(Winston-Salem Chronicle. Courtesy of Winston-Salem African American Archive-vertical file)*

North Carolina's first all-black programmed and manned radio station WAAA went on the air on October 29, 1950 in the heart of what was the booming black business district in downtown Winston-Salem. "The first commercial broadcast was a play by play of the A&T State College – Morgan State Bears football game broadcast direct from the stadium. Togo West and Bruce Miller were the announcers for the game." [143] The broadcast was sponsored by Reads Drug Store of Winston-Salem and the Coca Cola Bottling Company.

The station's studios and business office were in the Atlantic Building on the corner of Church and Third Streets in Winston-Salem, with the transmitter located on Beth Street in the Southern part of town.

Early personalities of WAAA were Leroy Johnson, Larry Williams, Bernard Baker, the Sensational Southlanders, Lucille Douthit, Velma Hayes Friende, Bruce Miller and Oscar Alexander. Oscar Alexander was the popular DJ "Daddy-Oh on the Patio,"[144] whose show aired from Ray's

COMMUNICATIONS

Roadside Drive-In on New Walkertown Road. As an on-air personality for WAAA his poetic rap style made him an institution in Winston-Salem for three decades.

Other popular announcers on WAAA during the station's early years included Larry Williams, Fred "Steady Freddie" Allen, and Robert "Bobcat" Roundtree.

WSMX Radio

"WSMX is on the air" were the first words spoken by deejay Paul S. Johnson, June 23, 1982, announcing that the first and only all black gospel radio station in Winston-Salem had begun broadcasting.

There were early gospel broadcast radio stations in the area, but they were not accommodating to African Americans. It wasn't until 1937 that E. E. Tanner's gospel program began on WAIR. In the late 1940's the African American gospel ensemble, the Camp Meeting Choir, could be heard on WSJS.

WSMX advertisement
(*Winston-Salem Chronicle*. Courtesy of Winston-Salem African American Archive-vertical file)

Owned and operated by Gospel Media Radio, a subsidiary of Macedonia True Vine Pentecostal Holiness Church of God, INC., the first full time gospel station in Winston-Salem, WSMX was the first of its kind in the city and was at the beginning of the explosion of the gospel music genre of the 1980's radio stations.

WSMX ranked higher than any other Christian music format station in the area. It came in "#12 out of 20 top stations in the triad." [145]

The station was originally located on Link Road in Winston-Salem and later moved to the business offices owned by Macedonia True Vine Pentecostal Holiness (TVPH) Church, INC. on Kinard Dr. The transmitter was on New Walkertown Road in the city.

WSMX operated from sunup to sundown Monday through Sunday on the 1500 AM radio band, with a transmitting power of 10,000 watts directional signal.

The station's extensive reach included not only various parts of North Carolina, but also reached into Virginia, Tennessee, and West Virginia. Its format was gospel music from traditional to contemporary. It featured various religious broadcasts from local and national ministers, news, information, and a Saturday sports show.

Early personalities of WSMX were veteran on air personality, Al Martin (The Godfather of Gospel), was morning; gospel singer and minister, Nancy Baker Caree (Wilson), (the Gospel Song Bird), was afternoon; and Paul S. Johnson, known as the Man with the Million Dollar Voice, sent listeners home during the evening drive time.

Al Martin began his radio career in Huntersville, Alabama in 1966. A graduate of Atkins High School, he attended Russell Commercial School and graduated with a special honor from New York's School of Announcing and Speech.

His first job was at WAAA, and later at WAIR. He joined WSMX in 1982, where he was announcer, music and religious director, and station coordinator.

WSMX is where he received his tag the Godfather of Gospel from station manager, Jay Springs.

Nancy Caree Wilson, a singer and minister, had a featured 30-minute segment called Prayer and Praise. She was also cohost of Gospel Expo, a local program at WGHP TV in High Point, North Carolina on Sunday mornings.

Paul Johnson, evening announcer and News Director at WSMX is originally from Bluefield, , West Virginia. He attended Marshall University in Huntington, West Virginia and majored in Mass Communication and Journalism.

He began his broadcast career in 1980 at WHEZ radio, a local radio station in Huntington, and at WMUL the University radio station, while a student at Marshall University. He had a successful weekly weekend radio show at the school called Disco 88.

Other early personalities of WSMX were Leonard "Tippy" Calloway and Mother (Mary) Bryce who continued the Prayer and Praise program.

Top Left to right: Paul Johnson, Al Martin . Bottom: Nancy Caree Wilson (Winston-Salem Chronicle 1983. Courtesy of Winston-Salem African American Archive-vertical file)

First African American Radio Announcer

Webster Bernard Baker, Jr.
(Courtesy of Mr. Webster Bernard Baker, Jr.)

The first African American radio announcer in Winston-Salem is Webster Bernard Baker, Jr. He was a disc jockey at WTOB radio station, with popular programs on Saturday afternoons.

Baker began his career with Mutual's WTOB in 1947. In 1948, he was one of two African American radio announcers in the state of North Carolina.

He sponsored his shows by writing his own commercials and selling advertising time to African American businesses in the city. His shows were popular due to his showcasing singers from Northern night clubs, and popular band leaders on the show.

Baker was a 1944 graduate of Atkins High School where he served as President of the student body. From Atkins he attended Morehouse College where he pursued a major in English and minor in Spanish. He also attended the North Carolina College in Durham. In Durham, he was employed at various radio stations ; WDUK, WHHT, and WSSB. There he had programs titled Records at Reveille, After Hours, and Late-Night Rendezvous.

During the War, Baker worked in Washington, DC, for the Census bureau, the Bureau of Naval Personnel, and the War Production Board.

After returning to Winston-Salem, he worked as a reporter for The Peoples Spokesman, a local black newspaper. He later became Program Director at the all black programmed radio station WAAA, in Winston-Salem.

First African American Woman to Own a Radio Station

Mütter Evans
(Courtesy of Billy Rich.)

When Mütter Evans purchased WAAA radio from Media Broadcasting Corporation for $1.04 million in 1979, becoming its general manager and owner, she became the youngest in the country, to own a broadcast radio station. She was also the first African American woman in North Carolina, and one of the first African American women in the country, to own a broadcast operation.

As general manager of WAAA, she began the commemorative observance of the birthday of Dr. Martin Luther King, Jr. in Winston-Salem, five years before it became a national holiday. It is one of the oldest commemoration events for Dr. King in the country. She also has established Mütter D. Evans Communications, a firm that aids in the areas of management, marketing, and public relations.

A graduate of Wake Forest University, Mütter Evans has served as an adjunct instructor at Winston-Salem State University, where she taught courses in mass communications.

Mütter Evans
(Courtesy of Billy Rich)

The First African American Woman Television Anchor

Denise Franklin
(Winston-Salem Journal. Courtesy of Winston-Salem African American Archive-vertical file)

The First African American woman to co-anchor local news in the city was Denise Franklin. She co-anchored the news at WXII Television in Winston-Salem. Franklin later became General Manager for radio station, WFDD FM 88.5 which is a part of Wake Forest University.

WXII advertisement *(Winston-Salem Chronicle. Courtesy of Winston-Salem African American Archive-vertical file)*

First from Winston-Salem to have a Syndicated Talk Show

Rolanda Watts
(Courtesy of the Bradshaw Estate)

Rolanda Watts is a successful journalist, talk show host and, actor. Born July 12, 1959 in Winston-Salem NC, she is the first African American from Winston-Salem to have an internationally syndicated talk show. Her show, titled *Rolanda*, was broadcast in 1994. Some called her the next Oprah Winfrey.

Rolanda Watts began her journalism career as a reporter for WFMY-TV2 in Greensboro, North Carolina.

She not only used her talents in journalism, she was also an actress in comedy and dramatic programing in such programs as, JAG, The West Wing, My Wife and Kids, Days of Our Lives, and The Bold and The Beautiful.

A graduate of Salem Academy in Winston-Salem, North Carolina, Magna Cum Laude graduate from Spellman College in Atlanta Georgia and journalism graduate from Columbia University, Watts also holds an honorary doctorate in Humane Letters from Winston-Salem State University.

Rolonda Watts is now CEO/President of her own production company, Watts Works Productions.

Chapter Eleven

Transportation

Transportation moves a community forward, but due to the restrictions of Jim Crow, African Americans out of necessity began a system of transportation when other modes of accommodations were not accessible to them.

Top Center : Jitney bus *(Courtesy of the Bradshaw Estate)*. Center Left: Elijah T. Miller with his Jitney circa 1926 *(Courtesy of the Bradshaw Estate)*. Center Right: Back of the garage and offices of The Safe Bus Company building on Church Street in Winston-Salem, N.C. *(Courtesy of Winston-Salem African American Archive-vertical file)*. Bottom: Safe Bus *(Courtesy of the State Archives of North Carolina)*

First African American Cab Service

Joe Martin provided the first cab service in 1927. He had a handsome carriage that provided service pick up for black riders at the train station.

First African American Operated Bus

"The very first black operated bus that came to Winston-Salem was purchased by Mrs. Jessie Hayes, a grocery store owner in Columbian Heights. The driver who drove the bus to Winston-Salem was Pete Sadler according to Mr. James Hayes who was living here at that time in the early 1920's."[146]

The First African American Owned Bus Company

Safe Bus picking up passengers
(Courtesy of the Bradshaw Estate)

Six years after Pete Sadler drove the first bus purchased by Mrs. Hayes to Winston-Salem, a group of 35 black business men in Winston-Salem, who owned small busses called jitney's, formed the Safe Bus Company to meet the growing transportation needs of the Black community. It was the only African American-owned city bus company in the nation and the world that ran a fixed route for the general public.

Their name came from their motto which was, Safety First. They promised the mayor, Thomas Barber, to operate a safe and organized transportation system.

Safe Bus, Inc. appeared before the board May 26, 1926 and "the State of North Carolina granted them a charter to acquire, own, maintain and operate buses, taxi cabs and trucks for the passengers for hire and to maintain plants and repair shop for the manufacture, repair and maintenance of said vehicles."[147]

Elijah T. Miller
(Courtesy of the Bradshaw Estate)

The busses were parked each night in front of Ralph R. Hairston's home of 1424 Cromartie Street."[148]

Some founder's and officers of the Safe Bus Company were Harvey F. Morgan, the first President; Jefferson Hairston, Vice-President; Charlie R. Peebles, Secretary/Treasurer; Clarence T. Woodland, Asst. Secretary.

Other names are George Ragsdale (G F. Ragsdale), Ralph R. Morgan (R. R. Morgan), John Adams (J.M. Adams), Elijah and Joseph Miller, Elliot Davis (E. A. Davis), George Dillahunt (G.L. Dillahunt), Fred McCall and C.R. Mosby.

Under the leadership of C. T. Woodland and Harvey F. Morgan, the company survived the depression and WWII.

In 1959 Mrs. Mary M. Burns, daughter of E. H. Miller became the first Woman to head the company when she was elected president of the Safe Bus Company. Six months later they elected Vice President, Mrs. Delphine

Morgan to succeed her as president. Mrs. Morgan was the widow of R. R. Morgan, a founder of the Safe Bus Company. She resided at 2401 North Patterson Avenue in Winston-Salem.

Mrs. Delphine Webber Morgan
*(North Carolina Room Forsyth County Central Library.
Winston-Salem Biography- vertical file)*

The company expanded between 1968-1972 as "Winston-Salem's sole transit line, employing several hundred blacks and becoming the largest black owned transportation company in the nation and known as the largest transportation business in the world. It maintained this position until it was purchased by the city of Winston-Salem in early 1972 becoming a part of the Winston-Salem Mass Transit Authority," [149] known as WSTA.

Mary Burns
(Courtesy of Winston-Salem African American Archive-vertical file)

Front of the garage and offices of The Safe Bus Company building on Church Street in Winston-Salem, N.C.
(Courtesy of Winston-Salem African American Archive-vertical file)

First African American Woman Bus Driver

Priscilla Stephens
(Courtesy of Winston-Salem African American Archive-vertical file)

Priscilla Stephens was trained in one day by Clark Campbell, the longtime bus driver for whom the downtown transportation Center is named. She went on to drive for RJ Reynolds Tobacco and Greyhound Bus Lines before retiring in 2012.

First Transportation Center Named for an African American

Clark Campbell Transportation Center Celebration
(Courtesy of Lester S. Davis)

The Clark Campbell Transportation Center on Trade and Fifth Street is the first building in downtown Winston-Salem and the only transportation center in the United States at this time, named for an African American.

The center was dedicated in March 2007 in honor of Mr. Clark Campbell, a bus driver who began his career with Safe Bus Company in 1944. Although officially retired from the Winston-Salem Transit Authority in 1992 he continued part time as a driver until 2006. His total years of service were 62 years and he logged over 3 million miles.

Representative Larry Womble said of Mr. Campbell at the dedication program; "to many of us he was a parent, a friend, a guardian angel." [150]

Top: Flyer for celebrating the naming of the Winston-Salem Transportation for Long time driver Clark Campbell *(Courtesy of Chenita B Johnson).*
Above: Clark Campbell *(Courtesy of the State Archives of North Carolina)*

Chapter Twelve

Community Institutions

"The intensification and hardening of racial segregation particularly after 1890 left the Negro with no alternative except to develop compensatory social relationships within their own group." (151) Institutions within these communities were developed to nurture and to give a sense of stability, well-being and belonging to those who previously had no such security.

YMCA

First Cemetery for African Americans

The first and oldest African American cemetery in Forsyth County was in Salem, North Carolina at the south end of Church Street, near what is known as the parish or stranger's graveyard. This was a place of burial for non-Moravians or strangers who died while staying or traveling through Salem.

In the beginning black and white Moravians were buried side by side in the God's acre cemetery, but this changed due to outward racial pressure, creating segregation in the community even in death, and a separate graveyard for blacks was created in the parish graveyard. One of the last to be buried in God's Acre was the infant son of Budney and Phoebe, in 1813. They were the enslaved couple who helped to found the first African church in their home in the Negro Quarter in Salem.

One hundred and eight of the black Moravians of Salem were buried in the parish graveyard from 1816-1859. In 1859 the cemetery closed, and another opened east of God's Acre.

Largest Historic African American Cemetery

The Odd Fellows Cemetery is the oldest and largest Historically African American cemetery in Winston, and 2nd oldest in Forsyth County. The cemetery opened in 1911. Odd Fellows was the only place that African American residents could be buried, in Winston until the opening of the first Evergreen Cemetery.

The "Old" Evergreen Cemetery was said to be part of the private property of local prominent African American landowner and farmer James Foy who sold some of the property around 1920. Until that time, the property called Foy Cemetery was used by the African American community for burials. Part of the sold property became part of the Evergreen cemetery that opened in 1928. The land backed up to Smith Reynolds Airport. With the expansion of Smith/ Reynolds Airport, over 700 graves were moved to the new Evergreen Cemetery which opened on New Walkertown Road in 1944. Some old graves still remain in the wooded area at the airport.

Oddfellows Cemetery was originally located in Winston Township (now Winston-Salem) and is on what is now Shore Fair Drive across from

Odd Fellows Cemetery Historic marker on Shore Fair Drive
(Photo taken by Chenita B. Johnson)

the Lawrence Joel Veterans Memorial Coliseum and Dixie Classic Fair Grounds, later renamed Carolina Classic Fair.

According to Doris Crosby, a long-time city resident, the area where the Odd Fellows Cemetery was located was farm area and was called Grunt Town because the farms raised pigs and hogs. She said the graves went all the way to where the rides on the fair grounds are today.

The cemetery is owned by the Odd Fellows Lodge. The 1884 Winston City Directory lists the Odd fellows Winston Star Lodge No. 2308 GUOOF with C. B. Cash as Secretary.

According to Mr. James Clyburn, OddFellows member and President of Friends of Odd Fellows Cemetery, Inc, as Odd Fellows members became older and began to die out, parts of the cemetery began to be sold without permission. One part of the cemetery was sold to Pine Hall Brick Company. It is said the company cleared the property and took the headstones from the cemetery and buried them. It is also said that the cemetery extended not only well into the current fairgrounds but also at Millbrook Apartments that backs up to the cemetery and where headstones were also discovered.

Later, the city of Winston-Salem wanted to buy the cemetery property to use as parking space for a sports complex but couldn't find all the relatives of those buried in the cemetery to obtain permission to remove the bodies. The OddFellows cemetery is the resting place of many notable veterans and residents such as members of the Hill family of Winston Mutual

Insurance, the File Family of Mt. Zion Baptist Church, Rev. Wentz of Wentz Memorial and WWII Fighter Pilot First Lt. Spurgeon Neal Ellington, a Tuskegee Airman awarded the Distinguished Flying Cross for his bravery as a pilot in 1944.

The OddFellows Cemetery now has historical designation and is being restored by the Friends of Odd Fellows Cemetery, Inc.

First YMCA / YWCA for African Americans

Second home of the YMCA in Winston-Salem
(Courtesy of the Bradshaw Estate)

Discussion concerning the first efforts to organize a YMCA for African Americans in Winston, took place in Winston on May 18, 1911. When it was considered feasible for a YMCA for African Americans, the community was challenged to raise $500 for funding of the first year.

September 1911 the African American branch of the YMCA was organized with a committee consisting of F. M. Kennedy, President; R. W. Brown (see chapters 2 and 5), Vice-President; F. M. Fitch, Secretary; J. H. Turner, Treasurer; Royal Puryear; C. H. Jones; L.O. Lee; C. B. Johnson; S. G. Atkins (chapter 2); E. W. Smith; and George Ragsdale.

"The YWCA was established January 1918"[152] in Pythian Hall on Chestnut Street. Miss Adele Ruffin, a representative of the national YWCA helped to organize 75 women into the YWCA, including
Mrs. Janie Melton, Mrs. E. O. Donoho and Mrs. Lillian B. Turner.
After moving from place to place, they settled in a brick garage on Chestnut near 7th street.

When the Depot Street School moved in 1926, the building was sold to the YMCA. When a fire destroyed the building, a new building was built, and by 1953 both the YMCA and the YWCA occupied the same building at the site of the Old Depot Street School on Patterson Avenue.
This new building was built due to the collaborative efforts of black workers, black residents, R. J. Reynolds Tobacco Company and Hanes Knitting Mills. The factory executives were approached by African American workers, and informed of the need for a new YMCA, and they agreed to match every dollar the workers could raise.
The workers did this by organizing workers of various Reynolds factories such as No. 8, No. 60 and No. 256, into basketball and baseball teams. Charging a 15-cent admission, the baseball games were played at a ballpark near Ferrell Street. Due to this effort, a new YMCA and YWCA building was erected on Seventh Street and Patterson Avenue on the former site of the Depot Street School.
Eventually due to urban renewal, the YMCA and the YWCA building on Patterson Avenue was torn down to make room for a parking lot. As of now, the lot is occupied by an Allegacy Credit Union and the Wake Forest BioTech Center. The area is now part of the Wake Forest Innovation Quarter.

The YMCA and the YWCA moved from the downtown building on Patterson Avenue to a new building on Water Works Road in 1983 and opened as the Winston Lake Family Y. It was renamed the Mo Lucas Senior Inclusive Recreation Center in honor of Moses "Mo" Lucas in 2016. Lucas was a family director and youth mentor with the Y for over 50 years beginning at the Patterson Avenue Y in 1954. There, he founded the Youth incentive program the drumline Boss Drummers and the Y-ettes majorettes.

COMMUNITY INSTITUTIONS

Drawing of YMCA AND YWCA at 6th Street and North Patterson Avenue (Courtesy of Winston-Salem African American Archive)

First Library for African Americans

East Winston Public Library Carver students 1955
(Courtesy of Winston-Salem African American Archive

The first organized library for blacks in Winston-Salem opened February 15, 1927 as a branch of the Carnegie Public Library, in the YWCA building on Chestnut Street, under the leadership of Mrs. Mary M. Hairston.

It was named the George Moses Horton Branch Library in "honor of a Negro slave poet born in North Carolina who in 1829 published his book of poems, *The Hope of Liberty*." (153) He was enslaved by William Horton in Northampton County, North Carolina and the poems were a protest of his enslavement.

"Mrs. M. Y. Ray, Alvan Jones, and Mrs. M. M. Hairston were volunteers that gave nearly one year of service of operations at the library so that blacks could have library privileges." (154)

November 14, 1954, a new library facility was built and opened on East Seventh Street on land provided by doctors H. D. Malloy, Sr., J. C. Jordan and H. Rembert Malloy (see *chapter 8*). It was renamed East Winston Branch Library.

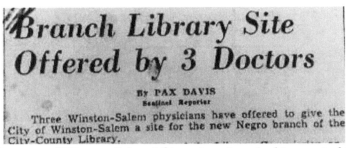

(Courtesy of Winston-Salem African American Archive-vertical file)

Mary Hairston
(Courtesy of Bradshaw Estate).

In 1998 it was designated as a Heritage Center, and on January 12, 2004 with a community program, the name was changed to Malloy-Jordan East Winston Heritage Center. Dr. Malloy was in attendance.

Notable Moments

George Horton wrote poems for the students at Chapel Hill and had been encouraged on his literary ambitions by students of the class of 1818, which included the future 11th President of the United States, James K. Polk.

Horton was the first African American poet in North Carolina and the first African American man in the south to be published. His poems were published while he was till enslaved.

Top: Langston Hughes at Horton Library February 6th, 1949 for the Negro History Week Book Fair. *Above:* Children at the George Moses Horton Branch Library, 1941 (*Courtesy of Forsyth County Public Library Photograph Collection, Winston-Salem, N.C.*)

 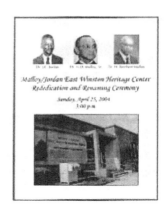

Dr. Malloy (left seated), Jackie Barber and Bobby Ray Wilson (on the right) at rededication and renaming ceremony. Above right: Program flyer of rededication, 2004 *(Courtesy of Chenita B. Johnson)*

First African American Boy Scout Troop

The First African American Boy Scout troop in the city, Troop No. 68, was established January 1934 at the First Baptist Church. The Troop was founded by Scout Masters T.F. Poag and G. F. Newell, both instructors at Atkins High School.

Boy Scout Troop #68
(Winston-Salem Journal, 1938. North Carolina Room, Forsyth County Central Library-vertical file)

The scout troop was organized with 17 charter members. The charter members were Robert Amson, Alton Butler, Spurgeon Ellington (see *chapter 13*), Clarence Glenn, Alphonse Greene, Joseph Haggler, Frederick W. Hairston, MacKay Hairston, John B. Henry, Marion Hauser, Charles Johnson, William Lyles, Russell March, James D. Pope, John D. Quick, Jr., J.C. White Jr. and Irvin Williams, Jr., Assistant Scoutmaster Frank O. Brown, Jr., with Clarence Grier, represented the troop at the 1937 Boy Scout Jamboree in Washington, DC.

A Troop Committee was named with the "responsibility of preserving the traditions and idealism of the scout movement and of the parent institution, and of stimulating the scoutmaster and aiding him in his work." [155]

The committee members were Ralph Morgan (see *chapter 5*), Attorney W. Avery Jones (see *chapter 7*), Clark S. Brown(see *chapter 3*), and Aladine Robinson (see *chapter 14*). Later Professor J.W. Paisley, Sr. (see *chapter 2*) Principal of Kimberley Park School joined the committee.

The First Playground in an African American Neighborhood

The first public playground for the black community was in the Happy Hills community. The playground was the first to be placed in an African American neighborhood in Winston-Salem. The idea for a playground came from resident and R. J. Reynolds Tobacco Company worker Wade Bitting and other residents who petitioned then Mayor R. J. Reynolds, Jr to clear undergrowth in the neighborhood to create a playground for the children.

It is said that the mayor liked the idea so much that he suggested that there be a playground in all African American neighborhoods.

Record Dedication of Community Recreational Centers in the African American Community

Winston-Salem set a state record Saturday January 17, 1942 when it accepted and dedicated three recreational centers, all in the African American community, at the same time.

Opening of the 14th Street swimming pool
(Courtesy of the Bradshaw Estate)

The three centers, Kimberley Park, Fourteenth Street and Happy Hill, were a three point $73,000 W.P.A. local project.

Earlier in 1940, a pool was built at Fourteenth Street with W.P.A. funding and $500 from the black community.

During the park dedication ceremony, "C.C. McGinnis, state W.P.A. administrator presented the centers to the city and Mayor Richard J. Reynolds accepted on behalf of the city." [156] "A.L. Butner gave the site for Kimberly Park and a cash donation of $1,000 and James A. Gray backed the sponsor's share of the project with $22,000." [157]

Fourteenth Street and Happy Hill received new playgrounds.

Other notables during this ceremony and presentation included Jack Atkins, Executive Secretary of the Winston-Salem Teachers College and individual representatives from each of the three centers.

Licensed Day Nursery for African American Children

In October 1938, Bethlehem House became the only licensed Daycare Nursery in the state of North Carolina for African American children. The Bethlehem Center was under the direction of Mrs. Marian Wooten who was asked to be director of the center in 1928.

Mrs. Marian Wooten
(Courtesy of Bradshaw Estate)

She was a graduate of Fisk University. She acquired special training in kindergarten work at Columbia University and had taken extension classes in education and supervision from UNC-Charlotte.

Under Mrs. Wooten, the center created the first community classes in nutrition, home beautification, writing for adults and the first Girl Scout Troop for African American Girls. She also began a well-baby clinic that was staffed by doctors and nurses at the center. Mrs. Wooten retired from the Bethlehem Center in 1973.

First Daycare for African American

The Goler Daycare Nursery was organized in 1942 during WWII by Mrs. Georgia Murray Marshall and Dr. A. L. Cromwell.

Mrs. Marshall was a graduate of Slater Normal and Industrial School. She taught at Salem Hill and Old Town schools.

The Goler Nursery was the first daycare nursery for African Americans in the community that was funded by the Community Chest. Children in this program were taught basic skills, and given nutritious meals as well as daycare. While funding for the program ended after the war, Mrs. Marshall did fundraisers, and continued the daycare until she retired in 1967.

Mrs. Georgia Murray Marshall
(Courtesy of Bradshaw Estate)

First to Collect African American Historic Information for Preservation

Joseph Elton Bradshaw, Sr.
(Courtesy of the Bradshaw Estate)

The father of African American History and Preservation in Forsyth County is said to be Joseph Elton Bradshaw, Sr. He was born in Winston-Salem in 1914. Graduating from Atkins High School in 1932, he continued his education and received his BA in Sociology from Lincoln University in Pennsylvania and a master's from Atlanta University.

After various employments, Mr. Bradshaw began teaching History in J. J. Jones High School in Surry County. In this occupation he realized the absence of African Americans from the history he was teaching, and he began collecting materials to use in class. This collection of local African American information which included photos and memorabilia, continued for 29 years.

Bradshaw had a vision to have a permanent home for this collection of local African American history.

In 1981 Mr. Bradshaw with the aid of Dr. William Rice, Dr. Lenwood Davis, Gloria Diggs Banks, James T. Diggs, Jr., Velma Hopkins, H. Rembert Malloy (see *chapter 8*) and others, The Society for the Study of Afro American History in Winston-Salem / Forsyth County was formed.

The Society for the Study of Afro American History in Winston-Salem/ Forsyth County

The first organization to collect, and preserve the history of African Americans in Winston-Salem and Forsyth County is The Society for the Study of Afro American History in Winston-Salem/ Forsyth County, Inc.

Formed in 1981 and officially organized in 1983, its mission was to document and preserve the history and chronicle the achievements and progression of African Americans in the Winston-Salem / Forsyth County area.

To more effectively market and document the history specific to the area nationally and internationally, the Archive committee of the SSAH eventually became *The Winston-Salem African American Archive.* This committee of the SSAH not only fulfilled the mission of the "Society" to educate the community of its African American history, but also acted as the repository and documenter of African American historical memorabilia of Winston-Salem and Forsyth County.

Currently the Winston-Salem African American Archive, no longer a committee of the Society, operates as a separate organization. It continues its mission of educating the public, as well as preserving, documenting, exhibiting and being a repository and resource for the community

Some Founding members of The Society for the Study of Afro American

History in Winston-Salem / Forsyth County, Inc. were Mr. Bradshaw, Dr. William Rice, Dr. Lenwood Davis, Gloria Diggs Banks, James T. Diggs, Jr., Velma Hopkins, H. Rembert Malloy, Mazie Woodruff, Harold L. Kennedy, Jr., Lester Davis, Billy Rich and Dr. Virginia Newell (*see chapter 4*).

First Citizens Review Board

A Citizens Police Review Board was voted on and approved by the Winston-Salem Alderman Board (City Council), June 15, 1992. The conception of a review board in Winston-Salem came from the encouragement of African American citizens in Winston-Salem to the Alderman Board concerning transparency and accountability of the police department to the community.

The vote to establish a review board came from a tie vote broken by Mayor Martha Wood. The vote split down racial lines with 4 African American Aldermen; Vivian Burke (see *chapter 4*), Nelson Malloy (see *chapter 4*), Virginia Newell (see *chapter 4*), and Larry Womble (see *chapters 3 and 4*), voting in favor and 4 White Aldermen; Robert Northington, Hugh Wright, Linda Sharpe, and Nancy Pleasants voting against. With the vote 5-4, the request was made to the Public Safety Committee to develop a plan for a Citizens' Police Review Board.

Although it was the second such board in the state of North Carolina, The Citizens Police Review Board in Winston-Salem was the first vehicle in the city that citizens could bring issues concerning police brutality for investigation.

With the contribution of interested citizens through public meetings, The Citizens Police Review Board plan was approved and adopted by the City Aldermen (City Council) on February 15, 1993.Its primary purpose is to act as a fact-finding body in cases involving unresolved citizen complaints against employees of the Police Department.

The Citizens Police Review Board consists of eleven Winston-Salem residents serving three-year terms. Members are appointed by the City Council after a recommendation by the mayor.

Chapter Thirteen

Military

Long before we were the United States of America and were simply 13 colonies fighting for independence from the British Empire, African Americans were standing and fighting alongside colonists although many were still enslaved.

There has been no war fought by the United States that African Americans did not shed blood and treasure on the battlefield. This includes the Revolutionary War where they were one-sixth of those who fought for freedom at Lexington, Concord and Valley Forge. There were 58 African American soldiers serving in the North Carolina Brigade under General George Washington.

African Americans fought the War of 1812; the Mexican-American War; the Civil War where around 220,000 blacks joined the ranks of the Union Army and Navy; the Spanish American War where twenty-two of the 330 sailors that went down with the Battleship Main were African American, as well as those who charged up San Juan Hill with "Teddy" Roosevelt and El Canay. They fought in World Wars I and II; the Korean Conflict; the Vietnam Conflict; the Gulf War; and the wars in Afghanistan and Iraq.

These loyal soldiers fought for their country and for the promise that is the United States of America, even when this promise seemed to be out of their reach.

WW I black soldiers in Winston-Salem, NC marching down Liberty Street
(Courtesy of Old Salem Museums & Gardens)

First Local African American Lieutenant of the Spanish American War

War veteran W. H. T. Powell is said to be the first resident of Winston, to have had the rank of Lieutenant in the Spanish American War.

Though Powell was not a native of Winston, he became a very active resident in the town concerning civic issues. When he died, he was commander of the Spanish American War soldier's organization in Winston.

First American Awarded the Croix De Guerre with Golden Palm

Sergeant Henry Johnson
"The Black Death" with Croix de guerre with Star and Golden Palm Leaf
(public domain/Wikipedia Commons)

Sergeant Henry Johnson (b.1892-d.1929), also known as William Henry Johnson, was an honored World War I soldier and hero. He was the first American soldier in World War I to be awarded by the French government with France's highest honor for bravery, the Croix de Guerre with Star and Golden Palm Leaf for extraordinary valor on the battlefield.

Henry Johnson was born in May 1892, in the town of Winston, North Carolina. When Henry was in his teens, his father moved the family to Albany, New York for work. Henry also worked in various jobs, and lived a relatively average life until April 6, 1917, when the United States declared war on Germany.

Henry Johnson was a small man, about 5 feet four inches tall and weighed 130 pounds, but two months after the declaration of war he enlisted in the U.S. army. His unit was a converted National Guard outfit which later became the 369th Infantry Regiment of the United States Army. This division later became known as the Harlem Hell fighters and trained in Spartanburg, South Carolina. While in South Carolina, an Alabama regiment of white troops was stationed near them, almost causing a fire fight between the two regiments.

This African American regiment was eventually sent to France, and although fully trained, these African American soldiers were used as menial laborers, such as digging latrines or as stevedores. The French military noticed the Americans were not using these soldiers on the battlefield and due to their heavy casualties, requested these soldiers for their regiment. Placed under French command the 369th Regiment was the first African American Unit to see combat.

On May 14th into May 15th, 1918, Henry Johnson and fellow soldier, seventeen-year-old Needham Roberts were on guard duty for the midnight to 4am shift when they came under attack by German soldiers. Hearing the wire of their perimeter being cut Johnson sent Roberts to get help. Under sniper fire he lobbed a grenade and a firefight ensued. He recalled Roberts, who became injured by enemy grenades. All he could do was hand Johnson grenades to lob at the Germans. In the conflict, Roberts was almost captured by two German soldiers, but Johnson fought them off although he was also injured.

After the grenades ran out, Johnson loaded his gun, but his French gun jammed when he inserted his American clip, so he used the butt of his weapon until it shattered. He then used his bolo knife in hand to hand combat and slashed in every direction. Johnson later mentioned one German kept bothering him, so he flipped him over his head and stabbed him in the ribs. This German soldier he said spoke in good New York English " *That black n----r got me.*"

He was still fighting, when reinforcements finally arrived an hour later and Johnson seeing them, passed out from his twenty-one wounds and from being shot three times. At the hospital, Johnson was treated for bayonet and knife wounds to his arm, back, feet and face. A steel plate was placed in his left foot. All of these were debilitating wounds.

Henry Johnson said of his encounter, that he just fought for his life, and a rabbit would've done that. Daylight however revealed more than that. Four Germans were found dead on the battlefield with evidence of thirty-two more in the fighting including thirty-eight bombs, riffles, bayonets and revolvers. Henry Johnson single handedly wounded or killed twenty-four enemy soldiers. He had defeated an entire platoon. This encounter was called the Battle of Henry Johnson.

The Germans called Johnson the *Black Death* and they designated African American troops the bloodthirsty Black Men. The French called them the Hell fighters, and the 369th became known as the Harlem Hell fighters. The 369th spent 191 consecutive days in combat, more than any American unit.

Both Johnson and Roberts were commended by General Blackjack Pershing and President Theodore Roosevelt. The entire French force in the area came to a ceremony to honor Privates Henry Johnson and Needham Roberts with the French Medal of Honor, the Croix de Guerre with citation.

They were the first Americans in World War I to be honored. However, for his valor on the battlefield, for rescuing a comrade and saving the lives of fellow soldiers, while wounded, Henry Johnson was awarded the Croix de Guerre, with star and Gold Palm. Both men were promoted to Sergeant.

After returning to New York there was a parade for the 369th which was attended by dignitaries including Mayor Al Smith. Henry Johnson rode in an open car to the cheers of those lining the streets.

Because of his popularity, Henry Johnson was enlisted to help sell Liberty Bonds and had a series of paid speaking engagements, however during one speaking engagement in St. Louis he told the truth about the treatment of Black soldiers by their white colleagues and their refusal to fight beside them. This created a racial backlash by whites, ending his popularity.

Unable to work due to his war injuries, he was almost penniless because his discharge papers did not mention he was wounded and he did not receive any benefits, but eventually he received a military pension.

Henry Johnson died in 1929 in a veteran's hospital in Washington, D.C. and was buried in Arlington National Cemetery with full military honors. He was posthumously awarded the Purple Heart in 1996, and the Distinguished Service Cross, the Army's second highest honor. But he had not yet been awarded the Nation's highest honor, the Congressional Medal of Honor. This was petitioned by Senator Charles Schumer of New York and Ronald Wynden of Oregon.

On June 2, 2015, President Barack Obama posthumously bestowed the Medal of Honor to Sgt. Henry Johnson. Accepting on his behalf was Command Sgt. Maj. Louis Wilson, of the New York National Guard. On June 3, 2015, Sgt. Henry Johnson along with Sgt. William Shemin, were inducted into the Hall of Heroes at the Pentagon in Washington, D.C.

Notable Moments

A postal facility at 747 Broadway was renamed for him, on September 4, 2007 and a charter school was dedicated in Albany New York, a
section of Northern Boulevard was named for him in New York, and a bronze statue of him was erected in Washington Park in Albany, New York in his honor, November 1991. It is inscribed: The Battle of Henry Johnson First American Awarded Croix De Guerre with Gold Palm for Valor.
Henry Johnson was used by the United States army for recruiting black soldiers after his death, which continued until 1976.

First Trained African American Marines

During the American Revolution, a few African Americans served in the Continental Marines, however the history of the United States Marine Corps has been exclusively white. This changed on June 25, 1941 when African Americans were accepted into the United States Marine Corps, after President Franklin Roosevelt signed the executive order to integrate the corps six months after the bombing of Pearl Harbor.

These first groups of African American marines were trained at Montford Point, a facility of Camp Lejeune, North Carolina.

Local Montford Marines
Left to Right- Back: Joseph Walker and Walter Lee Shipp. Front center: Josephus Carter *(Winston-Salem Journal. Courtesy of Winston-Salem African American Archive-vertical file)*

From August 26, 1942 until September 9, 1949, over 20,000 soldiers were trained there. They became known as the Montford Marines.
Some residents from Winston-Salem served as part of that first group of African American marines at Montford. They were Joseph Walker, Josephus Carter and Walter Lee Ship. They entered at various times in 1943 but served greatly together.

Segregation was still an issue in training these marines. While white marines were trained at Paris Island, South Carolina and San Diego, California, all African American marines were trained at Montford. The camp was later renamed Camp Johnson to honor Sergeant Major Gilbert "Hashmark" Johnson, one of the first African American drill instructors.

In June 2012, more than 400 Montford Point Marines were recognized for their service and sacrifice for their country, with the Congressional Gold Medal. The Congressional Gold medal bestowed by Congress is the highest civilian award of the United States.

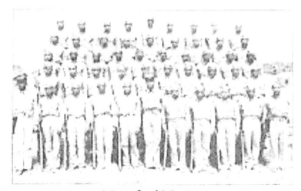

Montford Marines
(Winston-Salem Journal. Courtesy of Winston-Salem
African American Archive-vertical file)

First African American Fighter Pilot

Spurgeon Neal Ellington
(WSSU Archives-University Photograph Collection. Winston-Salem State
University Archives-C.G. O'Kelly Library)

First Lt. Spurgeon Neal Ellington was a Tuskegee Airman in World War II and was the first African American Fighter Pilot from Winston-Salem, North Carolina. A larger than life individual and flying Ace, Lt. Ellington was awarded the Distinguished Flying Cross for his bravery as a pilot in 1944.

He was born October 17, 1919 in Winston-Salem, to James A. and Emma Neal Ellington, who resided at 727 East Seventh Street. James Ellington was a successful businessman who had a profitable grocery business on Seventh and Linden Streets and had various investments.

After graduating from Atkins High School, Spurgeon Ellington attended and graduated in the 1939 class from Winston- Salem Teachers College and began his career as an elementary school teacher.

He enlisted in the United States Army at Fort Bragg, North Carolina in April 1942 and trained as a pilot at Tuskegee Army Airfield as a member of Colonel Benjamin O. Davis, Jr.'s fighter group. On May 28, 1943, he received his wings as a part of class 43-E-SE and was assigned to the 100th Fighter Squadron, 332nd Fighter Group. Excited about receiving his wings and wanting to show off his flying skills to the hometown, he flew home to Winston-Salem, flying down Main Street *on deck*, which means he was flying close to the ground. He was court martialed for this stunt and fined at Tuskegee. But he was forgiven and allowed to fly. He went with the 332nd when it moved to Michigan for advanced combat training.

Ellington's plane was the P-51 Mustang named the "Lollipoop II" and had a solid red tail. He flew with the 332nd Fighter Group, 99th Fighter Squadron. The 332nd squadron was depicted in the movie about the Tuskegee airmen, by Steven Spielberg titled "Red Tails".

After the war, Spurgeon Ellington was assigned as an instructor at a training base in Georgia. He was killed in 1945 with pilot, Lt. Richard Hall in a plane crash during a training exercise at Crystal Lake, Georgia and was buried at the Odd Fellows Cemetery in Winston-Salem.

Notable Moments

James Ellington built the Emma Building, a commercial building, in 1910. Named after his wife Emma, the building was located at 608-616 Patterson Avenue and housed various businesses such as a tailor, dry goods store, a variety store, barbershop and two large apartments with full bathrooms. Emma Ellington's mother, Mrs. Neal was the owner of several boarding houses in Winston.

The bulk of the black flyers were in the 99th fighter squadron. Being a highly decorated Fighter Squadron their campaigns included Sicily, Naples-Foggia; Anzio; Rome-Arno; Normandy; Northern France; Southern France; North Apennines; Rhineland; Central Europe; Po Valley; and Air Combat-EAME Theater.

There were a series of heritage paintings commemorating the service of the Tuskegee Airmen. Many depicted Spurgeon Ellington's plane flying in support of heavy bomber raids in Europe.

1ST Lt. Ellington's P-51 Mustang, "Lollipoop" was the favorite of almost every model plane manufacturer. Many of the models included decals to realistically reproduce the plane.

The plane was named for his wife, jazz singer Maria Antoinette Hawkins. He called Maria his "Lollipoop". He painted the name on his plane with an image of her wearing a red dress.

They were married in 1943 while he was still serving with the squadron. Maria was the niece of Charlotte Hawkins Brown, the founder of the Palmer Memorial Institute in Sedalia, NC. While Spurgeon Ellington was in Europe, Maria continued her career, singing with Count Basie's Orchestra and later as a singer with Duke Ellington's band. She later met and married singer Nat "King" Cole in 1948 and is the mother of singer Natalie Cole.

Congressional Medal of Honor

"Lawrence Joel bound up the wounds of his countrymen with no regard for their color or creed."- Alderman Martha Wood

Lawrence Joel with Congressional Medal of Honor
(Courtesy of Forsyth County Public Library Photograph Collection, Winston-Salem, N.C.)

Sergeant First Class Lawrence Joel (Feb.22, 1928-Feb.1984) was born to Trenton and Mary Ellen Joel, and grew up in East Winston. He was Winston Salem's only Congressional Medal of Honor winner and "the 1st Black man to receive the Medal of Honor for battlefield heroism."[158]

Joel began his military career at age 17 when he joined the Merchant Marines. In 1946 he enlisted in the army and except for a four-year interval, served until 1973.

Events that caused him to be honored occurred November 8, 1965 near Bien Hoa in South Vietnam when Company C, the first battalion 503 infantry 173rd Airborne Brigade, was on patrol and was ambushed and attacked by a Viet Cong force that killed or wounded nearly every man in the lead American squad.

Joel was an army paratrooper and medical aid specialist of this Company when they were attacked by the Vietcong. In the line of gunfire, he helped 13 wounded soldiers and saved the life of one with a serious chest wound. He was also shot but bandaged himself and continued to help not only his unit but those from another company until he was ordered to evacuate.

. Lawrence Joel was awarded the Silver Star and President Lyndon Johnson presented him with the Medal of Honor March 9, 1967. "He was the 1st African American to receive this honor, since the Spanish American War of 1898,"[159] and the first from Winston-Salem.

He was honored by his hometown of Winston-Salem with a parade April 8, 1967.

In 1986, after much public debate and controversy, the Winston-Salem Board of Aldermen voted to name the city's new coliseum for Lawrence Joel. It became the Lawrence Joel Veterans Memorial Coliseum and a repository to the memory of our fallen soldiers rests in the front of the coliseum.

Notable Moments

Joel is also recognized with several buildings and memorials bearing his name and dedicated in his honor throughout the United States. They include: The Joel Auditorium at Walter Reed Army Medical Center in Washington, D.C., the U.S, Army Clinics at Fort McPherson, GA. and Fort Bragg, N.C., and Joel Drive, of Blanchfield Community Hospital in Fort Campbell, KY.

His name is also honored in the song 8th of November by country artists Big and Rich.

Lawrence Joel married Dorothy Region and together they had 2 children, Tremain and Deborah Louise.

Parade in Winston-Salem for Lawrence Joel
(Courtesy of Forsyth County Public Library Photograph Collection, Winston-Salem, N.C.)

First African American General in the North Carolina National Guard

"I am privileged to serve." General James R. Gorham

James R. Gorham, a bank executive in Kernersville became the first African American officer to become Brigadier General in the North Carolina National Guard. He received his General Stars December 2, 2008.

James R. Gorham pinning ceremony
(Winston-Salem Journal. Photo by Tech Sgt. Brian E. Christianson. Courtesy of Winston-Salem African American Archive-vertical file)

Gorham joined the army after high school and served three years. Afterward he attended East Carolina University. It was there, during his sophomore year, he applied to officer candidate school at North Carolina Military Academy through the National Guard. He graduated with honors in 1980 and was commissioned a 2nd Lieutenant. He attended the Army War College and has commanded at every level.

In 2004, Gorham's guard unit, the 113-sustainment deployed to Iraq for 15 months instead of the normal two weeks. It was during this deployment he was promoted from Lieutenant Colonel to full Colonel.

J.R. Gorham became the Deputy Adjutant General for the guard. He was assigned to the Joint Forces Headquarters in Raleigh and responsible for the N.C. Military Academy and the Butner Training Facility.

When not serving in the guard, he worked as a business banker and Vice-President of First Citizens Bank in Kernersville, N. C.

The First African American Rear Admiral

The first African American Rear Admiral from Winston-Salem is Rear Admiral Walter Jackson Davis, Jr. who became Commandant of Navy District Washington, DC and later retired as Vice Admiral. Born in 1936, the Winston-Salem native is the son of Walter Jackson Davis, Sr. who worked at Western Electric in Winston-Salem and Inez May Stout.

Rear Admiral Walter Jackson Davis, Jr.
(Released to Public catalog.archives.gov/)

After Davis graduated from Atkins High School, he attended Ohio State University where he not only received a BS Degree in Electrical Engineering, he completed the Naval Reserve Officer Training Corps (NROTC) program at Ohio University and was commissioned in 1959.

In 1960 Davis was designated a Naval Aviator.

He had majored in electrical engineering because he wanted to have a degree in something that would make him always needed, but he excelled in the Navy, creating an unintended career which propelled him to the highest levels of the Navy.

As a combat pilot serving in Vietnam he accumulated over 3,500 flight hours and over 800 carrier landings, and his various operational assignments during his Navel career included squadron commander of the F-14 (VF-114), Aircraft Carrier Commanding Officer of the USS Ranger and Battle Group Commander.

His shore assignments included engineering positions as Navy Engineer for the F-14 aircraft and Naval Warfare IT (Information Technology).

The last Navel Assignment for Davis was Naval Deputy Chief of Naval Operations for Space Systems. He also was over Information Warfare systems, Command and Control Systems, and Modeling and Simulation where he developed, justified and directed the Navy's IT (Information Technology) budget.

Notable Moments

After retiring from the Navy, Davis used his engineering knowledge and served as President at BAE Systems and became co-founder of E-Fire. He later became a director at CommNexus.

First Resident Nominated and Appointed by Three United States Presidents for Government Positions

Togo Dennis West, Jr.
United States Secretary of Veteran Affairs
(public domain Wikipedia)

Togo Dennis West, Jr. was known as an exceptional individual. He is the only Winston-Salem Forsyth County resident to have been recognized and appointed by three sitting Presidents of the United States to government positions. The son of Togo West Sr., and Evelyn West, he was born in Winston Salem, North Carolina on June 21, 1942 and grew up on Cameron Avenue. His grandmother named Togo Senior, after Japanese Admiral Heihachiro Togo, hero of 1905's Russo-Japanese War. West graduated as valedictorian from Atkins High school in 1959 and continued his education at Howard University with an electrical and later

JD Degree. He later served in the United States Army as a judge in the Judge Advocate General Corps.

Due to his legal knowledge and exceptional and distinguished military service he was recognized by three presidents and appointed to government positions. Gerald Ford appointed him Deputy Attorney General of the U.S. Department of Justice in 1973; under President Jimmy Carter he was appointed as General Counsel to the Navy in 1979, he served as Deputy Secretary to the Secretary of Defense and General Counsel to the Department of Defense from 1980 to 1981.

All these appointments culminated to the nomination of West by President Bill Clinton, in September 1993, as Secretary of the Army.

After receiving Congressional confirmation, he was sworn in as the 16th Secretary of the Army. He held this position from 1993 to 1997.

In 1998, West was appointed by President Clinton as the United States Secretary of Veteran Affairs, succeeding Jesse Brown as the second African American to hold that position.

Chapter Fourteen

Entertainment

AFRICAN AMERICAN FIRSTS

Entertainment not only provided African Americans an escape from the stress of their lives, it created community spirit.

Legally unable to attend the various entertainment and cultural arts events and venues throughout the city without being relegated to a sectioned area of public auditoriums, African Americans in Winston-Salem Forsyth County became successful in providing entertainment for themselves and their community.

They did this by creating a duo cultural society to express themselves in various ways.

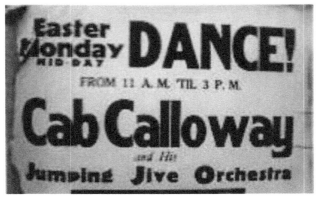

Top: Negro dance, early 1900s (*Courtesy of the State Archives of North Carolina*) Above: Cab Calloway advertisement (*Courtesy of the Winston-Salem African American Archive*)

FIRST BLACK FORSYTH COUNTY FAIR

African American leaders R.W. Brown (see *chapter 2*), J. H. Turner, James Timlic, J. S. Fitts and others formed the Piedmont Fair Association. This group sponsored the Forsyth County Fair which became The Piedmont Colored Industrial Fair or The Colored Fair. This African American County Fair usually followed the fair for white citizens and was "held in the area of Cleveland Avenue, where Piedmont Park houses are currently located."[160]

Colored fair 1945
(Courtesy of the Bradshaw Estate)

This event gave African Americans in Forsyth County an opportunity "to exhibit agricultural and household crafts as well as providing for them, a general outlet of recreation for the black community."[161]

It is said that educator, Booker T. Washington opened the first Piedmont Fair in 1900 accompanied by a parade. However, while there was a mile length parade and great community participation, the only dignitaries listed as speakers in the Union Republican newspaper were Mayor O. B. Eaton of Winston, and Rev. Dr. J. W. E. Bowen of Atlanta, Georgia.

The first Piedmont Colored Industrial Fair lasted for five days beginning Monday August 20, 1900 and ending Friday August 24, 1900. It included exhibits from Fort Slocum, N.Y., New Bern, Durham and Greensboro

Crowds were treated to horseback riders, climbing greased poles, bicycle races, ball games, band concerts and various other amusements. The only disappointment was the lack of transportation by Southern Railroad. The railroad initially reneged on a promise to provide train service for at least three days of the event, but at the last minute changed their minds and sent train cars, but the cars used were unfit and unsafe for the intended passengers, causing most not to use them.

The Colored Fair continued for years following the white fair, even when blacks and whites began to share the Dixie Classic Fair grounds in Winston-Salem. This practice of Jim Crow segregation continued until the Dixie Classic Fair integrated in 1964, with the James Strates Show. The Strates show came to Colored Fair at the fairgrounds but refused to come to the White Dixie Classic Fair unless it removed the Jim Crow segregation and allowed African Americans to attend.

The Piedmont Colored Industrial Fair or *The Colored Fair*. 1947 fair exhibit
(Courtesy of the Bradshaw Estate)

First African American Owned Park

Robinhood Park was completed and opened the summer of 1937. The park was developed by philanthropist and owner of Howard Robinson Funeral Home, It was the first of its kind in Forsyth County.

Lake and pavilion at Robinhood Park
(Winston-Salem Chronicle. Courtesy of Winston-Salem African American Archive-vertical file)

The Park Facilities covered 17 acres and was used by African Americans as far away as Danville, Virginia. A dance pavilion that projected over the lake was a favorite of the young people of the area and used for boating. There were also facilities for picnics, swimming and camping.

"Local bands played at the Park as well as National aggregations booked through the Morris Gale Booking Agency of New York. Jimmy Gunn was a frequent provider of music at the park featuring Al Harrington Guitarist. Al was the father of Jana Harrington, TV personality." [162]

The park was managed by Mr. George Booie.

George Booie and A. Robinson
(Courtesy of the Bradshaw Estate)

Mossell Hairston a contestant in Beauty Contest at Robinhood Park
*(Winston-Salem Chronicle. Courtesy of Winston-Salem African
American Archive-vertical file)*

First Theaters for African American Patrons

The creation of the Rex and Lafayette local theaters gave African American movie patrons the ease and opportunity to view movies without having to climb to the balcony entrance or relegated to a section in the theater as was the case in white owned theaters such as the Liberty and Carolina, due to Jim Crow laws in Winston-Salem Forsyth County, and in other Southern cities and counties.

The Rex Theater

The Rex Theater was the first theater for African Americans in the town that showed pictures in 1912. The theater was located at 104 East Fourth Street.

Rex Theater This photo from Fam Brownlee: Photoshopped for as much clarity as possible (*This enlarged picture is of the Rex Theater from a 1912 newspaper ad. Black Hollywood in the Twin City. Fam Brownlee, genealogy, history. NC Room, Forsyth County Central Library*)

Lafayette Theater

(Courtesy of Winston-Salem African American Archive)

The first to present movies and vaudeville shows in Winston-Salem was the Lafayette Theater. Opened in 1919 at 108 East Fourth Street. it brought in Vaudeville acts from Chicago, New York,

Philadelphia and Washington. On August 28, 1921 the Lafayette Theater was home to the 3-day world premiere of "*A Giant of His Race.*" This movie with a $50,000 budget was a "*race movie*" which was part of a genre that depicted successful black people on screen.

The North State Film Company formed by three white men of Winston-Salem was responsible for the movie being filmed in Winston-Salem. William Scales though not an official member was a consultant in planning. The movie used many local African Americans.

The film moved from Winston-Salem to the famous Lincoln Theater in Chicago for its second premier, from there to Harlem for a long run and other theaters across the country, receiving excellent reviews.

Mr. William Scales was the operator and owner of both the Lafayette and Rex Theaters. The Lafayette closed in 1926 and remained dark for a decade, reopening in October 1936. It closed for renovations in 1965 and never reopened.

Above: Ad from "Black Hollywood in the Twin City"
(Fam Brownlee, genealogy, history NC Room Forsyth County Library).
Below- Ad for Lafayette Theater *(Winston-Salem Journal March 8, 1925.*
Courtesy of Winston-Salem African American Archive-vertical file)

International Dancing Star and Entertainer

Harold Lloyd Nicholas
(Wikipedia photo)

Harold Lloyd Nicholas was the youngest of the phenomenal tap-dancing duo, the Nicholas Brothers who gained fame during the Harlem Renaissance, and broke the barriers to become one of the most popular show business acts in entertainment history.

Named after the silent screen actor Harold Lloyd, he was born March 21, 1921 in Winston-Salem, North Carolina. Harold Nicholas is the first known vaudeville and dance star from Winston-Salem. He and his older brother Fayard Nicholas had a career that began in childhood and spanned for almost 60 years. They called their dancing, classical tap, because it incorporated elements of ballet, tap as well as had a blend of acrobatics and used their entire bodies including arms and hands.

The brothers danced and sang on Broadway, on television, and Harold Nicholas appeared in more than 50 films. Their parents Ulysses and Viola Nicholas were college educated musicians and vaudeville orchestra directors.

Harold began his career, dancing on the black vaudeville stage at age 5 with his brother and sister Dorothy. Their act was known as the Nicholas Kids. The boys first appeared on the radio show Horn and Hardart Kiddie Hour. After being seen at the Lafayette Theater in New York City by a Warner Brothers producer, they appeared in a black vaudeville movie short titled *Pie Pie Blackbird* in 1932. That same year Harold at age eleven, and his brother Fayard, appeared at the Cotton Club in Harlem.

Samuel Goldwyn from Hollywood cast the brothers in Kid Millions two years later. They were in a London stage review in 1936 and were cast in various films such as The Big Broadcast of 1936, and Stormy Weather starring Bill "Bojangles" Robinson, Cab Calloway and Lena Horne where they performed their Jumpin' Jive dance routine, which Fred Astaire commented as the greatest movie musical number he had ever seen.

They also performed on Broadway in The Ziegfeld Follies of 1936, Babes in Arms in 1937, and St. Louis Woman in 1946 where Harold introduced the song, Come Rain or Come Shine.

Due to racial restrictions the brothers appeared on screen as guest artists. This would separate them from the movie plot and the screen time with white co-stars. These scenes could then be deleted for southern screening.

The last film that Harold Nicholas made with his brother was *The Pirate* in 1948. The movie starred Gene Kelly, who crossed the color line, when he danced with the Nicholas Brothers on screen.

He later became a solo performer. He went to live in France in 1950 and successfully performed throughout Europe and North Africa, appearing in the French film "L'Empite de la Nuit" in 1964 with Eddie Constantine. Back in the United States, he performed in such movies as "Uptown Saturday Night in 1974; Tap, in 1989 and the Five Heartbeats in 1991.

Notable Moments

Harold Nicholas married actress Dorothy Dandridge in 1942.

Harold and Fayard Nicholas in "Stormy Weather Jumpin' Jive dance routine" *(https://www.pinterest.com/pin/45317539970386141/)*

First Female Action Star

Pam Grier
(Public Domain. blackpast.org)

Winston-Salem Native, Pam Grier is said to be the first female action movie star and first bankable black actress in Hollywood. She is known for playing assertive female characters that did not lose femininity in her assertiveness and paving the way for many African American actresses. The Golden Globe and Emmy nominated actress was born May 26, 1949 in Winston-Salem, N.C. to Clarence and Gwendolyn Grier, Jr. Her mother was a nurse and her father was a mechanic for the United States Air Force. He was later stationed in Colorado, but she calls Winston-Salem her true home as many of her family still resides in the city.

While living in Colorado, Pam at age 18 was discovered by a talent scout when she entered a pageant at Colorado Springs hotel. She moved to California where her cousin Rosie Grier played for the LA Rams.

After years of hard work, she broke into show business with so-called Blaxploitation movies; Coffey, Foxy Brown, Sheeba Baby, Cool Breeze and later, in the Quentin Tarantino movie Jackie Brown. Her career has spanned over forty years and she is still revered as the woman who kicked down doors for women in action movies.

First Miss America from Winston-Salem

Nia Franklin
(Courtesy of James Franklin)

Nia Franklin, a native of Winston Salem, was crowned the 2019 Miss America in Atlantic City, New Jersey. She represented New York in the pageant. Franklin graduated from North Davidson High School in Welcome, North Carolina, and completed her undergraduate degree in music from East Carolina University and her master's degree in music composition from UNC School of the Arts where she earned the Campus Arts Scholarship and the Beth Stovall Music Scholarship, named after a former Miss North Carolina.

Notable Moments

In 2016, Franklin was crowned Miss Capital City in Raleigh and competed in the Miss North Carolina pageant. While at UNCSA, Franklin was selected for the 2017 William R. Kenan Fellowship with the Lincoln Center of the Performing Arts education division in New York City.

She was crowned Miss New York in June 2018 and Miss America on September 9, 2018. Her platform was of advocating for the arts.

Nia Franklin became the first Miss America in the post-swimsuit era.

Cultural Arts

Sculptor Selma Burke

Selma Burke at the Recorder of Deeds Building in Washington DC. with Plaque of FDR *(National Museum of the US Navy, PUBLIC DOMAIN)*

Famed artist and sculpture Selma Burke, "a graduate of Slater Industrial Academy and Slater Normal School (WSSU) is best known for her image of President Franklin Delano Roosevelt found on the dime."[163] She is the first known African American to be requested to do a sculpture image of a United States President.

She revealed a Bas Relief of Roosevelt at the Recorder of Deeds office in Washington DC in a ceremony on September 24, 1945. First Lady Eleanor Roosevelt attended the ceremony.

"According to the National Archives and records Administration of Franklin D. Roosevelt Library in Hyde Park, New York, the source of the Roosevelt image on the coin was the Sculpture of FDR done by Selma Burke."[164]

Selma Burke
(WSSU Archives-University Photograph Collection. Winston-Salem State University Archives-C.G. O'Kelly Library).

Nationally Recognized for 3-Dimensional Wire Sculptures

Haywood Oubre, The Master of Torque

Hayward Oubre, Chairman of WSSU Art Department 1965-1981 with two of his sculptures *(WSSU Archives-University Photograph Collection. Winston-Salem State University Archives-C.G. O'Kelly Library)*

Hayward L. Oubre (b.1916 - d.2003), was a sculptor, painter and educator, famously known not only for his paintings of the American Experience, but also for his artistic expressions of sculpture made from clothes hanger wire.

He is the first Winston-Salem resident nationally recognized for his unique artistic expression of 3-dimensional wire sculpture. His various creations made from colorful clothes hanger wire, pliers, and metal cutters include a rooster, horse, and the WSSU Ram which is in the O'Kelly library.

His artwork has appeared in various national museums, galleries and appeared in national magazines. Oubre also developed and copyrighted a color wheel that updated and expanded the 1810 color triangle developed by Johann Wolfgang von Goethe.

Originally from New Orleans Louisiana, Oubre received his undergraduate Arts Degree from Dillard University in 1939.

His continued education was interrupted while a student at Tuskegee when World War II began. He was drafted and worked as an engineer with the United States military during World War II. After he left the military, Oubre continued his education on the GI Bill and later received his master's Degree at the University of Iowa. His unique art works became known worldwide.

He then launched a career as an art educator, teaching first at Florida A&M University, then at Alabama State College, where he began creating his wire sculpture, and later at Winston-Salem State University (WSSU). There he became chairman of the Arts Department where he initiated a studio art program and continued his work in art sculpture.

He retired from WSSU in 1981 and was asked by renowned sculptor Selma Burke, a graduate of Slater Industrial Academy and Slater Normal School now WSSU, to become the curator of the Selma Burke Gallery which was formally at Winston-Salem State University.

The artwork of Haywood Oubre has more than 50 exhibits, including permanent collection status at Winston-Salem State University, Atlanta University, University of Delaware, The High Museum, and Metropolitan Museum of Art. He has earned numerous awards, including the U.S. Pentagon, Who's Who in American Art, being featured in various magazines, books, documentaries films, and earning North Carolina's highest honor, the Order of the Long Leaf Pine.

Notable Moments

As a Master Sergeant and Draftsman in the 97th Regiment he and 3,000 African American enlisted engineers helped to build the Alcan (Alaska - Canada) Highway used in the war effort.

This was the first time the military took steps to utilize black soldiers for other purposes than as stevedores, and ditch diggers.

The War Department officially considered black soldiers unsuitable for cold climates, and to be careless, shiftless, irresponsible and secretive. But with lack of personnel, Oubre and the other African American engineers were called to Alaska and Canada; and with the effort of black and white soldiers working together, the highway was opened November 20, 1940 to military traffic.

The highway (now known as the Alaska Highway), was opened to the general public traffic in 1948. It was also in that same year that President Harry S. Truman desegregated the US Armed Forces by Executive Order.

In 1993 the Pentagon honored Oubre and other surviving soldiers from the Alcan Highway battalion for their service.

Geraldine Pete, WSSC 1964 Class President with Ram sculpture created by Oubre. The sculpture was presented by the class of 1964 during the dedication of the C. G. O'Kelly Library in 1967.
(WSSU Archives- University Photograph Collection. Winston-Salem State University Archives-C.G. O'Kelly Library)

First Successful African American Comic Book Artist

Matt Baker

(Courtesy of Matt Baker Estate. Photo is property of the Estate of Matt Baker and may not be reproduced without permission from the Estate.)

Matt Baker, (December 10,1921-August 11, 1959) is considered the first successful African American in the comic book industry. Primarily a freelance artist, he mastered a wide variety of genre, such as westerns, crime, jungle adventures, and romance. He went on to become known as the master of the *Good Girl* style of comics during the 1940s and 1950s, the era known as the Golden Age of Comics. Good Girl is the style of drawing the female form. Baker was a master at drawing female characters more anatomically correct than his contemporaries. He also drew male characters in a graceful and fluid style.

In an industry dominated by white males, Matt Baker's extreme artistic talent broke through barriers, and his comics could be seen in newsstands across the country.

He was born Clarence Matthew Baker in Forsyth County, North Carolina, December 10, 1921, to Clarence and Ethel Baker. He had two brothers

Robert and John. The family later moved from North Carolina to Pittsburgh, Pennsylvania.

After Matthew Baker graduated from High School he moved to Washington, DC and worked for the government. He was unable to be drafted for military service due a heart ailment from battling rheumatic fever as a child.

He later moved to New York City to study art at the Cooper Union School of Engineering, Art and Design, a private college in the East Village. He had been an avid drawer and was inspired by his artistic heroes such as magazine illustrator Andrew Loomis, and comic book artists Will Eisner, Reed Crandall, Alex Blum and Lou Fine.

Baker began his career in New York as a background artist at S.M. Iger studio in 1944. The studio produced ready to print feature material for comic book publishers. He was given scripts to pencil but since his work was inked over by other artists, they were given the credit for his early work.

His first assignment was as a penciler and inker on the *Sheena Queen of the Jungle story in Fiction House's Jumbo Comics #69* in November 1944. He also did work through Iger Studio for Fox Comics, Fiction House, Quality Comics, and St. John Publications.

From 1944 to 1948 he was the principal artist on "Sky Girl", a regular feature in Fiction House's Jumbo Comics. December 1946, he illustrated the character, "Lorna Doone" for Classic Comics, and was assigned to Fiction House's comic feature called "Tiger Girl". His most well-known character was "Phantom Lady," a crime fighting Washington Socialite. He penciled and inked this character from 1947 to 1949. He drew her in blue short shorts with slits up the sides, a matching halter top with plunging neckline, a belt and scarlet cape.

In 1948, Matt Baker became the lead artist with St. John's Publications. It was there in 1950 he penciled the picture novel, "It Rhymes with Lust," what is considered to be the first modern graphic novel.

From 1952-1954, he produced "Flamingo," a syndicated comic strip for Phoenix Features.

Over the decade, Matt Baker created many popular characters such as "Canteen Kate" during the Korean War; and various teenage romance titles.

Baker later freelanced for Atlas Comics, which later became Marvel Comics. His work included Western themed comics, and later Science fiction comics such as "Strange Tales." His last confirmed work from Atlas/ Marvel was the Romance title: I Gave Up the Man I Love, in *"My Own Romance" #73* published posthumously in 1960.

From 1948 to 1954, Matt Baker produced over 1,000 comic pages and 200 comic covers. In 2009 he was inducted into the Will Eisner Comic Book Hall of Fame.

"Phantom Lady"
(Courtesy of Matt Baker Estate. Photo is property of the Estate of Matt Baker and may not be reproduced without permission from the Estate.)

Diggs Art Gallery

Diggs Art Gallery
(Winston-Salem State University)

One of the largest exhibition spaces for African art and African American Diaspora in North Carolina is the Diggs Gallery located on the campus of Winston-Salem State University. The gallery is the first of its kind in the city. It was named for Winston-Salem State University alumnus, James Thackery Diggs, a Professor of art at Winston-Salem State University. A renowned artist, "he was one of the founders of the Associated Artists of Winston-Salem and the Southeastern Center for Contemporary Art (S.E.C.C.A.)." [165]
The Diggs gallery opened October 2, 1990.

James Thackery Diggs
(Courtesy of the Bradshaw Estate)

Organizer of the First African American Community Theater

Flonnie Anderson was born in 1930 to Henry and Janie Thomas, and grew up at 1609 Clark Avenue in Winston-Salem, North Carolina. After attending West Virginia State and graduating in 1949 in Theater, she became the first African American Thespian and Director with the Little Theater of Winston-Salem, and organized the first African American community theater in the south during the 1950's.

Anderson taught drama classes at Atkins, Anderson, and Parkland High Schools. After the schools integrated, she taught drama and English at Parkland. It was at Parkland that she began the first integrated school theater program, and became the first teacher to direct a production that featured both white and black students in Forsyth County. She retired in 1989 after 34 years or teaching.

On her 86th birthday, Saturday March 8, 2016 the auditorium at Parkland High School was renamed to honor Flonnie Anderson.

First Professional African American Theater Company and National Black Theater Festival

Larry Leon Hamlin
(Courtesy of Winston-Salem African American Archive)

Larry Leon Hamlin is founder of The NC Black Repertory Company in 1979.[166] It is the first professional Black theater company in the state.
The mission is to foster, promote, and create cultural and educational activities nationally and internationally, focusing on making Black theater accessible on a national level to all citizens of the United States, especially the minority, disfranchised, and underserved communities.

Hamlin again made history by creating and organizing the First National Black Theater Festival in Winston-Salem in 1989. This organization was created to sustain and develop black theater around the world.

The National Black Theater Festival is a bi-annual event held in Winston-Salem, North Carolina, attracting entertainers from the United States and various countries around the world.

Left to right: Larry Leon Hamlin founder of The N.C. Black Repertory Company, Jennie Johnson, actress Ella Joyce, and Sylvia Sprinkle-Hamlin
(Courtesy of Dr. William Rice Collection)

The Oldest Professional African American Dance Company

Otesha Creative Arts Ensemble

Amatullah Saleem
(Courtesy of Miss Amatullah Saleem)

The Otesha Creative Arts Ensemble is the oldest professional African American dance company in North Carolina. It was founded by Miss Amatullah Saleem, with Ron Dutch and Gilbert Young in 2010.

Miss Saleem, who was raised in Winston-Salem, NC, and Harlem New York, trained and performed in New York, with artist Katherine Dunham. After traveling with this dance troupe, she returned to the United States, and opened the Pyramid Dance Studio in SoHo-East, New York, NY.

Miss Saleem came back home to Winston-Salem and accepted the position of Dance/Music Specialist for the City Recreation Department of Winston-Salem, NC. In this position, she produced the African Folk Arts Festival, an annual citywide project, for six years and became the founding Artistic Director of the regional dance troupe, Otesha Dance and Music Ensemble which introduces African American children to the music and dance of West Africa.

AFRICAN AMERICAN FIRSTS

Members of the Otesha Creative Arts Ensemble dance in the opening gala procession of the National Black Theatre Festival. *(Journal File Photo)*

Drummers with Otesha Creative Arts Ensemble,
(Journal photos by Andrew Dye/Journal)

First Local Resident to Recite Poem at Presidential Inauguration

Dr. Maya Angelou, poet, scholar, and local resident of Winston-Salem became the first African American to give poetic recitation at a Presidential Inauguration. She recited her poem *On the Pulse of Morning*, at the 1993 Inauguration of Bill Clinton. At that time, she was the first poet since Robert Frost in 1961, to recite at an inauguration. President Clinton called her the black woman's poet laureate.

Dr. Angelou has served on 2 presidential committees and awarded 3 national medals: The Presidential Medal of Arts in 2000, The Lincoln Medal in 2008 and The Presidential Medal of Freedom in 2011, presented by President Barack Obama.

Dr. Maya Angelou
Maya Angelou reciting her poem "On the Pulse of Morning" at President Bill Clinton's inauguration, January 1993
(Wikipedia, the free encyclopedia public domain)

President Barack Obama, presenting Dr. Maya Angelou with the Presidential Medal of Freedom, 2011
(Office of the White House public domain, via Wikimedia Commons)

First African American Music Promotions

According to the Twin City Sentinel May 4, 1935, early in the 20th century Mrs. C. B. Cash was the first to break the silence in the promotion of music aspirations in the city.

Mrs. Cash was also the first piano player and music teacher, and she was among the first local schoolteachers in Winston.

First African American Music Teacher

Mrs. Coral Hickerson was the first Black Twin City music teacher who was from the city.

First African American Musical Organization

The Twin City Glee Club paved the way for the major musical organizations in this city prior to World War I, according to the Twin City Sentinel.

The Glee Cub was headed by Phil W. Jeffries, Sr.

First Local group to Perform for the King and Queen of England

The Nell Hunter Choral Society of Winston-Salem was part of a select group to perform in Washington DC in 1939. They were the first local group to perform for the King and Queen of England.

This Winston-Salem choral group performed earlier for President Franklin Roosevelt at The University of North Carolina campus.

Their performance in Washington DC was at a *Celebration of America* event given by President Franklin D. Roosevelt, where they sang for King George VI of England and his wife Queen Elizabeth.

The choral group also made two recordings, one for President Franklin Roosevelt and one for the King and Queen to take back to England.

ENTERTAINMENT

The Nell Hunter Choral Society
Front row left to right: Mrs. Laura E James, Mrs. Leather Hill, Mrs. William Pearson, Misses Odessa Malone and Eloise Hodson, Mrs. Virginia Turner and Mrs. Carrie M. Smith. Back row: left to right. Mrs. Thelma Cobb, James Lark, William Stinson, Lee Miller, Gaither Miller and Mrs. Lillian Gambrell.
(Winston-Salem Journal. Courtesy of Winston-Salem African American Archive-vertical file)

First Successful R & B Singing Group

The Five Royals

The Five Royals of Winston-Salem was the first successful R&B group in America."[167] The Group originally began as the gospel group the Royal Sons, but soon they became a part of the new soul sounds emerging in the 1960's. Their major hits included, *Courage to Love; You know, I know, You know*; and *Baby Don't Do It*. Other artists sang some of their songs, such as: "Think," sung by James Brown and "Dedicated to the One I love," the love anthem written by Lomond Pauling to his wife, was sung by the Shirelles, the Mamas and Papas and the Stylistics.

Initial group members were: Jimmy Moore, Johnny Holmes, John Tanner, Lomond Pauling, Otto Jeffries and Obadiah Carter.

The Five Royals was honored in their hometown with a street named after the group in Winston-Salem called Five Royals Drive. In 1992 the group received the North Carolina Folk Heritage Award and has a permanent booth located at the North Carolina Historical Museum in Raleigh.

In 2015 the Five Royals were inducted into the Rock N Roll Hall of Fame in Cleveland, Ohio.

The Five Royals
Left to right Obadiah Carter, Lomond Pauling. Top: John Tanner, James Moore, and Otto Jeffries.
(Courtesy of Winston-Salem African American Archive and Fred Tanner)

First Auditorium to Hold a Swing Concert

The first Swing concert ever performed at a black college was at the Fries Auditorium on January 18, 1938 with Jimmy Launceford and his band.

The Fries Auditorium was built in 1939 and located on the campus of Winston-Salem Teachers College, now Winston-Salem State University. It had a seating capacity of 1,000 and was a focal point for entertainment in the community, hosting various national and internationally known entertainers such as tenor, Roland Hayes.

Fries Auditorium was named for Henry Elias Fries, who served as Chairman of the Board of Trustees of the school since its beginning.

Fries was the founder of Fries Manufacturing and Power Company. When he died in 1949 at age 92, he had been with the Board for 50 years.

The auditorium was in the pit area in front of Diggs Gallery but a torrential rain in 1970 collapsed the roof and destroyed everything inside except a grand piano. The O'Kelly Library was built on its site. The only remnant left of the Fries auditorium is a handrail that leads to the Diggs Gallery parking lot. It was replaced by the Kenneth R. Williams Auditorium constructed in 1975 and located on campus at Martin Luther King, Jr Blvd.

Fries Auditorium
(WSSU Archives-University Photograph Collection) Winston-Salem State University Archives-C.G. O'Kelly Library)

Current K.R. Williams Auditorium
(WSSU Archives-University Photograph Collection. Winston-Salem State University Archives-C.G. O'Kelly Library)

Chapter Fifteen

Sports

Sports and competition provided the African American Community an outlet to escape the stress of life and a way to create community bonding.

Sports were used by factory workers to raise money to build a YMCA, and it was sports that brought one of the greatest college basketball coaches to Winston-Salem, creating a dynasty for a generation.

Winston-Salem Athletics-one of many early Baseball teams in Winston-Salem. Left to right: standing-John McLoyd, p; H. Raymond, rf; Frank Boweaver, p; R. Harris, p,; Ed Hall,3b; Sam Moore, lf; Sam Clark, cf. Seated:-I.A Scales,2b and manager; Howard Lundlow, cf; Frank Wade, ss; John Hicks, p.; and T. Long,c
(WSJ newspaper. North Carolina Room Forsyth County Central Library)

Oldest Semi-Professional Baseball Team

Winston-Salem Pond Giants
(Courtesy of Winston-Salem African American Archive)

The Old Prince Albert Pond Giants in Winston-Salem is "the nation's oldest semi-professional baseball team."[168] The team began in 1914, taking its name from a section of the city along Northwest Blvd and North Cherry Street which had been nicknamed the Pond due to the reservoir that broke in 1904 covering the area with water. The team later became the Winston-Salem Pond Giants. They played games at the Old Southside Park and sometimes at the former Ernie Shore Field located at 401 Deacon Boulevard.

The Pond Giants originally played in the Negro National League and their tenure extended over three decades. After the team integrated in 1956 some players went to the Major Leagues.

Star players of the Pond Giants over the years were: Gilbert "Rags Gwyn," Dave Campbell, Nathaniel Campbell, Will Thompson, Raymond Wallace, James Crump, County Glenn, Slick Coleman, and Willie "Chick" Carter who joined the team as a bat boy in 1938 and later became a pitcher and outfielder.

The contemporary manager for the Pond Giants was Mr. Nelson Petree.

Pond Giants *and* Southside Ball Park
(Courtesy of the Bradshaw Estate)

First African American NCAA Coach of the Year

Clarence E. "Big House" Gaines
Naismith Basketball Hall of Fame presented to Coach Gains
(WSSU Archives-University Photograph Collection. Winston-Salem State University Archives-C.G. O'Kelly Library)

College basketball legend, Coach Clarence E. "Big House" Gaines came to Winston-Salem State Teachers College (Winston-Salem State University) from Morgan State University in 1945.

At Morgan State he gained recognition as an All-American football player and participated on the basketball and track teams.

It was there he was given his famous nick name when according to oral accounts the school's business manager took one look at the 6 ft. 3in., 265lb Gaines and declared Boy, "*I never seen anything bigger than you but a house.*"

Graduating in 1945, with a B.S. Degree in Chemistry, Gaines was on track to become a dentist however, he was asked to go to the Winston-Salem Teachers College in Winston Salem to assist Coach Brutus Wilson also a Morgan State Alumnus, who coached all the sports at the school.

This temporary assignment became permanent when Coach Wilson departed for Shaw University in 1946, making Gaines the head football and basketball coach, athletic director, trainer, and ticket manager.

Gaines coached football from 1946-1949 and was proficient as a coach. He was named CIAA (Central Intercollegiate Athletic Association) Football Coach of the Year after leading the RAMS to an 8-1 season in 1948. But in the following year 1949, he only coached basketball, and served as Athletic Director. During his tenure as head basketball coach at WSTC, he coached greats such as Cleo Hill and Earl the Pearl Monroe and "his teams won more games during his career than any active coach ranking him 5th on the NCAA's list of basketball coaches with the most wins with his record of 828-446." [169] These wins include 12 CIAA Championships and the NCAA College Championship in 1967 which is the first time in NCAA history that a historically black college or university has won this national championship. He was named NCAA Coach of the Year in 1967 and he is the first African American coach to be honored with this title.

In 1983 Coach "Big House Gaines" was inducted into the Naismith Basketball Hall of Fame, named in honor of James Naismith, the inventor of basketball.

When Coach Gaines retired, his win/loss record of 828/446 made him the winningest active coach in NCAA history and the second winningest in college basketball behind University of Kentucky coach, Adolph Rupp. In retirement, he was moved to fourth when surpassed by his friend Jim Phelan of St. Mary's College. He and Phelan were surpassed by still active coaches Bobby Knight and Mike Krzyzewski, Coach Gaines now has the sixth All-Time wins in the NCAA.

Notable Moments

In 1950 Gaines received his master's Degree in Education from Columbia University.

The C. E. Gaines Center on the campus of Winston-Salem State University is named for him and he was also honored by the city of Winston-Salem through the efforts of Rep. Larry Womble (see chapters 3), Council Member Joycelyn Johnson and with the approval of the City Council, by having a street named for him. The street is off New Walkertown Road in Winston-Salem, North Carolina.

Coach Clarence E. "Big House" Gaines, in 1945, the year he came to Winston-Salem Teachers College as an assistant coach.
(WSSU Archives-University Photograph Collection. Winston-Salem State University Archives-C.G. O'Kelly Library)

First African American Football Coach in the ACC

Bill Hayes
(Courtesy of Billy Rich. Winston-Salem African American Archive)

Bill Hayes, a Former Winston-Salem State head football coach and director of athletics is one of the first African American coaches in the Atlantic Coast Conference (ACC) and the first at Wake Forest University. He began his coaching career as a running backs coach in 1973-1975, as part of the coaching staff at Wake Forest University.

He continued his coaching career at Winston-Salem State University and NC A&T State University. As coach at WSSU he won three CIAA titles and two division- II playoff appearances 1978 and 1987. Under his leadership as coach at NC A&T the school won three MEAC titles and two Division I-AA playoff appearances 1992 and 1999.

Hayes became Athletic Director at Winston-Salem State University and retired in 2014. He has been inducted into eight halls of fame, including the North Carolina Sports Hall of Fame, in 2018.

First African American Head Football Coach in the ACC

Jim Caldwell
(*Courtesy of Wake Forest University Athletics Department*)

On 1993, Jim Caldwell was named head football coach at Wake Forest University and became the first African American head football coach in the ACC (Atlantic Coast Conference). After his career at Wake Forest he began coaching in the NFL in 2001 as a quarterback coach with the Tampa Bay Buccaneers, and later with the Indianapolis Colts and Baltimore Ravens.

He became head coach with the Detroit Lions in 2014.

First Woman Assistant Commissioner in the Atlantic Coast Conference (ACC)

In 1988, Winston-Salem State University alum, Delores Todd became the first woman and African American, to serve as Assistant Commissioner in the Atlantic Coast Conference (ACC). She was a woman of many firsts and successful throughout her sports career.

Delores Todd
*(Winston-Salem State University - WSSU Hall of Fame
WSSU Dept. Of Athletics)*

Not only was she successful in sports, in 1980, as a model for Fashion Fair cosmetics, she became the first African American to be featured on the Kellogg's Corn flakes cereal box.

Originally from New Jersey Todd graduated with honors from Winston-Salem State University in 1972, with a degree in Health and Physical Education. She received her master's degree in Human Relations and Psychotherapy from Governor's State University in 1981.

Afterwards she served as head coach for four years at Northwestern University, where she earned the 1983 Cross Country Big Ten Coach of the Year honors.

She joined the staff at Georgia tech in 1985 and became its first fulltime woman track and cross-country coach, becoming the first African American head coach man or woman in the ACC in track and field. There she was three-time Georgia State Coach of the Year while winning the Georgia State Intercollegiate Championship in three consecutive years, of 1985, 1986 and 1987.

Returning to North Carolina, Todd became the first woman and the first black person to Chair the Greensboro Parks and Recreation Commission, when she was appointed to the position in in 1994. In September 2006 she became the first woman to serve on the NCAA Division 1 Baseball Committee.

In 2001, Todd was inducted into the Central Intercollegiate Athletic Association (CIAA) Hall of Fame and in Winston-Salem State University's Hall of Fame in 2002.

On May 4, 2005 NC A&T University named Delores Todd as the University's Director of Intercollegiate Athletics.

She is now the director/head coach at Heritage High School in Wake Forest, N.C.

Delores Todd on Kellogg's Corn Flakes box *1980*
(Courtesy of Delores "Dee" Todd)

First NBA Draft Pick

It is said that before there was Michael Jordan, there was Cleo Hill. He had hook shots from either hand, a jump shot, a high vertical leap and could dunk from the free throw line.

Born in New Jersey May 9, 1938, Hill attended Winston-Salem Teachers College from 1957-1961 and was coached by the iconic Clarence "Big House" Gaines.

When he graduated from WSTC in 1961, Hill was considered the best player in the country.

Cleo Hill

Left to right :Cleo Hill as St Louis Hawks member and at WSTC. *(WSSU Archives-University Photograph Collection. Winston-Salem State University Archives-C.G. O'Kelly Library)*

He was selected by the St. Louis Hawks in the first round National Basketball Association draft in 1961. He was only the fifth African American from a Historically Black College and University to be drafted in the first round, and the first from Winston-Salem.

Despite scoring 26 points during his first NBA appearance, Hill played only one season in the NBA.

Due to his talent overshadowing his white team-mates in scoring and performance, the St. Louis Hawks team management ordered the team coach, Paul Seymour, to diminish Hill's defensive role during the 1961-1962 season so the white stars of the team, Bob Pettit, Cliff Hagan, and Clyde Lovellette, would receive more shot attempts. When the coach refused to do this, he was fired. Another coach, Harry Gallatin, replaced Seymour. He reduced Hill's playing time and had him spend more time on the bench. This seriously reduced Hill's scoring average which went from double digits to 5 points per game. After that season he was released from the Hawks, and never played again in the NBA because no NBA team would take him. His former coach and supporter, Seymour used the words *white balled* to describe Hill's predicament.

Cleo Hill went on to become a successful head coach at Essex County in Newark, New Jersey where in his 24- year career he has won 489 games.

Cleo Hill at WSTC
(*WSSU Archives-University Photograph Collection. Winston-Salem State University Archives-C.G. O'Kelly Library*)

First NBA Star from Winston-Salem

Harold "Happy" Hairston L.A. Lakers 1974
(*Wikimedia Commons-Public domain*)

The first NBA star from Winston-Salem was Harold "Happy" Hairston. Born in Winston-Salem May 31, 1942 he was called "Happy" because he smiled a lot.

Happy graduated from Atkins High School and attended college at New York University. The 6 feet 7 inches tall Hairston went into the NBA draft in 1964 and was first drafted by the Cincinnati Royals. He then played for the Detroit Pistons, and later became a player for the Los Angeles Lakers in 1969, with players such as Wilt Chamberlain. He was a starting forward for the Lakers during the 1971-1972 season, pulled 1,045 rebounds and was 11th in the Lakers all-time leading rebounder that season. His teammate Wilt "*the Stilt*" Chamberlain pulled down 1,572 and led the Lakers team. These numbers helped the Lakers win a record 33 games in a row in 1971-1972 season.

In 1973-1974 Hairston led the league in rebounds and in 1974-1975 Happy Hairston set the NBA record for the most defensive rebounds of 13 in one quarter when they played the Philadelphia 76's. Happy Hairston is 57th of all time in the league history.

During his basketball career, Hairston managed to do some acting, appearing in such shows as "Sanford and Son," "Fame," "Knots Landing" and, "Happy Days." He also managed golf courses in the Los Angeles area. After he retired from the NBA, "Happy" Hairston established the Happy Hairston Youth Foundation which paid for the education of underprivileged children.

First African American Scholarship Player at Wake Forest University

Norwood Todman
(*Courtesy of Wake Forest University Athletics Department*)

In 1966 Norwood Todman became the first African American scholarship player on the freshman basketball team at Wake Forest University.

Norwood Todman shooting the ball
(*Courtesy of Wake Forest University Athletics Department*)

NBA Hall of Fame

Vernon Earl "The Pearl" Monroe
(*Winston-Salem State University WSSU Dept. Of Athletics –
WSSU Hall of Fame*)

Originally from South Philadelphia, Vernon Monroe, attended Winston-Salem State College from 1963-1967, and was the force that helped to lead the Mighty Rams to the 1967 National NCAA College Division II Basketball Championships CIAA Championship(Central Intercollegiate Athletic Association) and Chicago Invitational Tournament Championship.

Because of his scoring performance, he was given his nickname, "Earl the Pearl" by The Sentinel columnist Luix Overbea.

The Winston-Salem State College All American graduated in 1967 and was drafted in the second round by the Baltimore Bullets NBA team. He was later traded to the New York Knicks. Monroe played in the NBA for 13 years and retired in 1980. In 1989 he was elected to the Naismith Basketball Hall of Fame.

First African American ACC Player of the Year

Charlie Davis
(*Courtesy of Wake Forest University Athletics Department*)

In 1971, Wake Forest University basketball player, Charlie Davis became the first African American basketball player to be named ACC (Atlantic Coast Conference) Player of the Year. Originally from New York City, Davis attended Wake Forest from 1969-1971. He earned first team All-ACC honors for three straight years and was the 8th draft pick in 1971 by the Cleveland Cavaliers, where he had a stellar career.

In 1984, Charlie Davis was inducted into Wake Forest's Hall of Fame. He was chosen as one of the all-time best players of the ACC and was on the 50th Anniversary team. He later returned to Wake Forest in 1989 to work in the athletic administration where he later became Assistant Athletic Director.

Davis continued in athletic administration as Athletic Director at Bowie State University in Maryland and at North Carolina A&T University in Greensboro, North Carolina.

Left: Charlie Davis. Right: Wake Forest Team Co Captains: Dicker Walker and Charlie Davis *(Special Collections & University Archives/Wake Forest University)*

First Woman Professional Basketball Player from Winston-Salem

Camille Little

(UNC-Chapel Hill. 2006-2007 Womens Basketball Roster. Gohills.com)
https://goheels.com/sports/womens-basketball/roster/camille-little/7316

The first woman professional Basketball player from Winston-Salem, North Carolina is Marissa Camille Little. She was born in Winston Salem, North Carolina, to Robert and Elaine Little. . She has an older sister, Brandi Little.

Little graduated from Carver High School and attended the University of

North Carolina at Chapel Hill. While at Carver she was an athlete who excelled in the classroom as well as on the basketball court. She was a member of the National Honor Society in her sophomore through senior years and she was honored as A.P. Player of the Year as a sophomore in 2001, when she led Carver to a 30-0 record and a State Championship.
She was Associated Press (A.P.) North Carolina Player of the Year as a senior in 2003 and she was a McDonald's All-American that same year. During her career at Carver, she Scored a school-record 2,168 points.
At UNC-Chapel Hill, Little and fellow All-American Ivory Latta led the Tar Heels to two Final Four appearances in her four years. She was voted the 2004 ACC Freshman of The Year and was named to the 2007 ACC All-Defensive Team. In her career at UNC, she has scored 1,773 points and averaged 12.8 points per game with 5.9 rebounds per game.

Camille Little became a professional basketball player after becoming the 17th overall pick in the 2007 WNBA Draft, by the San Antonio Silver Stars. She has since played for the Atlanta Dream, and the Seattle Storm. Little helped the Seattle Storm win their second championship in 2010. On January 28, 2015 WNBA draft, Little was traded along with Shekinna Stricklen to the Connecticut Sun.

First NCAA Champs from a HBCU (Historically Black College and University)

The Mighty Rams of Winston-Salem State College (Winston-Salem State University) won the 1967 National NCAA College Division II Basketball Championships and were CIAA Champions and Chicago Invitational Tournament Champions. They are the "1st team in NCAA history from a historically black college or university to win a national championship."[170] The team posted a game winning record of 31-1 for the 1967 season.
WSSC senior, Earl Monroe, not only led the nation in scoring with 41.5 points per game, he won the national Scoring Championship and set the Division II scoring record with 1,329 points.
In Winston-Salem's evening newspaper The Sentinel, columnist "Luix Overbea referred to Monroe's scoring as Earl's Pearl's."[171]

From that day forward Vernon Earl Monroe became *Earl the Pearl* Monroe through the duration of his professional basketball career with the Baltimore Bullets and the New York Knicks. He was inducted into the Naismith Memorial Basketball Hall of Fame in 1990.

The Mighty Rams 1967 NCAA Championship Team:
Left to Right Front row: Johnny Watkins, Alan McManus, William English, James Reid, Earl Monroe, Donald Williams and Eugene Smiley. Left to right back row: Ralph Funches, Steven Smith, David Green, Frank Hadley, John Lathan, Ernest Brown, Percy Lesure, and Vaughn Kimbrough.
(WSSU Archives-University Photograph Collection. Winston-Salem State University Archives-C.G. O'Kelly Library)

The 1967 National NCAA College Division II Basketball Championships
(*Courtesy of the Bradshaw Estate*)

First College to Integrate in the Atlantic Coast Conference (ACC)

Wake Forest College (Wake Forest University) in Winston-Salem was the first college in the Atlantic Coast Conference, (ACC) to integrate its football program with the enrollment of three African American players; Robert Grant, Kenneth Henry, and Willie Smith to the roster in 1964.

Robert Grant and Kenneth Henry were later drafted into the NFL.

Robert Grant *(l)* and Kenneth "Butch" Henry (r)
(*Courtesy of Wake Forest University Athletics Department*)

First in Football Hall of Fame from Winston-Salem

Carl Eller was born in Winston-Salem, North Carolina, January 25, 1942. He was the First NFL star and NFL Hall of Fame winner from Winston-Salem. He was inducted into the Pro Football Hall of Fame August 8, 2004.

Eller attended Atkins High school where as a player he helped Atkins win the North Carolina High School Athletic Conference state title in 1959. Affectionately known as "Moose", Eller was a well-rounded student who was also President of his senior class and was voted "Best Personality." After graduation from Atkins High School in 1960, Eller attended the University of Minnesota. There he became an all-star player and helped them to win the Rose Bowl in 1961.

Carl Eller
(*Winston-Salem Chronicle. Courtesy of Winston-Salem African American Archive-vertical file*)

He was drafted to the NFL in 1964 as a first-round draft pick of two leagues, the National Football League's Minnesota Vikings and the Buffalo Bills of the American Football League.

Eller played for the Minnesota Vikings, 1964-1978. At 6 feet 6 inch, 247-pounds he was a defensive end for the team and part of the famed *Purple People Eaters* defensive line. He led the Vikings to 10 Central Division Titles as well as the 1969 championship.

Eller later played for the Seattle Seahawks in 1979.

He retired from the NFL that same year, after 16 seasons that included four Super Bowls, six Pro Bowls, and a total of 133 1/2 career sacks. During his football career, Eller also starred in the Blaxploitation movie, The Black Six. This 1974 film starred various football players and was one of the first films to depict Black Bikers.

In 1980, Carl Eller worked for NBC as an NFL sports analyst. He later became a licensed drug and alcohol counselor and in 1986 founded a group of substance-abuse clinics in the Twin Cities of Minnesota, called Triumph Life Centers.

First African American Quarterback in the ACC

Freddie Summers became the first African American quarterback in the Atlantic Coast Conference (ACC) and at a historically white southern college.

In 1967 he was recruited and attended Wake Forest College (Wake Forest University) in Winston-Salem where he set records at the school in passing and scoring. He became Co-captain with Carlyle Pate in 1968.

Originally from South Carolina, Freddie Summers first attended McCook Nebraska Junior College prior to transferring to Wake Forest College. Summers was drafted by the Cleveland Browns in the fourth round in 1969 as a defensive back.

Freddie Summers
(Courtesy Special Collections & University Archives/Wake Forest University)

Freddie Summers (number 7)
(Courtesy of Wake Forest University Athletics Department)

First African American Running Back at Wake Forest University

Larry Hopkins
(*Courtesy of Wake Forest University Athletics Department*)

Lawrence David Hopkins ("Hoppy") of Panama City Florida was the first Black running back at Wake Forest College in Winston-Salem, North Carolina.
Rushing more than 100 yards in games on 10 occasions, he helped Wake Forest win their first ACC Championship in 1970 when he scored the winning touchdown against North Carolina with a 14-13 victory. He twice rushed 200 yards in a game.

Hopkins' career rushing yards totaling 2,212 yards is untouched and ranks him eighth among the school's rushing leaders.

As a student, Hopkins made the Dean's List in all four of his semesters at Wake Forest and although an exemplary athlete, and student, he encountered discrimination from professors who didn't believe that black athletes deserved A's. Hopkins was a member of Gamma Sigma Epsilon, the national honor society for chemistry and made A's in chemistry yet, his professor would only give him a B because a black football player could not have earned an A and must have cheated.

After graduation from Wake Forest and a stent in the air force, earning the rank of Major, Hopkins returned to Winston-Salem in 1983, continuing his pursuit of his medical career.

On December 3, 2010, Larry Hopkins was selected to represent Wake Forest University as one of the Class of 2010 Dr. Pepper ACC Football Championship Legends. Hopkins was one of 12 ACC players selected to be honored.

Notable Moments

Dr. Larry Hopkins, M.D. served on the Board of Trustees at Wake Forest University and became Assistant Professor of General Gynecology.

Larry Hopkins
(*Courtesy of Wake Forest University Athletics Department*)

First Woman Football Coach in North Carolina

According to the N.C. High School Athletic Association, Angela Lambson, head coach for the Winston-Salem Prep JV team, became the first known woman to coach a high school football team when the Jr varsity Football teams of Winston Prep and Parkland High school met on the field on September 3, 2015 at Deaton-Thompson Stadium in Winston-Salem.

Angela Lambson
(Winston-Salem Chronicle. Courtesy of Winston-Salem African American Archive-vertical file)

She is now known as "Queen" throughout the city of Winston-Salem. From 2000 to 2003, Lambson was a member of the Carolina Cougars, a local Women's Professional Football team located in Greensboro, N.C. In 2013 she became coach of the Winston-Salem Tiny Rams, an 8th grade Unlimited Division team. Under her leadership they won the American Youth Football League (AYFL) National Championship.

Notable Moments
On September 24, 2015, Coach Lambson and the Winston Prep JV Football team defeated Walkertown 50-0, to win their first conference game of the season.

First Heavyweight Boxing Champion from Winston-Salem

The first boxing champion from Winston-Salem, North Carolina was Joseph Weldon McFadden.

Born in Kingstree, South Carolina in 1927, McFadden later resided in Winston-Salem and attended Atkins High School where he excelled in football.

Prior to turning Professional in boxing in 1950, McFadden had and won 30 armature bouts. He won the South Pacific Heavyweight Championship while serving in the Army Air Force.

Joe McFadden with Joe Louis.
Left to right: J.L. Davis, Joe McFadden, Joe Louis, unknown soldier. Back row: Lonzo Funches, Willie Wyfall, and unknown soldier.
(Courtesy of Lester S. Davis. Winston-Salem African American Archive)

In 1948 he boxed in the Olympic Trials in Chicago. Professionally he boxed in New York City where he fought Cuban Heavyweight Champion Nino Valdez and heavyweight contender Roland LaStarza. One of his greatest opponents of his boxing career was Joe Louis.

After his boxing career, Joe McFadden joined the Winston-Salem Police Department and retired as a corporal after a thirty-year career.

Joe McFadden was inducted into Atkin's High School Sports Hall of Fame in 2006 and Carolina's Boxing Hall of Fame in 2013.

Joe McFadden Boxing in the ring with Roland Lastarza (1952)
(*Courtesy of Winston-Salem African American Archive*)

Joe McFadden
(City of Winston-Salem Police Department. Public Photo)

First Black ACC Tennis Player

Audley Bell
(Courtesy of Wake Forest University Athletics Department)

In 1969, Audley Bell, a Jamaican student attending Wake Forest College (Wake Forest University) in Winston-Salem, N. C., became the first black tennis player to play tennis in the Atlantic Coast Conference (ACC).

Audley excelled in his sport regardless of The Old Town Country Club closing its doors to the tennis court to keep from admitting Bell on the court.

He later played in the Davis Cup for his home country.

Notable Moments

Bell attended Boston College and received his B.S. degree in Management, graduating cum laude. Also, an alumnus of Wingate University, Bell was inducted into the Wingate University Sports Hall of Fame in 2008.

He is now Chief Audit Officer at World Vision International, a non-profit located in Monrovia, California.

Track and Field

First Black College or Small University to Win Penn Relays

The Penn Relays 480-yard shuttle hurdle team of Winston Salem State Teachers College won the 1957 Penn Relays with a winning time of 59.8 seconds. The school was the "first small college and or historically black college to win this event at the Penn Relays."[172]

Noted team members were Joe Middleton, Francis Washington, Elias Gilbert, and Carl Brown.

AFRICAN AMERICAN FIRSTS

Winston-Salem Teachers College relay team won at the Penn Relays, c. 1957. Left to right: Joseph Middleton, Elias Gilbert, Carl Brown, and Francis Washington. *(WSSU Archives-University Photograph Collection. Winston-Salem State University Archives-C.G. O'Kelly Library)*

The 1959-60 Winston-Salem Teacher's College Rams track & field teams was the best in the nation as they took home the National Association of Intercollegiate Athletics (NAIA) Men's Outdoor Track & Field National Championships. Under the guidance of legendary head coach Wilbur Ross, the Rams took home the national titles in both seasons.
(WSSU Archives-University Photograph Collection Winston-Salem State University Archives-C.G. O'Kelly Library)

World Record Holder

Elias Gilbert
(WSSU Archives-University Photograph Collection. Winston-Salem State University Archives-C.G. O'Kelly Library)

In 1959 Elias Gilbert of Winston-Salem Teachers College held the world's Record in the 220 low hurdles and set the world's record in the 120-yard-high hurdles.

Two years earlier in 1957, Elias Gilbert twice defeated Olympic high hurdles Champion Lee Calhoun. It was at that tournament Gilbert and the hurdle team of Winston Salem State Teachers College won the 1957 Penn Relays.

A three-time national champion and two-time NAIA All-American Gilbert captured the 1958 110-yard high hurdles (13.6), the 1959 120-yard high hurdles (14.6) and the 440-yard high hurdles (53.6), national championship during his illustrious career.

He captured the Herbert B. Marrett Outstanding Performer award from the NAIA in both 1956 and 1958.

Elias Gilbert, world record holder in 220 hurdles at the time of this photograph and predicted to be one of the greatest hurdlers of his era, c. 1959. *(WSSU Archives-University Photograph Collection. Winston-Salem State University Archives-C.G. O'Kelly Library)*

Golf

First African American PGA Member

Jerry Jones
(Courtesy of Winston-Salem African American Archive vertical file)

W inston Lake golf pro "Jerry Jones was the first Black member of the North Carolina Chapter of the PGA. He was the coach of golfers Lee Elder and Jim Dent and founded the first Pro-Am tournament at Winston-Lake Golf Course."[174] Lee Elder became the first African American to qualify for the Masters Tournament in 1975 and was the first African American to be on the Ryder Cup Team.

First African American Golf Tournament Winner

Joe Johnson
(*Courtesy of Winston Lake Golf. Photo taken by Chenita B. Johnson at Winston lake golf field house*)

J oe Johnson became the first African American to win the Forsyth Invitational Golf Tournament."[175] In 1966 the Winston-Salem Recreation Department announced it would accept 3 three black golfers into the previously all white 3-day tournament.
Distinguishing himself with wins at the Asheville, Gate City, and Winston Lake Opens as well as 24 other amateur tournaments, Johnson was one of

the 3 golfers selected by Winston Lake Pro Jerry Jones to participate in the tournament. Joe Johnson topped a field of 156 players. Following his tournament win he turned professional and played part-time.

First Golf Course for African Americans in Forsyth County

Winston Lake Golf
(City of Winston-Salem Recreation and Parks Department. Public photo)

The Winston Lake Golf Course is the first golf course for African Americans in Forsyth County. It was part of a park proposal in 1952. The Allen Organization developed a master plan for Winston Lake Park which included a lake, picnic facilities, playgrounds swimming pool, nature trail and an 18-hole golf course.

The first 9 holes opened four years later, on June 16, 1956. The golf course was an immediate hit with black golfers in Winston-Salem and from throughout the regional area. On May 31, 1962, golf course architect Ellis Maples was brought in for the construction of 9 additional holes to expand the course to 18 holes These additional holes opened for play on April 15, 1964.

Because it was one of the few golf courses with 18 holes open to blacks, this expanded course became more of a regional draw for black golfers.

According to the Parks and Recreations Department, Winston Lake Golf Course became a regular stop on the black golf tour. For more than 10 years in the 1970s and 1980s, Winston Lake was home to the E. Jerry Jones Pro-Am Golf Tournament, named for the golf pro at the course during those years.

This event attracted some of the best black golfers of the era, including Charlie Sifford, Lee Elder, Pete Brown and Calvin Peete. Joe Johnson, a Winston-Salem native and part-time professional golfer, also played in the tournament.

In 2001, the entire course underwent a $1.4 million refurbishment that brought a new 4,500 square-foot clubhouse, new practice greens, and an irrigation system for the fairways, greens and tees. The new club house was completed in 2002 and named after E. Jerry Jones, former Golf Professional at Winston Lake Golf course.

Programs at Winston Lake Golf Course have expanded over the years to include the Senior Golf Association, the Junior Golf Program, the First Tee of the Triad and the Ladies Axillary Group.

This historic golf course was inducted into the National Black Golf Hall of Fame March 27, 2010 in Tampa, Florida. It was selected for the Hall of Fame in the special category of Organization and Locations.

E. Jerry Jones
(*Courtesy of Winston Lake Golf. Photo taken by Chenita B. Johnson at Winston lake golf field house*)

Winston Lake Club House
(*Courtesy of Winston Lake Golf. Photo taken by Chenita B. Johnson at Winston lake golf field house*)

NOTES

1. Lenwood G. Davis et al., *African Americans in Winston-Salem/Forsyth County: A Pictorial History* (Virginia Beach: The Donning Company Publishers, 1999), 15.

2. Sharrie Harless, *"Study Uncovers Salem's Black History,"* Donated by Jon Sensbach, Old Salem Researcher, 16 Feb.1990.

3. Adelaide Fries, Stuart Thurman Wright and J. Edwin Hendricks, *Forsyth: The History of a County on the March, Revised Ed.* (Chapel Hill: The University of North Carolina Press, 1976), 256.

4. Alan Willis, "Blacks in Winston - A History Emerging from Obscurity," *Winston-Salem Sentinel*, 10 Feb. 1983, 1.

5. *Old Salem: African Americans in Salem Walking Tour,* pamphlet, Winston-Salem, North Carolina.

6. Larry Edward Tise, *Winston-Salem in History, vol.10, The Churches* (Winston-Salem: Historic Winston, 1976), 32-33.

7. Phillip Africa, *"*Slave Holding in the Salem Community 1771- 1851," *NC Historical Review* 54, 3, July (1977), 275.

8. Fries, *Forsyth (revised), 272.*

9. *The Chronicle,* "*Black Presence Dates Back to 1769,"* 13 Jan. 1979, 6.

10. Ibid., *6.*

11. Frank V. Tursi, *Winston-Salem: A History* (Winston-Salem: John F. Blair Publisher, 1994), 82.

12. *The Chronicle,* Black Presence, 6.

13. Jennifer Bean Bower, *Images of America: Moravians in North Carolina* (Charleston S.C.: Arcadia Publishing, 2006), 107.

14. Tursi, *Winston-Salem,* 82.

15. Frank Tursi, "Archeologists working to trace History of Salem's Black Church," Winston-*Salem Journal, 28 July* 1991, E1.

16. Sharyn Bratcher, "Early Black Churches in Winston-Salem," *Winston-Salem Chronicle*, 3 Feb. 1979, 13.

17. Adelaide Fries, et al., *Forsyth: The History of a County on the March* (Chapel Hill: The University of North Carolina Press, 1949), 77-79

18. Bratcher, *Chronicle,* 3 Feb. 1979.

19. Fries, *Forsyth,* 77-79.

20. Winston-Salem Chronicle, "St. Paul United Methodist Church celebrates its 144th anniversary," 21 May 2015 http://www.wschronicle.com/2015/05/st-paul-united-methodist-church-celebrates-144th-anniversary/

21. Steele, *Key Events in the African American Community 1870-1950* (Old Salem: North Carolina, 1994), 11.

22. E. Louise Murphy, *History of Winston-Salem State University 1890-1995* (Virginia Beach: The Donning Company Publishers, 1999), 30.

23. Hugh Victor Brown, E-Quality Education in North Carolina Among Negroes (Raleigh, North Carolina: Irving Swain Press, INC., 1961), 21.

24. Davis, *African Americans,* 53.

25. Ibid., 54.

26. George Booie, "Roots of Black Winston-Salem: Making it through the depression ," *The Chronicle,* 24 Feb. 1979, 16.

27. The Chronicle, "Forsyth County's seal was designed by Carver student in 1949," 14 Feb. 2019.

28. Fries, *Forsyth revised,* 319.

29. Tursi, *Winston Salem,* 250.

30. The *Chronicle,* "WSSU *Grad 1st In* Country To *F*inish," 22 Jan. 1977, 9A.

31. *Old Salem: African Americans.*

32. Murphy, The *History of Winston-Salem State,* 29.

33. Joan S. Rodgers, *"Salem Blacks Built Schoolhouse in 1867,"* *Winston-Salem Journal,* 19 Apr. 1992, B1.

34. Yvette N. Freeman, "Facts About Areas First School for Blacks Uncovered," *Winston-Salem Chronicle,* 16 Apr. 1992.

35. Juanita Jarrett, "History of Blacks in Winston-Salem," *Winston-Salem School System Schools*, Central School Office, 1991.

36. Murphy, *History of Winston-Salem State*, 35.

37. Fries, *Forsyth (revised)*, 272.

38. Steele, *Key Events*, 22.

39. *The Chronicle*, "Winston-Salem Negro High School", 24 Feb. 1979, 13.

40. Betty J. Reed, *The Brevard Rosenwald School* (Jefferson: McFarland and Company, INC., 2004), 28.

41. Ibid., 1.

42. Edward Everett Hill, Carver High School: *Society for the Study of African American History Calendar of Educators*, 3rd ed. 1992.

43. *The Chronicle*, "Black Senior High Schools Disappear," 31 Mar. 1979, 5.

44. Phillip N. Henry, PhD. and Carol M. Speas, PhD., *The Heritage of Blacks in North Carolina,* vol. 1, (Raleigh: NC African American Heritage Foundation, Inc., 1990), 7.

45. Murphy, *The History of Winston-Salem State*, 21.

46. News and Observer, *"Winston-Salem State started at Academy,"* 16 May 1964 and 10 Apr. 1966.

47. Frenise A. Logan, *The Negro in North Carolina 1876-1894* (Chapel Hill: University of North Carolina Press, 1964), 215-216.

48. Steele, *Key Events*

49. Gary Dorsey, "The shame that Winston tucked away," *Sentinel*, 24 Jan. 1980, 1, 15.

50. Robert W. Neilson, *History of Government City of Winston-Salem North Carolina All American City 1766-Bicentennial 1966, vol.1* (Winston-Salem: Community Government Committee, 1966) 472.

51. *The Chronicle*, "A riot to save a black life," 3 Feb. 1979, 14.

52. Tursi, *Winston-Salem*, 249.

53. Ibid., *249.*

54. Ibid., *249.*

55. Ibid., *249*

56. John Railey, *"*In Winston Sit In Help End Segregation,*"* *Winston-Salem Journal*, 2 Feb. 2000.

57. Ibid.

58. Sharyn Bracher, "You Can if You Think You Can,*"* *The Chronicle*, 2 Dec. 1978, 7.

59. Yvette McCullough, "Appreciation Service - A Queen in Our Midst,*"* *The Chronicle*, 10 Feb. 1979, 16.

60. Logan, *The Negro in North Carolina,* 216.

61. Jeffrey J. Crow, Paul D. Escott, and Flora J. Hantely, *A History of African Americans in North Carolina* (Raleigh: NC Office of Archives and History, 2002), 117.

62. Tursi , Winston-Salem, 162.

63. Jarrett, "History of Blacks," 26.

64. McCullough, "Appreciation Service," 16.

65. Robert W. Neilson, *History of Government City of Winston-Salem, North Carolina All American City 1766 Bicentennial 1966, vol. 2* (Winston-Salem: Community Government Committee, 1966) 855-856.

66. Tursi, *Winston-Salem,* 272.

67. *Ram Pages,* "Montgomery Wins City Council Seat as WSSU Senior." Winston-Salem State University, http://www.wssurampages.com/archives/2438,(accessed 15 Dec. 2009).

68. Tursi, *Winston-Salem,* 272.

69. *Winston-Salem Chronicle,* "200 Years of Progress in Winston-Salem," 31 Mar. 1979.

70. Neilson, *History of Government,* v.1, 415.

71. Chuck Milligan, *"Early Black Firefighters of North Carolina,"* Annotated http://legeros.com/history/ebf/index.shtml/ (accessed 15 June 2010).

72. Neilson, *History of Government v.2,* 628-629.

73. Ibid.*,* 885-886.74. *The Chronicle,* "29 Years Pay Off," 16 Aug. 1980, 1.

75. City of Winston-Salem, *Black Police Officers Discussed*: *Meeting Notes, 1940-1949* (*City of Winston-Salem Government,* Winston-Salem, N.C.*),* 1-2. http://www.cityofws.org/, (accessed 2012).

76. *Winston-Salem Chronicle*, "Profiles of Black City officials," 24 Nov.1988, A3.

77. *Winston-Salem Journal*, "Officer who helped Break Racial Barriers in W-S Police Department Dies, "25 Sept. 1988

78. Marilyn Sprague-Smith, M.Ed., *The Journal for Women*, July 2004. http://www.ncjournalforwomen.com/months/2004/months/july04/july04smith2.htm (accessed 2010)

79. *Winston Salem Chronicle*, 28 Feb. 1979, 14.

80. Fries, *Forsyth (revised)*, 264.

81. Ibid., 264.

82. The Chronicle, "Roots of Black Winston-Salem," 17 Mar. 1979, 17.

83. *Winston -Salem Chronicle*, "200 Years of Progress," 5.

84. *Winston-Salem City Line* "Beaty Public Safety Training and Support Center Opens," Winston-Salem Marketing and Communications Department, Fall 2009, 1.

85. Winston-Salem Chronicle, "History Making Carmon Sworn In," 10 Jan. 2008, A1, A11.

86. *Winston-Salem Chronicle*,27 Jan. 1979, A12.

87. *Press Release,* "Appointment of Judge Roland H. Hayes,"1, http://www.aoc.state.nc.us/www/public/aoc/pr/hayes.html (accessed 21 Jan. 2010).

88. Robin B. Barksdale, "Loretta Biggs Her Dream Came True Early, *Winston-Salem Chronicle*, 19 Feb. 1987, A1, A3.

89. Gray Dorsey, "They're Big Trees Now, "*Sentinel*, 31 Oct. 1981, 15, 18.

90. Fries, *Forsyth (revised)*, 256-257.

91. Davis, *African Americans*, 67.

92. Logan, *The Negro in North Carolina*, 215.

93. *Winston-Salem Chronicle*, 3 Feb. 1979, 13.

94. Jarret, *History of Blacks*, 2.

95. Ibid., 2.

96. Ibid., 2.

97. Winston-Salem *City Directory*, 1915, 584.

98. Yvette N. Freeman, "Ola Mae Forte Looks Back Over Her Career," *The Chronicle*, 28 May 1992, B 5.

99. Fries, *Forsyth (revised)*, 262.

100. Malcolm A. Pharr "Black Business Community has long History," *The Phoenix*, Jan-Feb ca 1998, 17.

101. *Winston-Salem Journal*, 21 Feb. 2000, B-1 & B3.

102. Davis, *African Americans*, 68.

103. Davis, *African Americans*, 71.

104. Winston-Salem *Chronicle*, 31 Mar. 1979.

105. Davis, *African Americans*, 105.

106. *The Chronicle*, "20th Century Opens with Black Business Upsurge," 10 Feb. 1979, 7.

107. *The Chronicle*, 12 Feb. 1977, 14.

108. *The Chronicle*, 31 Mar. 1979, 7.

109. Ibid., 7.

110. Davis, *African Americans*, 92.

111. Twin City Sentinel, "Half Century of Negro Progress in Twin City," 4 May 1935, 29.

112. Malcolm A. Pharr, Black Business, 17.

113. *The Chronicle*, 3 Mar. 1979, 6.

114. Fries, *Forsyth (revised)*, 262.

115. Fries, *Forsyth (revised)*, 259 - 260.

116. Ibid., *260*.

117. Davis, *African Americans*, 79.

118. Steele, *Key Events*, 5.

119. Obituary, James J. Sanson, 1.

120. Davis, *African Americans*, 109.

121. Ibid., 109.

122. Ibid., 114.

123. Henry, PhD., *The Heritage of Blacks*, 410.

124. Ben Steelman, "James Shober A Carolina Healer," *The African American Registry,* Wilmington Star,(S C, USA), 2003. http://wwwaaregistry.org/historic_events/view/james-shober-first-black-doctor-graduat-north-carolina (accessed 2 Feb 2010).

125. Richard W. Prichard, MD, *Winston-Salem in History, vol. II Medical* (Winston-Salem: Historic Winston, 1976), 19.

126. Steele, *Key Events,* 24.

127. *The Chronicle,* "Dr. Malloy Made Medical History in 1948, "10 Mar. 1979, 20.

128. *Twin City Sentinel,* "Half a Century of Negro Progress,"4 May 1935.

129. Fries, *Forsyth (revised),* 266.

130. Robert W. Prichard, MD, "Winston-Salem's Black Hospitals prior to 1930," *Journal of The National Medical Association* 68, no.3 (1976), 240-249.

131. Davis, *African Americans,* 99.

132. *North Carolina: The Old North State and the New* Vol. IV, (Chicago: The Lewis Publishing Company, 1941), 24.

133. *Digital Forsyth,* "Negotiated Segregation. A separate African American Church, A school and a community near Salem," (Forsyth County, North Carolina) http://www.digitalforsyth.org/photos/stories/negotiated-segregation (accessed Aug. 2012)

134. Ibid., "Negotiated Segregation."

135. Old Salem *African Americans in Salem Walking Tour,* Winston-Salem, North Carolina.

136. Ibid., "Negotiated Segregation."

137. Murphy, *History of Winston-Salem State University,* 26.

138. Town of Winston Directing Board: Meetings Notes Town of Winston, (City of Winston Government 1907-1913)

139. Steele, *Key events,* 21.

140. Manly Wadel Wellman and James Howell Smith, *Winston-Salem in History,* vol. 8, *Industry and Commerce 1896-1975* (Winston-Salem: Historic Winston)

141. Steele, 28.

142. Jarret, *"History of Blacks in Winston-Salem."*

143. *The Chronicle*, "We Haven't Made It Yet," 31 Mar. 1979, 6-7.

144. *Winston-Salem Journal*, 23 June 1988, 13.

145. *Winston-Salem Chronicle*, 8 Aug. 1985, A1.

146. Pharr, Black Business Community, 17.

147. Steele, *Key Events*, 28.

148. Fambrough L. Brownlee, *Winston-Salem A Pictorial History*, (Donning Publishers 1977), 168.

149. Steele, *Key Events*, 28

150. *TWU* (transportationworkerunion),"Clark Campbell Mourned," twu.org/international/article/clark_campbell_mourned/(accessed 2010).

151. Logan, *The Negro in North Carolina*, 218.

152. Davis, *African Americans*, 131

153. *Winston-Salem Journal*, "City's Library Facilities for Negroes," Sept. – Oct. 1938.

154. Ibid., *Winston-Salem Journal*.

155. Leroy Davis, "Negro Scouts Have Record of Helpful Service Since Organization Here in '34," *Winston-Salem Journal*, 4 Sept. 1938, 29.

156. Oliver Crawley, "Three Negro Parks Are Dedicated," *Winston-Salem Journal and Sentinel*, 18 Jan. 1942.

157. Ibid.

158. H. G. Jones, *The Heritage of Blacks in North Carolina Vol. 1*, ed. Phillip N. Henry, PhD. and Carol M. Speas, PhD. (Raleigh: NC African American Heritage Foundation, Inc., 1990) 297.

159. Keith Tilley, "So you think you know Lawrence Joel," *Forsyth Family Magazine*, May 2009, 6.

160. Davis, *African Americans*, 139

161. Steele, *Key events*, 7-8

162. *The Chronicle*, "Picturesque People From Days Past," 24 Feb. 1979, 14-16.

163. Carter Cue and Lenwood Davis, Winston-*Salem State University,* 52.

164. Darlene Clark Hine, ed., *Encyclopedia of Black Women in America: Dance, Sports, and Visual Arts* (New York: Facts On File, Inc., 1997), *3:* 182.

165. Frank Tursi, "The People who wrote history," Winston-Salem Journal, 25 Feb. 1988, 20. Vertical files Afro American History-
biographical collection, NC Room Winston-Salem Central Library.

166. Davis, *African Americans, 137.*

167. Davis, *African Americans,* 146.

168. *The Chronicle,* "The Nation's Oldest Semi-Pro baseball team", 14 Apr. 1979, 13.

169. Wade G. Dudley, *Historic Photos of Winston-Salem,* (North Carolina: Turner Publishing Company, 2008), 181.

170. Cue, *Winston-Salem State University,* 83

171. Ibid., 104.

172. Ibid., 80.

173. *Winston-Salem African American Historical and Cultural Guide,* (Winston-Salem: North Carolina Convention and Visitors Bureau) 22.

174. *Winston Lake Golf* Public information from Winston Lake Golf Club.

175. *Winston Lake Golf* Public information from Winston Lake Golf Club.

BIBLIOGRAPHY

"A History of First Baptist Church, 1879-Present." Accessed December 22, 2015. http://www.fbcwinston.org/church-history/

"A Riot to Save a Black Life." *The Chronicle* (Winston-Salem, NC), February 3, 1979, 14.

A Salute to the African American Woman and Her Contribution to Winston-Salem Forsyth County From 1900-1950. Calendar The Society for the Study of Afro American History in Winston-Salem / Forsyth County, 1995.

About Our Founder Marshall B. Bass. THE MARSHALL B. BASS CHILDREN'S FUND.2013. http://bassforchildren.org/?page_id=205

"ACC Announces 2010 Football Championship Game Legends Class." *Atlantic Coast Conference.* http://theacc.com/news/2010/8/3/51d0c33ca0ee267cf05f6eb4_131481045 149764324.aspx?path=general.

Adams, Robin. "Black Oriented Radio Stations Make Gains-WAAA-WAIR-WSMX Make Top 20 Ratings." *Winston-Salem Chronicle* (Winston-Salem, NC), August 8, 1985, A1+.

Adams, Robin. "County's First Black. Hayes Appointed District Court Judge." *The Chronicle* (Winston-Salem, NC), August 30, 1984, "n.pag."

Adams, Robin. "Financially troubled radio station will come back strong, says Sumler." *Winston-Salem Chronicle* (Winston-Salem, NC), April 19, 1984, A1.

"Addie Morris Mission." *Walsh's Directory of the Cities of Winston and Salem, N.C. and Suburbs for 1902-03.* Charleston, SC: The W. H. Walsh Directory Company 1902

"Adelphia Ice Cream Company." *Winston-Salem NC City Directory.* Vol. XVIII. Asheville, NC: Commercial Service Company, Inc. publisher, 1920.

African American Caucus of the Forsyth County Democratic Party. Chenita Johnson, personal knowledge..

African American Neighborhoods in Winston-Salem 1890-1850. Calendar The Society for the Study of Afro-American History .in Winston-Salem / Forsyth County, 1997.

Africa, Phillip. "Slave Holding in the Salem Community 1771-1851." *North Carolina Historical Review* 54, no.3 (July 1977):275+.

Alford, Natalie. "Historic African American Owned Safe Bus Company On Exhibit." *North Carolina Transportation Museum*. February 4, 2008. Accessed May 19, 2015. http://www.nctrans.org/media/Releases/Historic-African-American-owned-Safe-Bus-company-0.aspx.

"Alston, Eldridge D." *Winston-Salem Journal Obituaries* (Winston-Salem, NC), December 30, 2016. http://www.journalnow.com/obituaries/alston-eldridge-d/article_e0c58d3b-3bea-5ef4-ba0b-db4d8c97202c.html.

Amash, Jim and Eric Nolen-Weatherton, ed. "Matt Baker: The Art of Glamour." *The Comics Journal*, January 18, 2013. http://www.tcj.com/reviews/matt-baker-the-art-of-glamour/.

"Angelou among Presidential Medal of Freedom Recipients." *Winston-Salem Journal (Winston-Salem, NC)*, February 16, 2011. Accessed August 4, 2011. http://www.journalnow.com/news/local/angelou-among-presidential-medal-of-freedom-recipients/article_c33c7cbc-4113-5580-8587-f73647ce24ad.html.

Archer, Marlee. "How Jill Brown-Hiltz Paved the Way for Black Female Pilots in the U.S. Airline Industry." *Atlantic Black Star*, June 4, 2015. http://atlantablackstar.com/2015/06/04/how-jill-brown-hiltz-paved-the-way-for-black-female-pilots-in-the-u-s-airline-industry/.

"Assistant Police Chief Catrina A. Thompson Appointed Chief of Police." *City of Winston-Salem, NC*. August 25, 2017. http://www.cityofws.org/Departments/Police/News/ID/20364/Assistant-Police-Chief-Catrina-A-Thompson-Appointed-Chief-of-Police.

"Atkins, Hannah Diggs." *Winston-Salem Journal* (Winston-Salem, NC), July 1, 2010. Accessed May 5, 2015. http://www.legacy.com/Obituraries.asp?Page=LifeStory&PersonId=143862169

"Atkins High School." *Winston-Salem Journal* (Winston-Salem, NC), April 3, 1931, "n.pag."

Barber, Jacquelyne. Personal interview by Chenita Johnson. Winston-Salem, NC, December 6, 2006.

Barber, Keith. "Winston-Salem commemorates 50th anniversary of sit-in victory." *YES WEEKLY* (Greensboro, NC), May 26, 2010. Accessed March 3, 2011. http://yesweekly.com/Winston-Salem-commemorates-50th-anniversary-of-sit-in- victory-a13637/.

Barksdale, Robin. "Carver's First Graduating Class Honored At Round Up." *Winston-Salem Chronicle* (Winston-Salem, NC), September 7, 1989, B1.

Barksdale, Robin. "Godfather of Gospel bids farewell to off-air duties". *Winston-Salem Chronicle* (Winston-Salem, NC), June 22, 1989, B6.

Barksdale, Robin B. "Loretta Biggs - Her dream came true Early." *Winston-Salem Chronicle* (Winston-Salem, NC), February 19, 1987, A1+.

"Barr Makes History." Editorial Letters to the Editor, *Winston-Salem Chronicle* (Winston-Salem, NC), December 29, 2014. Accessed May 6, 2015. http://www.wschronicle.com/2014/12/editorial-letters- editor/.

Bernard Baker. Personal interview with Chenita Johnson

"Bernard Baker." *Press Release - WAAA Radio. W Triple – A's Program Director.*

"Best Choice Center." *YWCA of Winston-Salem.* Accessed June 5, 2014. http://www.ywcaws.org/best-choice-center/.

"Bethel, W.L. Pastor Presbyterian Church." *Turner's Fifth Annual Winston and Salem City Directory for the Years 1891 and 1892.* Yonkers, NY: E.F. Turner and Publishers 1891.

"Bethel, W.L. Pastor Presbyterian Church." *Turner's Fifth Annual Winston and Salem City Directory for the Years 1891 and 1892.* Yonkers, NY: E.F. Turner and Publishers 1891.

Black Churches of Winston-Salem and Forsyth County 100 Years or more. Calendar - The Society for the Study of Afro-American History in Winston-Salem/ Forsyth County, Inc., 1994.

"Bobby Kimbrough sworn in as new Forsyth County sheriff." Staff Report: The *Clemmons Courier* (Clemmons, NC), December 13, 2018. Accessed December 18, 2018. https://www.clemmonscourier.net/2018/12/13/bobby-kimbrough-sworn-in-as-new-forsyth-county-sheriff/.

Brady, A. and Vernon J. Ehlers. *Black Americans in Congress 1870-2007*. Washington, DC: U.S. Government Printing Office, 2008.

"Black Presence dates back to 1769." *The Chronicle* (Winston-Salem, NC), January 13, 1979, 6.

"Black Senior High Schools Disappear." *The Chronicle* (Winston-Salem, NC), March 31, 1979, 5.

"Black Society Booms with rest of City." *The Chronicle* (Winston-Salem, NC), February 17, 1979, 11-12.

Blunt, Theodore "Ted". *Our Campaigns*. January 25, 2008. Accessed March 7, 2017. https://www.ourcampaigns.com/CandidateDetail.html?CandidateID=174590.

Booie, George. "Do You Remember When." *The Chronicle* (Winston-Salem, NC), February 12, 1977, 14.

Booie, George. "Making it Through the Depression." *The Chronicle* (Winston-Salem, NC), February 24, 1979, 13+.

Booie, George. "Picturesque People from Days Past." *The Chronicle* (Winston-Salem, NC), February 24, 1979, 16. .

Bower, Jennifer Bean. *Images of America: Moravians in North Carolina*. Charleston, SC: Arcadia Publishing, 2006.

Bracher, Sharyn. "You Can if You Think You Can." *The Chronicle* (Winston-Salem, NC), December 2, 1978, 7.

Bragg, Michael. "Our all-female school board now led by an African-American woman. Members of Winston-Salem/Forsyth board say they want to focus on equity." *Winston-Salem Journal.* . (Winston-Salem, NC), December 14, 2018. Accessed December 19, 2018 .https://www.journalnow.com/news/local/our-all-female-school-board-now-led-by-an-african/article_584b8d93-4366-556f-80d4-6519c63b5276.html

Brewer, Lisa De Maio. "North Carolina Police Chief Wears Christ Well." *Christian Chronicle*, Sept. 2005. Accessed August 8, 2009.http://www.christianchronicle.org/article/ north-carolina-police-chief-wears-christ-well.

Brown, Hugh Victor. *A History of the Education of Negroes in North Carolina*. Raleigh, North Carolina: Irving Swain Press, INC., 1961.

Brown, Hugh Victor. *E-Quality Education in North Carolina Among Negroes*. Raleigh, North Carolina: Irving Swain Press, INC, 1964.

Brownlee, Fambrough L. *Winston-Salem: A Pictorial History*. Norfolk, Va. The Donning Company, Inc., 1977.

"Cameron Avenue Trail". *Compiled by Andrea Howard from writings of Langdon Opperman, and William Rice*. Vertical File: Winston-Salem African American Archives. Winston-Salem, NC.

"Camille Little." Carolina Women's Basketball. Accessed February 6, 2016. http://www.goheels.com/ViewArticle.dbml?ATCLID=205677437.

Campbell, Ed. *Twin City Sentinel* (Winston-Salem, NC). April 16, 1962, 7.

"Captain Walter Jackson Davis, Jr." *Commanding Officers of USS Ranger*. 2011. Accessed January 28, 2016. http://www.uss-ranger.org/Captains/25Davis.html.

"Carl Eller returns to Winston-Salem for Hometown Hall of Famers Plaque Ceremony." *Pro Football Hall of Fame*. March 21, 2013 Accessed November 3, 2014. https://www.profootballhof.com/news/carl-eller-returns-to-winston-salem-for-hometown-hall-of-famers-plaque-ceremony/.

"Carl Eller." *Pro Football Hall of Fame*. 2004. Accessed October 22, 2016. https://www.profootballhof.com/players/carl-eller/.

"Carl 'Moose' Eller." The National Football Foundation and College Hall of Fame, Inc., 2006. Accessed November 10, 2014. https://www.footballfoundation.org/ Programs/CollegeFootballHallofFame/SearchDetail.aspx?id=90111.

"Carl Russell: Long Term Service to Blacks in Winston-Salem." *Winston-Salem Chronicle* (Winston-Salem, NC), March 24, 1979, 6

Carlson, Elizabeth "The influence of radio: The rise of three radio stations in the North Carolina Piedmont." Music History of North Carolina Chapter VII 1930—1960: p20. Carolina Music Ways. Accessed August 8, 2015. http://www.carolinamusicways.org/pdf/mHistory.pdf.

"Carver High School Yearbook: Hi-Lite 1949." *Brief History of the School*. Accessed May 5, 2015. http://library.digitalnc.org/cdm/singleitem/collection/yearbooks/id/22575/rec/1.

Caswell, Tyler. "USNA Hosts First African American Marines- 'Saluting Montford Point Marines'." *CHIPS: The Department of the Navy's Information on Technology Magazine*. February 27, 2015. Accessed March 6, 2015. https://www.doncio.navy.mil/chips/ArticleDetails.aspx?ID=6084.

"Catrina Thompson appointed chief of police for Winston-Salem Police Department." *WXII News 12*. August 25, 2017. Accessed August 26, 2017. https://www.wxii12.com/article/Catrina-thompson-appointed-chief-of-police-for-winston-salem-police-police-department/12094774.

"Celebrate African American Artists From North Carolina This Month." *North Carolina Arts Council*. February 12, 2013. Accessed June 5, 2016. https://www.ncarts.org/blog/2013/02/ celebrate-african-american-artists-from-north-carolina-this-month.

"Celebrate Black History". *North Carolina Room Word Press* (blog). January 19, 2012. Accessed March 7, 2012. https://northcarolinaroom.wordpress.com/2012/01/19/celebrate-black-history-2012/.

Chamberline, Gaius "Matt Baker." *Great Black Heroes*. Entertainment Hero. January 14, 2016. https://www.greatblackheroes.com/entertainment/matt- baker/.

"Chambers, Daisy. African American Politicians and Public Officials." *Calendar - The Society for the Study of Afro American History in Winston-Salem Forsyth County*. Winston-Salem, NC., 1999.

Charlie Davis. *Digital Forsyth*. Forsyth County North Carolina http://www.digitalforsyth.org/photos/stories/ charlie-davis.

"Chas. B. Wilson." *Winston-Salem City Directory.*
Asheville, NC: Commercial Service Company, Inc. Publishers, 1918. 513.

Cherrie, Victoria. "Lillian Bonner, city's first black female officer, dies." *Winston-Salem Journal (Winston-Salem, NC),* January 14, 2000, B1+.

"Chief Buffalo Child Long Lance." Accessed August 28, 2011. http://fomaparty.blogspot.com/2011/08/chief-buffalo-child-long-lance.html.

"Chief Buffalo Child Long Lance: NC's Most Famous Lumbee Native." *Candid Slice.* June 30, 2016. Accessed October 12, 2016. http://www.candidslice.com/chief-buffalo-child-long-lance-ncs-most-famous-lumbee-native/.

Chief Sylvester Clark. "Chief Buffalo Child Long Lance." *Find A Grave.* September 16, 2006. Accessed October 18, 2011 https://www.findagrave.com/cgibin/fg.cgi?page=gr&GRid=15771003.

City of Winston-Salem Directing Board. City of Winston-Salem Government Meetings Notes. City of Winston-Salem 1980-1989. *Black Phillips Smith Government Center.* Winston-Salem, NC : Winston-Salem Marketing and Communications Department, July 17, 1989. Accessed April 8, 2015.
http://www.ci.winston-salem.nc.us/ portals/0/pdf/marketing-and-communications/Winston-Salem%201980-1989[1].pdf

City of Winston-Salem Directing Board. City of Winston-Salem Government Meetings Notes. City of Winston-Salem: 1940-1949. *Black Police Officers Discussed.* Winston-Salem, NC: Winston-Salem Marketing and Communications Department. Accessed October 15, 2012.
http://www.cityofws.org/portals/0/pdf/marketing-and-communications/History/Winston-Salem%201940-1949.pdf.

City of Winston-Salem Directing Board. City of Winston-Salem Government Meetings Notes. City of Winston-Salem:1940-1949. *John Joyce.* Winston-Salem, NC: Winston-Salem Marketing and Communications Department. http://www.cityofws.org/portals/o/pdf/marketing-and-communications/History/Winston-Salem%201940-1949.pdf.

City of Winston-Salem, NC - History of the Winston-Salem Police Department. *Police Chief History, Pat Norris.* http://www.cityofws.org/departments/police/history/police-chief-history.

City of Winston-Salem Directing Board. City of Winston-Salem Government Meetings Notes. City of Winston-Salem: 1913-1919. *Request for Black Officers.* March 7, 1919. Winston-Salem, NC: Winston-Salem Marketing and Communications Department. Accessed April 7, 2012. http://www.cityofws.org/portals/o/pdf/marketing-and-communications/Winston-Salem%201913-1919.pdf.

"City's Library Facilities for Negroes." *Winston-Salem Journal* (Winston-Salem, NC), Sept-Oct 1938.

"City Names First Negro as Clerk." *Sentinel* (Winston-Salem, NC), February 18,1963,14.

City of Winston-Salem, North Carolina.
"Early African American Firefighters." Accessed November 6, 2014. http://www.cityofws.org/Departments/Fire/WSFD-History/Early-African-American-Firefighters.

City of Winston-Salem, NC. Winston-Salem Law Enforcement 1859-1913. *The History of Winston-Salem Police Department:1-2.* City of Winston-Salem, NC. Accessed December 2, 2015. http://www.cityofws.org/departments/police/history/winston-law-enforcement-1859-1913.

"Civil Rights Movement Begat Change in Winston-Salem." *The Chronicle* (Winston-Salem, NC), March 24, 1979, 5.

"Clark Campbell Mourned." TWU (transportationworkersunion).Washington, DC, 2010. Accessed May 5, 2011. http://www.twu.org/international/article/

Clayton, Eli brick mason. *Turner & Co.'s Winston and Salem City Directory for the Years 1889-1890.* Yonkers, N.Y.: E.F. Turner and Publishers, 1889.

"Cleaning Was Way to A Better Life." *The Chronicle (Winston-Salem, NC),* March 3, 1979, 6.

Clodfeltor, Tim. "Denise Franklin out as general manager for WFDD." *Winston-Salem Journal* (Winston-Salem, NC). March 26, 2012. Accessed January 2, 2014. http://www.journalnow.com/business/denise-franklin-out-as-general-manager-for-wfdd/article_3e8498c7-0f81-54ad-a5fd-708ef0695d34.html.

Clodfeltor, Tim. "A Marvtastic Start: Festival Kicks off With Gala, Awards." *Winston-Salem Journal* (Winston-Salem, NC). August 1, 2017. Accessed January 3, 2018. https://www.journalnow.com/news/local/a-marvtastic-start-festival-kicks-off-with-gala-awards/article_d2382479-68b4-52df-8924-75e960245abf.html.

Clyburn, James. President of Friends of Odd Fellows, Inc. Personal Interview with Chenita Johnson. Winston-Salem, NC, December 6, 2006.

"Coach Big House Gains inducted into the National Basketball Hall of Fame." *Winston-Salem Journal (Winston-Salem, NC),* February 25, 1988, "npag."

Colin, Emily and Lynn P. Roundtree. *N.C. Bar Association: The Changing Face Of Justice. A Look At The First 100 Women Attorney's In North Carolina.* Cary, NC: NC Bar Association, 2004.

Lewis-Colman, David. "Review: Civil rights unionism: Tobacco workers and the struggle for democracy in the mid-twentieth century south." by Robert Rodgers Korstad. August 27, 2012. Accessed September 15, 2014. https://libcom.org/history/review-civil-rights-unionism-tobacco-workers-struggle-democracy-mid-twentieth-south.

Conatz, Juan. "Review: Civil rights unionism: Tobacco workers and the struggle for democracy in the mid-twentieth century south" by Robert Rodgers Korstad. August 27, 2012. Accessed September 15, 2014. https://libcom.org/history/review-civil-rights-unionism-tobacco-workers-struggle-democracy-mid-twentieth-south.

"Conversations with Artists. 'Amatullah Saleem'." National
 Endowment for the Arts 50th Anniversary Archive, Washington, DC.
 2015. Accessed June 15,
 2016.https://www.arts.gov/accessibility/accessibility-
 resources/leadership-initiatives/arts-aging/mini-conference-creativity-
 2.

"County Grand Jury." *Winston-Salem Chronicle* (Winston-Salem,
 NC), February 29, 1979, 14. Vertical Files: Afro American History.
 North Carolina Room Winston-Salem Central Library.
 Craver Richard.

Crawley, Oliver. "Three Negro Parks Are Dedicated." *Winston
 Salem Journal and Sentinel (Winston-Salem, NC),* January 18,
 1942, 14\

Crow, Jeffrey J., Paul D. Escott and Flora J. Hantely. *A
 History of African Americans in North Carolina*. Raleigh: NC
 Office of Archives and History, 2002.

Cue, Carter B. and Lenwood G. Davis. *Winston-Salem State
 University.* Charleston, South Carolina: Arcadia Publishing, 2000.

Cunningham and Young. *Winston-Salem, N.C. City Directory.*
 Asheville, NC: Commercial Company Inc., Publishers, 1921. 528.

Cynthia S. Durham. *Winston-Salem NC City Directory.*
 Winston-Salem, NC: Polk City Directory 2001.

Daniel, Fran. "Nine-year-old NC girl turns wish into candy Store."
 SCNow (Florence, SC) May 23, 2013. Accessed July 15, 2014.
 http://www.scnow.com/news/article_886fca5a-c3d1-11e2-971b-
 0019bb30f31a.html.

Daniel Fran. "Eli's Pack & Ship to leave Thruway." *Winston-Salem
 Journal (*Winston-Salem, NC), December 25, 2013. Accessed April 16,
 2016.
 https://www.journalnow.com/business/eli-s-pack-ship-to-leave-
 thruway/article_fee6f25a-6d07-11e3-8524-0019bb30f31a.html.

"Dash to Honor Pond Giants Tonight with Throw Back Jerseys."
 BallPark Business. August 6, 2011. Accessed November 5, 2016.
 https://ballparkbiz.wordpress.com/tag/winston-salem-pond-giants/

Davis Lenwood G., William J. Rice, and James H. McLaughlin. *African Americans in Winston-Salem/Forsyth County: A Pictorial History*. Virginia Beach, VA: The Donning Company Publishers, 1999.

Davis, LeRoy. "Wheatley Home President Dies. Activities Of Colored People." *Winston-Salem Journal and Sentinel* (Winston-Salem, NC), April 24,1938,10.

Davis, LeRoy. "Negro Scouts Have Record of Helpful Service since Organization here in "34". *Winston-Salem Journal* Winston-Salem, NC), September 4,1938, 229

Davis, LeRoy. "Royalty Entertainers Leave. Activities of Colored People." *Winston-Salem Journal* (Winston-Salem, NC), June 7, 1939.

Davis, Lester. Co-Director of the Winston-Salem African American Archive. Personal interview with Chenita Johnson. June 3, 2015.

Decker, Stefanie Lee. "Atkins, Hannah Diggs (1923-2010)." In *Encyclopedia of Oklahoma History and Culture*. Oklahoma City, OK :Oklahoma History Center,2009. Accessed September 8,2015. https://www.okhistory.org/publications/enc/entry.php?entry=AT002.

Death notice of Anna Maria Samuel. Bethabara Church Book 1798.

"Dedicate New School Today." *Winston-Salem Journal* (Winston-Salem, NC), April 2, 1931.

"Dee Todd, First African-American Woman to Appear on Kellogg's Corn Flakes Box, to Keynote Empowered Girls of NC 4th Annual High Tea." *Yes Weekly* (Greensboro, NC), October 9, 2017. Accessed November 2, 2017. http://yesweekly.com/Dee-todd-first-african-american-woman-to-appear-on-kelloggs-corn-flakes-box-to-keynote-empowered-girls-of-nc-4th-annual-high-tea/.

Dell, John. "Ram Ramblings: WSSU Hall of Fame class announced and it's a good one." *Winston-Salem Journal (Winston-Salem, NC)*, June 6, 2012. Accessed February 4, 2014. http://www.journalnow.com/sports/colleges/ ram-ramblings-wssu-hall-of-fame-class-announced-and-it/article_b28a0da0-8e7c-510e-a3ff-1b96e71b1284.html

Department: Recreation & Parks. *Winston Lake Golf Course Selected for National Black Golf Hall of Fame.* City of Winston-Salem: Marketing and Communications. March 15, 2010. http://www.cityofws.org/Departments/Recreation-Parks/News/ID/11122/Winston-Lake-Golf-Course-Selected-for-National-Black-Golf-Hall-of-Fame.

"Depot Street: Patterson Avenue near Liberty." *Winston -Salem's African American Neighborhoods 1970-1950.* Architectural and Planning Report: Winston-Salem's African American Resources.1993.

"DelWatts Radio and Electronics." *Hill's Winston-Salem City Directory 1949-50.* Richmond, VA: Hill Directory Co., INC. Publishers, 1949.

"Diggs Gallery. The Legacy of Gordon Hanes and James Thackeray Diggs" *Winston-Salem State University. October 1, 2005 - December 17, 2005.* https://www.wssu.edu/academics/colleges-and-departments/college-of-arts-sciences-business-education/arts-humanities/diggs-gallery/exhibitions.html.

"Dillahunt, George." *Hill's Winston-Salem, NC City Directory, 1946.* Richmond, VA: Hill Directory Co., Inc. Publishers.

Dillahunt, George. *Hill's Winston-Salem, NC City Directory, 1947-1948.* Richmond, VA: Hill Directory Co., Inc. Publishers.

"Diversity in the Medical Society." *The North Carolina Medical Association – 150 Years of Leadership*, (2004):8. Accessed August 8, 2013. http://www.ncmedsoc.org/wp-content/uploads/2013/08/NCMS_history_brochure1.pdf.

"Diversity @ Wake." *Wake Forest University :Intercultural Center.* Accessed March 4, 2016. http://interculturalcenter.wfu.edu/diversity-wake/.

Dorsey, Gary. "The shame that Winston tucked away.*" The Sentinel* (Winston-Salem, NC), January 24, 1980, 1+.

Dorsey, Gary. "They're Big Trees Now." *The Sentinel* (Winston-Salem, NC), October 31, 1981, 15+.

Douglas, Craig. "BRA board chairman 'Jeep' Jones to retire after 32 years." *Boston Business Journal* (Boston, MA), September 13, 2013. Accessed August 7, 2015. http://www.bizjournals.com/boston/blog/mass_roundup/2013/09/bra-board-chairman-jeep-jones-to.html.

Drabble, Jenny. "Bishop with Winston-Salem ties to preach at royal wedding next weekend." Winston-Salem Journal. https://www.greensboro.com/news/local_news/bishop-with-winston-salem-ties-to-preach-at-royal-wedding/article_af9b22dc-eac8-5dad-a314-3220ca5da605.html. May 12, 2018.

"Drew: Unraveling the Mystery." *The Chronicle* (Winston-Salem, NC), February 13, 1992, A1+.

"Dr. Bruce Soda". *Twin City Sentinel* (Winston-Salem, NC), May 4, 1935.

Dr. Cynthia Durham. (Winston-Salem, NC), https://www.wellness.com/dir/432943/chiropractor/nc/winston-salem/cynthia-durham-durham-chiropractic-acupuncture-clinic-pc-dc#referrer.

Dr. Harvey Allen. Retired physician. Personal interview with Chenita Johnson. August 28, 2013.

"Dr. Malloy Made Medical History in 1948." *The Chronicle* (Winston-Salem, NC), March 10, 1979, 20.

Dudley, Wade G. *Historic Photos of Winston-Salem.* Nashville, TN.: Turner Publishing Company, 2008.

Dunning, Jennifer. "Harold Nicholas, Dazzling Hoofer, Is Dead at 79." *The New York Times* (New York), July 4, 2000, B7. https://www.nytimes.com/2000/07/04/arts/harold-nicholas-dazzling-hoofer-is-dead-at-79.html.

Durham Chiropractic-Acupuncture Clinic, PC. http://www.wellness.com/dir/432943/chiropractor/nc/winston-salem/cynthia-durham-durham-chiropractic-acupuncture-clinic-pc-dc#referrer.

Dwiggins, Don. "African American Women in History and Culture." *Black History Month at the Library. Forsyth County North Carolina.* January 25, 2012. Accessed March 3, 2012. http://www.co.forsyth.nc.us/article.aspx?NewsID=17308.

"1870-1900: Years of Transition." *Winston-Salem Chronicle* (Winston-Salem, NC), February 3, 1979, 13.

E. Jerry Jones. Public information - Winston Lake Golf Club. Winston-Salem, NC, June. 2010.

Eaon, Hubert A. "Winston-Salem Native the First Black
        Doctor in State". *Winston-Salem Chronicle* (Winston-Salem, NC),
        February 18, 1982, 1+.
"Edward Everette Hill. Principal of Carver in 1936." Paper
        submitted by Geneva Cook Hill. Vertical File in Winston-Salem
        African American Archive.
"Edwill, James S." *Chas. Emerson & Co's Winston, Salem &
        Greensboro NC Directory 1879-80.*
Eller, Robert. "Pond Giants Open 65th." *The Chronicle* (Winston-
        Salem, NC), April 4, 1979, 13.
"Eli's Pack and Ship: from Point A to Point B (and everywhere in
        between)." *Winston-Salem Chronicle* (Winston-Salem, NC),
        November 30, 2012. Accessed April 10, 2015.
        http://www.wschronicle.com/2012/11/elis-pack-and-ship-from-
        point-a-to-point-b-and-everywhere-in-between/
Evans, Meghann. Forsyth County Promotes Tatum to Assistant
        County Manager. *Winston-Salem Journal.* December 11, 2014.
        https://www.journalnow.com/news/local/forsyth-county-promotes-
        tatum-to-assistant-county-manager/article_74fd2492-8165-11e4-bee5-
        27a6bcdfd995.html
"Exhibit features safe bus company." NC Department of cultural
        Resources news. *NC Department of Cultural Resources.* February 5,
        2008. Accessed March 3, 2009. http://news.ncdcrLgov/2008/02/05/
        exhibit-features-safe-bus—company/.
"Experiment In Self Reliance." *Mission and Vision.*
        Accessed February 1, 2015. http://eisr.org/who-we-are/mission-
        vision/.
Fair, T. Willard. " T. Willard Fair was the Muhammad Ali of
        black Dade County." *Miami Herald* (Miami Florida), October 6,
        2013. Accessed October 28, 2013.
        https://www.miamiherald.com/news/local/community/miami-
        dade/miami-stories/article1955947.html.
Fam. "Black Hollywood in the Twin City". *North Carolina Room
        Word Press* (blog). March 14, 2017. Accessed May 5, 2017.
        https://northcarolinaroom.wordpress.com/
        2017/03/14/black-hollywood-in-the-twin-city/.

Fam. "Black Police Officers. The Forgotten Story." *North Carolina Room Word Press* (blog). February 25, 2010. Accessed February 15, 2012. https://northcarolinaroom.wordpress.com/2010/02/25/black-police-officers-the-forgotten-story/

Fam. "Happy Hairston. Black is Back." *North Carolina Room Word Press* (blog). February 22, 2014. Accessed May 8, 2014. https://northcarolinaroom.wordpress.com/tag/happy-hairston/.

Fam. "Lollipoop II...a saga...." *North Carolina Room Word Press* (blog). June 19, 2014. Accessed February 10, 2015. https://northcarolinaroom.wordpress.com/tag/spurgeon-ellington/.

Fam. "The Battle of Henry Johnson." *North Carolina Room Word Press* (blog), February 23, 2012. Updated June 3, 2015. Accessed April 10, 2014. http://northcarolinaroom.wordpress.com/2012/02/23/the-battle-of-henry-johnson/.

Fam. "Black Police Officers. The Forgotten Story." *North Carolina Room Word Press* (blog). February 25, 2010. Accessed February 15, 2012. https://northcarolinaroom.wordpress.com/2010/02/25/black-police-officers-the-forgotten-story/.

"Farm for retired slaves now site of fine homes." *Winston-Salem Journal and Sentinel* (Winston-Salem, NC), April 10, 1966, K21.

Fearnbach, Heather. "Boston Cottage: One of North Winston's Earliest Subdivisions." *Black Business, INK.,* March 2003.

Fearnbach, Heather. "Salem Plantation - Liberia - Happy Hill." *Black Business, INK.,* January 2013. +.

Fearnbach, Heather. *Winston-Salem's Architectural Heritage*. City of Winston, North Carolina: Forsyth County Historic Resources Commission. 2015.

"File, Mossella E." *Miller's Winston-Sarem N. Carolina City Directory*. Asheville, NC: Piedmont Directory Co.,INC. Publishers, 1928.

"File, Mossella E." *Miller's Winston-Salem NC City Directory 1930*. Winston-Salem, NC and Asheville, NC:

"First Black City Personnel Director." *The Chronicle* (Winston-Salem, NC), October 29, 1977, 1-2.

"First Lt. Spurgeon Neal Ellington." *Find a Grave.* July 24, 2010. Accessed January 9, 2016. https://www.findagrave.com/cgi-bin/fg.cgi?page=gr&GRid=55388800.

"First in Senate". *Winston-Salem Journal* (Winston-Salem, NC), November 6, 2012.

"First Negro Clerk". *The Sentinel* (Winston-Salem, NC), February 18, 1963

"First black woman elected to Oklahoma House dies." *The Oklahoman.* NewsOk (Oklahoma City), June 18, 2010. Accessed October 5, 2015. https://oklahoman.com/article/3469435/first-black-woman-elected-to-oklahoma-house-dies.

Fish, Carson. "Noteworthy Firsts: Karen L. Parker." University Archives *UNC University Library* (Blog). February 16, 2017. https://blogs.lib.unc.edu/uarms/index.php/2017/02/carolina-firsts-karen-l-parker/.

Fitts, John Shephard. *Turner's Winston and Salem City Directory for the Years 1894 and 1895.* Yonkers, NY: Turner and Company Printers and Binders, 1894.

"Five Downtown Stores close Lunch Counters." Winston-Salem Journal (Winston-Salem, NC), February 10, 1960, 1.

Forsyth Savings and Trust Building 408 Church. The *Winston-Salem NC City Directory, 1915.* Asheville, NC: Hackney and Moale Co. Printers.

Forsyth Savings and Trust Co. 410 N. Church. The *Winston-Salem N.C. City Directory, 1915.* Asheville, NC: Hackney and Moale Co. Printers.

Fox, Janet. *Winston-Salem: A Cooperative Spirit.* Winston-Salem, North Carolina: Old Salem, INC.,1994.

Francis, Charles E. *The Tuskegee Airmen: The Men who Changed a Nation,* Fifth edition. The University of Michigan: Brandon Books Publishing Company,2008.Accessed March 15, 2015. https://books.google.com/books?id=gv8LAQAAMAAJ&source=gbs_Book_other_versions.

Franklin, Denise. "Celebrate Black History." *North Carolina Room Word Press* (blog). January 19, 2012. Accessed March 7, 2012. http://northcarolinaroom.worgpress.com/2012/01/19/celebrate-black-history—201..

Freeman, Yvette N. "Facts about Areas First School for Blacks Uncovered." *Winston-Salem Chronicle* (Winston-Salem, NC), April 16, 1992.

Fries, Adelaide L., Mary Callum Wiley, Douglas L. Rights, Harvey Dinkens, Charles N. Siewers, Flora Ann Lee.
Forsyth: The History of a County on the March. Chapel Hill USA: The University North Carolina Press, 1949

Fries, Adelaide, Stuart Thurman Wright and J. Edwin Hendricks.
Forsyth: The History of a County on the March (Winston-Salem, NC). Chapel Hill: The University of North Carolina Press, 1976.

Gaddy, Hugh. "Edward Diggs". BLACK IN TIME: A Moment in Our History. April 22, 2011. Accessed August 6, 2012. http://www.blackintime.info/black-in-time-a-moment-in-our-history/e-odiggs

Galindo, Dan. "An interest in Policing led to a breakthrough move." *Winston-Salem Journal* (Winston-Salem, NC), November 24, 2007. Accessed December 9, 2015.
http://www.journalnow.com/news/local/an-interest-in-policing-led-to-a-breakthrough-move/article_a36f1c4e-e2b7-56d7-ac5f-196e49ea7883.html.

Garms, Layla. "City's second black police chief takes oath." *Winston-Salem Chronicle* (Winston-Salem, NC), July 4, 2013. Accessed November 7, 2015.
http://www.wschronicle.com/2013/07/citys-second-black-police-chief-takes-oath/.

"Gates, Alex." *Chas. Emmerson and Co.'s Winston, Salem and Greensboro North Carolina Directory, 1879 -'80.* Raleigh, NC: Edwards, Broughton, and Co. Printers and Binders, 1879.

Gillespie, Michele. *Katherine and R. J. Reynolds: Partners of Fortune in the Making of the New South.* Athens GA: University Press of Georgia, October 1, 2012. Accessed April 5, 2015. https://books.google.com/books/about/Katharine_and_R_J_Reynolds.html?id=lQOpAAAAQBAJ

Gilmer, Susan. "Daily Reminder Calendar brings City's black history to life." *Winston-Salem Journal* (Winston-Salem, NC). February 20, 1997, A1+.

Giunca, Mary. "In with the New(er). Volunteers bring life to old Cherry." *Winston-Salem Journal* (Winston-Salem, NC), April 23, 2009, B1+.

Gray, Jenny. "Police chief named in Littleton." The Daily Herald (Roanoke Rapids, NC). July 2, 2014. Accessed September 14, 2017. http://www.rrdailyherald.com/news/ police-chief-named-in-littleton/article_3c53cb86-020e-11e4-a89d-0014bcf887a.html.

Gray, Lozie Ann. "Moments in Black History." Excerpts from a short program at United Metropolitan Baptist Church. February 14, 1993.1-3.Vertical File

Green, Anne Wooten. "7 over Seventy Senior Awards." *SPARK Magazine*, August 6, 2016. Accesed September 5, 2016. http://www.journalnow.com/spark/ over-seventy-senior-awards/article_e446ac02-5bdd-11e6-a61a-134b98d7b10b.html.

"Grier, Pam. Biography." *IMDB*. January 12, 2015. https://www.imdb.com/name/nm0000427/bio.

Gutierrez, Bertrand M. "City Picks its Attorney." *Winston-Salem Journal* (Winston-Salem, NC), May 2010. Accessed May 6, 2012. http://www2.journalnow.com/news/local/article.

Gutierrez, Bertrand M. "50 years later, it's a grand reunion. Group recalls pioneer days at WSSU nursing school." *JournalNow* (Winston-Salem, NC). November 4, 2007. Accessed 2010. https://www.journalnow.com/news/local/years-later-it-s-a-grand-reunion-group-recalls-pioneer/article_aa2ffc6e-095c-59d6-ade1-45b2b44c9980.html.

"Half A Century of Negro Progress in Twin City." *Twin City Sentinel* (Winston-Salem, NC), May 4, 1935, 25-28.

Hall, Brian. "Dash to Honor Winston-Salem Pond Giants." wfmynews2 digitriad. 22 Aug. 2011. Accessed August 25, 2012. http://www.digitriad.com/news/article/185542/13/dash-to-wear-replica-jerseye-/.

"Hall, H. H. Dr." *Turner's Fifth Annual Winston and Salem City Directory for the Years 1891 and 1892.* Yonkers, NY: E.F. Turner and Publishers.

"Hall, H. H. Dr." *Walsh's Directory of the Cities of Winston and Salem, NC for 1902-03.* Charleston, SC: The W. H. Walsh Directory Company Charleston, SC 1902.

Hall, Melissa. "First Black General in N.C. National Guard." *Winston-Salem Journal* (Winston-Salem, NC), December 25, 2008. B1+.

Hannah Diggs Atkins. Obituary. *Winston-Salem Journal* (Winston-Salem, NC) July 1,2010. Accessed May 7, 2015. http://www.legacy.com/obituries/winston-salem.

Hanes, Frank Borden. "Disc Jockey Sells Own Show; 'Best Job I Ever Had,' He Says." *Sentinel* (Winston-Salem, NC), March 25, 1948.

"Happy" Hairston. A L.A. Laker and Man of the Community. African *American Registry.* Accessed May 8, 2014. https://aaregistry.org/story/happy-hairston-a-l-a-laker-and-man-of-the-community/.

Hardman, Peggy. "LANIER, RALPHAEL O'HARA." *Handbook of Texas Online*, Texas State Historical Association. June 15, 2010.Accessed August 12, 2013. http://www.tshaonline.org/handbook/online/articles/fla88.

Harless, Sharrie. "Study Uncovers Salem's Black History." Donated by Jon Sensbach, Old Salem Researcher. February 16, 1990.

Harold (Happy) Hairston. *Basketball Reference.* Accessed May 2014. https://www.basketball-reference.com/players/h/hairsha01.html.

Harold 'Happy' Hairston. Biography. Accessed May 8, 2014. https://www.imdb.com/name/nm0354376/bio.

"Harold Nicholas." Biography. Accessed May 8, 2016. https://www.imdb.com/name/nm0629389/bio.

Harrison, Anthony. "Story of glory: Two women who revolutionized women's basketball." *Triad City Beat* (Winston-Salem, NC), March 9, 2016. https://triad-city-beat.com/story-of-glory/.

Harry, Cheryl Streeter. *Winston-Salem's African American Legacy (Images of America)*. Charleston, SC: Arcadia Publishing, 2012.

"Hawkins Bound for Seattle." *The Chronicle* (Winston-Salem, NC), August 26, 1978, 6.

Haywood Oubre (1916-2006). The Johnson Collection, LLC. Spartanburg, SC. http://thejohnsoncollection.org/hayward-oubre/.

"Haywood l. Oubre peerless artist and master of torgue." Articles about Haywood L.Oubre (blog). January 10, 2006. https://haywardoubre.blogspot.com/2006/01/.

"HBCU of the Week on AJC Sepia: Winston-Salem State University's Notable Graduates." *Atlanta. News. Now.* https://www.ajc.com/news/local-education/hbcu-theweek-ajc-sepia-winston-salem-state-university-notable-graduates/FmfXYS4BdDDXoh0YzORCM/.

Hearn III, Thomas K. *Wake Forest University*. Charleston, SC: Arcadia Publishing, March 16, 2004. https://www.arcadiapublishing.com/Products/9780738515908.2015.

Henderson, Archibald. *North Carolina The Old North State and the New Vol.IV*. Chicago: The Lewis Publishing Company, 1941.

"Sgt. Henry Johnson Medal of Honor Recipient." Arlington National Cemetery. June 10, 2015. Accessed November 3, 2015. https://www.youtube.com/watch?v=aUpvLDU6i5g

Henry, Phillip N., PhD and Carol M. Spears, PhD *The Heritage of Blacks in North Carolina*. Raleigh, NC: African American Heritage Foundation, NC, 1990.

Herron, Arika. "Parkland auditorium to be named for long-time teacher." *Winston-Salem Journal* (Winston-Salem, NC) December 31, 2015.
Accessed January 15, 2016. http://www.journalnow.com/news/local/parkland-auditorium-to-be-named-for-long-time-teacher/article_3c1fd660-abb2-52a8-84d1-1b82ffe2ab9b.html

Hill, Edward Everett. *Educators Whose Names are Identified with Public Schools*. Calendar - Society for the Study of Afro American History in Winston-Salem / Forsyth County, 3rd ed. 1992.

Hill, Edward Jr. "Spreading gospel over the air". *The Chronicle* (Winston-Salem, NC), November 25, 1982, 15.

Hines, Darlene Clark, ed. "The Sculptors." In *Facts on File Encyclopedia of Black Women in America—Dance, Sports, and Visual Arts* Vol.3, New York: Facts On File, Inc., 1997.

Hinton, John. "Bobby Kimbrough Jr. sworn in as sheriff of Forsyth County, becoming first black person to hold the job in the county's history." *Winston-Salem Journal* (Winston-Salem, NC), December 4, 2018. Accessed December 18, 2018. https://www.journalnow.com/news/local/bobby-kimbrough-jr-sworn-in-as-sheriff-of-forsyth-county/article_4e22aad0-0f95-5ca0-a7a8-5365f0e12e57.html.

Hinton, John. "Campbell, longtime city bus driver dies this Week." *Winston-Salem Journal* (Winston-Salem, NC), December 31, 2008. Accessed February 13, 2010. http://www.journalnow.com/news/local/campbell-longtime-city-bus-driver-dies-this-week/article_24b0aaa4-2a0c-5a8b-9c37-271677043aed.html.

Hinton, John. "First Black in North Carolina Senate." *Winston-Salem Journal* (Winston-Salem, NC), November 6, 2012, 1.

Hinton, John. "Our company: Safe Bus, started in 1926, was source of pride in Winston-Salem's black community." *Winston-Salem Journal* (Winston-Salem, NC), June 16, 2013 Accessed July 10, 2015. http://www.journalnow.com/news/local/our-company-safe-bus-started-in-was-source-of-pride/article_5613c018-d6f3-11e2-8657-0019bb30f31a.html.

Hinton, John and Laura Graff. "A legacy of sweat and brick." *Winston-Salem Journal* (Winston-Salem, NC), October 30, 2011. Accessed March 2, 2015. http://www.journalnow.com/news/local/a-legacy-of-sweat-and-brick/article_bba40383-8ce2-589c-ba54-274eba70f038.html.

Hinton, John. "Overbea, trailblazing black journalist, dies." *Winston-Salem Journal* (Winston-Salem, NC), July 14, 2010. Accessed September 8, 2014. http://www.journalnow.com/news/local/overbea-trailblazing-black-journalist-dies/article_757fc840-d054-544d-b1f1-0553e855d308.html.

Hinton, John. "Saint Paul United Methodist Church celebrates its 142nd anniversary." *Winston-Salem Journal* (Winston-Salem, NC), May 24, 2013. https://www.journalnow.com/news/local/saint-paul-united-methodist-church-celebrates-its-nd-anniversary/article_e109da02-c4da-11e2-93d4-0019bb30f31a.html.

"History Making Carmon Sworn In." *The Chronicle* (Winston-Salem, NC), January 10, 2008, A1+.

"HISTORY OF THE NURSING DIVISION General Nursing Information 4 History of the Nursing." *Course Hero*. https://www.coursehero.com/file/p6uefoh/General-Nursing-lnformation-4-HISTORY-OF-THE-NURSING-DIVISION-The-Nursing/.

Hoang, Khai. "Bowens introduced as Littleton's new police Chief." *The Daily Herald* (Roanoke Rapids, NC), August 20, 2014. Accessed September 14, 2017. http://www.rrdailyherald.com/news/bowens-introduced-as-littleton-s-new-police-chief/ article_b490a20a-2887-11e4-aac0-0019bb2963f4.html.

Holiness Review. *Walsh's Directory of the Cities of Winston and Salem, NC for 1902-03.* Charleston, SC: The W. H. Walsh Directory Company, 1902.

"Holland's Seeds Sprout." Winston-Salem Chronicle (Winston-Salem, NC). February 16, 1980, 215.

Horton, Bunny. "Palmer Gill Friende Obituary." January 19, 2004 Accessed February 5, 2016. https://www.ancestry.com/boards/localities.northam.usa.states.nort hcarolina.counties.forsyth/10465/mb.ashx.

Howard, Ike. President of Forsyth County NAACP. Personal interview with Chenita Johnson. Winston-Salem, NC, August 8, 2015.

Howard, Ruthell. "Deejay is Minister of the Airwaves."
    Winston-Salem Chronicle (Winston-Salem, NC), December 2, 1982.

Howse, Jordan. "County's First Black Sheriff's Deputy, Eldridge
    Austin, dies at 88". *Winston-Salem Journal* (Winston-Salem, NC),
    December 28, 2016.
    Accessed December 31, 2016.
    http://www.journalnow.com/news/local/county-s-first-black-
    sheriff-s-deputy-eldridge-alston-dies/article_9df1eed4-089b-5b97-
    8606-3017241807c3.html.

"Hyman, John Adams (1840-1891)." *History, Art & Archives:
    United States House of Representatives.* Accessed December 6, 2016.
    http://history.house.gov/People/Detail/15549.

"It Was Time. Part of the Series - Blacks in Winston-Salem:
    A Past Overlooked." *Winston-Salem Journal* (Winston-Salem, NC)
    February 25, 1988, 222.

Jackson, James. "Diggs Gallery celebrates 20 years with 'Pride and
    Dignity' exhibit," *The News Argus* (Winston-Salem, NC),
    October 26, 2010. Accessed June 5, 2011.
    http://www.thenewsargus.com/news/view.php/402783/Diggs-
    Gallery-celebrates-20-years-with-P.

James Sansom, Jr. Obituary. Submitted by the Family to Chenita
    Johnson, 2010.

"James Shober First Black Doctor To Graduate From A North
    Carolina Medical School." *University Medical Center library online.*
    Accessed October 8, 2013.
    http://www.ncmedboard.org/embed/timeline_content/1878_dr._sh
    ober_practice_in.

Jarrett, Juanita. *History of Blacks in Winston-Salem.*
    Winston-Salem, North Carolina: Central School System
    Office, 1991: 1-9.

"Jim Caldwell." *Pro football history.com*
    Accessed January 3, 2017. https://pro-football-
    history.com/coach/49/jim-caldwell-bio.

"Jim Peace: Life as an entrepreneur." *Afro American* (Baltimore,
    MD): googlenews.com, July 26, 1988, 4D. Accessed August 4, 2014.

"Joe Johnson." Winston Lake Golf Club, Winston-Salem, NC. May 6, 2010.

Joe McFadden. Carolinas Boxing Hall Of Fame. Accessed March 5, 2015. http://www.carolinasboxinghalloffame.com/joe-mcfadden.

John Joyce. *Hill's Winston-Salem City Directory.* Richmond, VA: Hill Directory Co., Inc., Publishers, 1945.

"John W. Paisley." *Educators Whose Names are identified with Public Schools.* Calendar - Society for the Study of Afro American History, 3rd ed., 1992.

Johnson, Dianne and Dorothy Carpenter. *Medical Archives Wake Forest Medical School African-Americans in Medicine Melting Pot III for Cultural Awareness Committee.* Wake Forest school of medicine February 6, 2012. Accessed August 12, 2014. http://www.wakehealth.edu/uploadedFiles/User_Content/SchoolOfMedicine/Library/Archives/Documents/african_american_highlights_bowman_gray_rev_w.pdf.

Johnson, Michelle. "His Rightful Place." *Winston-Salem Journal* (Winston-Salem, NC), February 23, 1960,1.

Jones, Frank. "George Washington Slept Here." Winston-Salem Journal (Winston-Salem, NC), February 21, 1959.

Jones, Jae . "Bill Wilkerson: One of the First Black Pilots in the Country with US Airways." *Black then. Discovering Our History.* February 9, 2017. https://blackthen.com/bill-wilkerson-one-first-black-pilots-country-us-airways/.

Jones, Morgan. "Karen Parker: A Woman to Remember." *News and Perspectives from University Archives and Records Management Services.* March 18, 2013. https://blogs.lib.unc.edu/uarms/index.php/2013/03/karen-parker-a-woman-to-remember/.

Jordan, Ronald. "Famed Indian Chief Really Winston-Salem Man." *Winston-Salem Journal* (Winston-Salem, NC), August 29, 1976, Sect. C.

Jordan, Ronald. "Bittersweet Memories". *Winston-Salem Journal* (Winston-Salem, NC), August 30, 1992, B1+

Joseph Weldon McFadden. *Atkins High School Sports Hall of Fame.* Accessed November 14, 2015. http://www.wsfcs.k12.nc.us/Page/93291.

Kamara, Margaret. "Winston-State University Teams up with NASCAR for a Degree Program." *Diverse: Issues in Higher Education.* Fairfax, Va.: *CMA publication.* June 19, 2007. https://diverseeducation.com/article/7606/.

Killian, Joe. Black sheriffs make history in sweep of seven largest NC counties. The PROGRESSIVE PULSE November 7, 2018. pulse.ncpolicywatch.org

Kimberley Park School. *Winston-Salem, N. Carolina City Directory.* Asheville, NC 1926: The Miller Press, (Inc.) Printers, 1926.

"Larretta Rivera-Williams." *Global Sisters Report: a project of National Catholic Reporter.* National Catholic Reporter publications:ncronline.org. Accessed May 3, 2018. https://www.globalsistersreport.org/authors/larretta-rivera-williams

"Larry Hopkins Named 2010 ACC Football Legend." *Wake Forest University Athletics.* August 3, 2010. Accessed December 8, 2010. https://godeacs.com/news/2010/8/3/Larry_Hopkins_Named_2010_ACC_Football_Legend.aspx.

"Larry Leon Hamlin made History by bringing First National Black Theater Festival to Winston-Salem." *Winston-Salem Chronicle* (Winston-Salem, NC), January 25, 1990, "n.page." Vertical files. North Carolina Room Forsyth County Central Library.

Lash, Whilemena. Personal interview with Chenita Johnson.(Winston-Salem, NC),June 6, 2015.

Laughlin, Jeff. "Heroes of the Hardwood." *Winston-Salem monthly* (Winston-Salem, NC), February 27, 2014.http://www.journalnow.com/winstonsalemmonthly/heroes-of-the-Hardwood/article_8ef94708-9a4e-11e3-b23c-0017a43b2370.html.

League Grocery Store. *Walsh's Winston-Salem North Carolina City Directory for 1904-05* Charleston, SC: The W. H. Walsh Directory Company. 1904.

Lena Tillett. "Six black women leading major NC police departments make
    history." *WRAL.com*. September 7, 2017. Updated July 13, 2018.
    Accessed September 14, 2017. http://www.wral.com/six-black-
    women-leading-nc-police-Departments/16930938/.

Lee, Cleon O. *The Winston-Salem, NC City Directory*. Asheville,
    NC: Piedmont Directory Company Publishers,Inc.,1915.

Lee, Cleon Oscar. *Walsh's Winston-Salem North Carolina City
    Directory for 1906*. Charleston, SC: The Walsh Directory Company.

Lee, Cleon Oscar. *Winston-Salem North Carolina City and
    Suburban City Directory,* Asheville, NC : Piedmont Directory
    Company, Publishers, Inc., 1910.

"Legal Briefs of Son of WSSU Founder Given to Yale Law Library."
    Winston-Salem State Archway Magazine, May 2004. WSSU Archives
    Digital Collection. Accessed August 12, 2014.
    http://cdm17140.contentdm.oclc.org/cdm/compoundobject/collecti
    on/p17140coll7/id/3999/rec/1.

Lewis, Henry S. Jr. "Daily Reminder Calendar brings city's
    black history to life." Winston-Salem Journal(Winston-Salem, NC),
    February 20,1997.

"Librarian Education: Eliza Atkins Gleason, First African American to Earn
    PhD in Library Science." *Little Known Black Librarians Facts*.
    September 8, 2011.
    Accessed November 15, 2015.
    http://littleknownblacklibrarianfacts.blogspot.com/2011/09/librarian
    -education-eliza-atkins.html.

"Listing of Black Churches by Period of Founding."
    The Chronicle (Winston-Salem, NC), January 26, 1980.

"Local Group to Sing for King and Queen." *Winston-Salem
    Journal and Sentinel* (Winston-Salem, NC), June 4, 1939,33.

"Local Man First Negro to Head Hampton School." *Winston-
    Salem Journal and Sentinel* (Winston-Salem, NC), January 24,
    1943,33.

"Local Teacher Awarded 'Who's Who' Certificate Miss Naomi C.
    McLean." *The Chronicle* (Winston-Salem, NC), February 5,1977,10.

Logan, Frenise A. *The Negro in North Carolina, 1876-1894*. Chapel Hill, North Carolina: University of North Carolina Press, 1964.

"Long Remembered Strike lasted 38 Days." *Winston-Salem Chronicle* (Winston-Salem, NC), March 10, 1979, 17.

Long, Walter. *Winston-Salem, NC City Directory 1925*. Asheville, NC: The Miller Press, 1924.

Long, Walter L. *Miller's Winston-Salem, N. Carolina City Directory, 1928*. Asheville, NC: The Miller Press, 1927.

Longworth, Jim." Womble Leaves Big Shoes to Fill." *YES Weekly* (Greensboro, NC), April 4, 2012, 1.

"Loretta Copeland Biggs." *BallotPedia*. Accessed August 11, 2015. https://ballotpedia.org/Loretta_Copeland_Biggs.

Lowe, Kegan. "High School football coach makes her own way at Winston-Salem Prep." *Winston-Salem Journal* (Winston-Salem, NC), October 20, 2015, Section D. Accessed December 5, 2015. http://www.journalnow.com/sports/prepzone/football/high-school-football-coach-makes-her-own-way-at-winston/ article_37ff0727-d8d2-5f55-9da2-8a0baed98447.html.

Lt. Spurgeon Neal Ellington. Find A Grave. Accessed July 24, 2010. http://www.findagrave.com/cgi-bin/fgi?page=gr&Grid+55388800.

Luck, Todd. "City Council honors new Miss America's Winston-Salem roots." *The Chronicle* (Winston-Salem, NC). September 20, 2018. http://www.wschronicle.com/2018/09/city-council-honors-new-miss-americas-winston-salem-roots/.

Luck, Todd. "First Ladies Speak." *The Chronicle* (Winston-Salem, NC), March 1, 2012, A1+.

Luck, Todd. "Former drivers recount experiences at historic Safe Bus Co. of Winston-Salem." The Chronicle (Winston-Salem, NC), February 18, 2016. Accessed May 6, 2016. http://www.wschronicle.com/2016/02/former-drivers-recount-experiences-historic-safe-bus-co-winston-salem/

Luck, Todd. "Moore becomes WSFD's first black female battalion Chief." *Winston-Salem Chronicle* (Winston-Salem, NC). December 3, 2015, A4. Accessed January 1, 2016. http://www.wschronicle.com/2015/12/moore-becomes-wsfds-first-black-female-battalion-chief/.

"Luix Overbea Remembered for Ties to Black Community." Maynard Institute. July 15,2010. Accessed October 24, 2014. http://mije.org/richardprince/why-media-arent-giving-obama-credit#Overbea.

"Machine Preserves Organs." *Winston-Salem Journal* (Winston-Salem, NC), August 24, 1968.

Mack, Angela. "James Shober paved the way for black physicians in Tar Heel State." *Star News ONLINE* (Wilmington, NC), February 12, 2007. Accessed February 8, 2010. http://www.starnewsonline.com/news/20070212/james-shober-paved-the-way-for-black-physicians-in-tar-heel-state.

"Making it Through the Depression." *The Chronicle* (Winston-Salem, NC), February 24, 1979,14.

"Malloy Made Medical History in '48." *The Chronicle* (Winston-Salem, NC), March 10,1979,20.

"Marissa Camille Little." Nike FIBA World Ranking. Euro Cup Women. https://www.fiba.basketball/eurocupwomen/17-18/player/Marissa-Camille-Little.

"Marshall Bass to Speak at Voorees Assembly." *The Times and Democrat* (Orangeburg, SC), September 8, 2004,4A. www.TheTandD.com https://www.newspapers.com/image/?clipping_id=24186597&fcfToken=eyJhbGciOiJIUzI1NiIsInR5cCI6IkpXVCJ9.eyJmcmVlLXZpZXctaWQiOjMoNjE3MjQyNiwiaWFoIjoxNTc2MDQ1NTE3LCJleHAiOjE1NzYxMzE5MTd9.zTS301yJIjn9WEih0omh7_3HrWwm8AmAosrlb9jAXWc.

Marshall B. Bass. *Prabook. World Biographical Encyclopedia, Inc.* https://prabook.com/web/marshall_b.bass/53570.

Martin, Stephen. "Striking Out Against Big Tobacco: A movement extinguished: A Duke historian chronicles the short life of Local 22, a feisty tobacco union." *Duke Magazine,* March 2004. Accessed

January 15, 2015. http://dukemagazine.duke.edu/articla/striking-out-against-big-Tobacco.

Martin, Tony. "Henry Johnson (1891-1929). *American National Biography*. October 2008. Accessed October 20, 2014. http://www.anb.org/articles/20/20-01908.html.

Massaquoi, Hans J. "The New Navy Trying To Put The Past Behind." *Ebony Magazine*, September 1, 1989. Accessed January 5, 2015. https://books.google.com/books/about/Ebony.html?id=2MwDAAAAMBAJ.

Mason, Scott. "Cereal Box makes history." *TarHill Traveler* WRAL.com January 21, 2009. http://www.wral.com/lifestyles/travel/video/4373015/.

Mayfield, A.A. "Forsyth County's Only Negro High School." *Winston-Salem Journal* (Winston-Salem, NC), November 13, 1938.

Mays, Raqiyah. "Pam Grier to be honored at Black Enterprise Women of Power Summit: Hollywood's first female action star to receive Legacy Award for her work in film and business." *Black Enterprise Magazine,* October 17, 2014. https://www.blackenterprise.com/pam-grier-2015-legacy-award-honoree-women-of-power/.

McCabe, Catlin. "Profiles in Black Cartooning: Matt Baker." *Comic Book Legal Defense Fund*. February 5, 2016. http://cbldf.org/2016/02/profiles-in-black-cartooning-matt-baker/.

McConney, Christopher. *Miller's Winston—Salem, N. Carolina City Directory, 1928*. Ashville, NC: Miller publishers, Inc., 1927.

McCullough, Yvette. "Appreciation Service-A Queen in Our Midst." *The Chronicle* (Winston-Salem, NC), February 10, 1979, 16.

McDowell, Ian. "Piedmont-Born Comic Book Pioneer Matt Baker." *Yes Weekly* (Greensboro, NC), May 31, 2017. Accessed March 2018. http://yesweekly.com/piedmont-born-comic-book-pioneer-matt-baker/.

McKenzie, Samantha. "A People's Victory." *Winston-Salem Chronicle* (Winston-Salem, NC), June 18, 1992, A1+.

"McLean's Stenographic." *The Chronicle* (Winston-Salem, NC), March 31, 1979, 6-8.

Mebane, Lillie. The *Winston-Salem, N.C. City Directory*.
    Asheville, NC : Hackney and Moale Co.,Printers,1915.
Mebane, Lillie. *Winston-Salem, N.C. City Directory*. Asheville,
    NC: Commercial Company Inc., Publishers,1916.
Mebane, Lillie. *Winston-Salem, N.C. City Directory*. Asheville,
    NC: Commercial Service Company, Inc. Publishers, 1920.
"Meet the Expert: Lafayette Jones, president and CEO of SMSi-
    Urban Call Marketing, Inc. and publisher of Urban Call."
    Multicultural
Marketing Resources, Inc. May 16, 2012.
    Accessed June 3, 2014. http://multicultural.com/multicultural-
    articles/meet_the_expert_lafayette_jones_president_and_ceo_of_sm
    si-urban_call_marketing-_inc_and_publisher_o .
Melas, Chloe. "Miss America 2019 is Nia Franklin." CNN.
    September 10, 2018.
    https://www.cnn.com/2018/09/09/entertainment/miss-america-
    winner-nia-franklin/index.html.
"Memorial Industrial School. Public, Private Welfare
    Agencies Provide for Needy Among Negroes." *Winston-Salem Journal
    and Sentinel* (Winston-Salem, NC), April 24,1938,14,Sec.8.
Metas Restaurant. Accessed 8 Feb. 2016.
    https://www.facebook.com/pg/MetasRestaurant/photos/
    ?ref=page_internal.
"Methodists Also Celebrating A 200th Birthday This Year."
    Bicentennial Edition:16. Vertical files (African American Churches-
    Methodists). North Carolina Room Winston-
    Salem Central Library.
"Migration to the Factories." *The Chronicle* (Winston-Salem, NC),
    February 3,1979,13.
Milligan, Chuck. "Early Black Firefighters of North
    Carolina, Annotated." June 15, 2010. Accessed August 25, 2010.
    http://legeros.com/history/ebf/index.shtml/.
Mitchell, Vickie Davis. "Colored Baptist Orphanage-Waughtown-
    Belview." *AfriGeneas States Research Forum*. September 27,2005.
    Accessed September 11, 2012. http://www.afrigeneas.com/forum-
    states/index.cgi/md/read/id/1409/sbj/nc-colored-baptist-orphanage-
    waughtown-belview/.

Mizelle, Erin. Special to The Chronicle. "Loretta Biggs becomes U. S. judge." *The Chronicle* (Winston-Salem, NC), March 12, 2015. Accessed September 5, 2015. http://www.wschronicle.com/2015/03/loretta-biggs-becomes-u-s-judge/.

Molina, Camila. "Royal Wedding: North Carolina's Bishop Michael Curry quotes MLK, invokes spirit of American slaves." MAY 19, 2018. UPDATED MAY 21, 2018. Accessed June 6, 2018. https://www.newsobserver.com/entertainment/article211495389.html.

"Montgomery Wins City Council Seat as WSSU Senior." *RamPages.* December 15,2009. Winston-Salem State U.(Winston-Salem, NC). Accessed October 21, 2010. http://www.wssurampages.com/archives/2438.

Moore, Kathleen. "Bishop Michael Curry of the Diocese of North Carolina will be the next presiding bishop." June 27, 2015 News. https://deputynews.org/bishop-michael-curry-of-the-diocese-of-north-carolina-has-been-elected-and-confirmed-as-the-next-presiding-bishop-of-the-episcopal-church/.

Morgans Cleaning System. *Winston-Salem, NC City directory.* Asheville, NC: Commercial Service Co., Publishers, 1922.

Morgan-Hoffman. *Winston-Salem, NC City Directory.* Asheville, NC : Commercial Service Co., Publishers, 1923.

Morton, Lorrain Hairston. NORTHWESTERN UNIVERSITY LIBRARY. Accessed September 12, 2015. http://findingaids.library.northwestern.edu/catalog/inu-ead-nua-archon-1581.

Moss, Mark R. "The Rapid Ascent of Mutter Evans." *Black Enterprise,* December 1980. Accessed October 2, 2015. https://books.google.com/books?id=ZBxM.

"Mrs. Burns President of Safe Bus Company." *WS Afro American History (Winston-Salem, NC)* 1959. (A-K)-Vertical file North Carolina Room. Winston-Salem Central Library.

Mulhern, Mike. "No. 800 for Big House Gains Reaches Milestone in his Illustrious Career as WSSU Basketball Coach." *Winston-Salem Journal* (Winston-Salem, NC), January 25,1990,1+

Murphy, E. Louise. *The History of Winston-Salem State University 1892-1995*. Virginia Beach, VA: The Donning Company Publishers, 1999.

Mütter D. Evans. *The History Makers*. August 15, 2014. Accessed September 6, 2015. http://www.thehistorymakers.com/biography/mütter-evans.

"My Day by Eleanor Roosevelt." October 2, 1945. Accessed January 18, 2010. https://www2.gwu.edu/~erpapers/myday/displaydoc.cfm?_y=1945&_f=md000145.

Nance, Chad. "Reflections on Winston-Salem's Local 22 Marker Dedication." *Camel City Dispatch* (Winston-Salem, NC), April 21, 2013 http://www.camelcitydispatch.com/reflections-on-winston-salems-local-22-marker-dedication/.

"Naomi C. McLean Leaves a Legacy Of Professionalism." *African-American Tymes-Winston-Salem Chronicle* (Winston-Salem, NC), November 1995

"NC A&T names new athletics director." *Onnidan Online*. May 4, 2005. Accessed 8, March 2015. https://onnidan.com/04-05/news/may/ncat0504.htm.

"Negro High School." *The Chronicle* (Winston-Salem, NC), February 24,1979,13.

"Negro High School Is Formally Dedicated." *Twin City Sentinel* (Winston-Salem, NC), April 2, 1931.

"1945-1950: Blacks Enter into Mainstream." *The Chronicle* (Winston-Salem, NC), March 10,1979,17.

"1950-1960: A Decade of Reckoning." *The Chronicle* (Winston-Salem, NC), March 17, 1979,l7.

"Negroes Run White Branch Bank in Winston-Salem." *Jet Magazine*, December 11, 1952,5.

"Negotiated Segregation. A separate African American Church, A school and a community near Salem." *Digital Forsyth*. August 2012. Accessed October 12, 2012. http://www.digitalforsyth.org/photos/stories/.

Neilson, Robert W. *History of Government- City of Winston-Salem, North Carolina The All American City - 1766-Bicentennial 1966 Vol.1 and 2*. Winston-Salem, N.C.: Community Government Committee, 1966.

"New Denominations Emerge In Winston, Forsyth." *The Chronicle* (Winston-Salem, NC), February 2, 1980, 18.

Newton, Huey P. *The Black Panther Intercommunal News Service*, June 30, 1973, 4.

"9-year-old business owner honored in Winston-Salem." May 16, 2013. Accessed November 11, 2014. http://www.wxii12.com/news/localnews/piedmont/9yearold-business-owner-honored-in-winstonsalem/20177346.

Noonan, Kevin. " A Victory for Diversity." *Out & About-Greater Wilmington. March 29, 2017.* https://outandaboutnow.com/2017/03/29/a-victory-for-diversity/

"North Carolina Medical Society 150 Years of Leadership." The History of the North Carolina Medical Society's Pioneering Physician Leaders." *North Carolina Medical Society*. 2004. Accessed December 3, 2016. http://www.ncmedsoc.org/ wp-content/uploads/2013/08/NCMS_history_brochure1.pdf.

Oak Street Colored School. *Winston-Salem, NC City Directory*. Asheville, NC: Commercial Service Company Publishers. 1918.

ODD FELLOWS- Winston Star Lodge No. 2308 GUOOF. *Directory of Greensboro, Salem and Winston*. Atlanta, GA: Interstate Directory Company. 1884.

"Odd Fellows Cemetery." The Historic Marker Program: Forsyth County Historic Resources Commission. Accessed March 3, 2015. http://www.cityofws.org/Portals/0/pdf/Planning/HRC/historic-marker-program/Marker-Sheets/19_OddFellowsCemetery.pdf.

O'Donnell, Lisa. "City to Recognize Black Panthers." *Winston-Salem Journal* (Winston-Salem, NC), October 14, 2012, A1+.

"Officer who helped Break Racial Barriers In W-S Police Department Dies." *Winston-Salem Journal* (Winston-Salem, NC), September 25, 1988.

"Old Salem - *African Americans in Salem." Walking Tour Pamphlet.* Winston-Salem, North Carolina.

Opperman, Langdon. "Winston-Salem's African American Neighborhoods: 1870-1950." *Architectural and Planning Report Forsyth County Joint Historic Properties Commission City of Winston-Salem and the North Carolina Division of Archives and History.* 1994.

Opperman, Langdon. "Winston-Salem's African American Neighborhoods: 1870-1950." *Forsyth County Joint Historic Properties Commission,* 1993.

Otterbourg, Ken. "Lillian Lewis made headway for blacks." *Winston-Salem Journal* (Winston-Salem, NC), March 10, 1998, B2.

Overbea, Luix. "First Negro at Reynolds - Gwen Bailey Will Graduate." *Twin City Sentinel* (Winston-Salem, NC), June 5, 1959,1+.

Owen, Jackie. "School Integration Rises." *Twin City Sentinel* (Winston-Salem, NC), August 29,1966,1+.

Holcomb-Pack, Judie. "Episcopal locals beam over first black top bishop". *Winston-Salem Chronicle* (Winston-Salem, NC) November 5, 2015.

"Pam Grier." *IMDb.* Accessed February 2, 2015. http://www.imdb.com/name/nm0000427/.

"Pam Grier Biography.com." Biography. Accessed April 2,2014. https://www.biography.com/people/pam-grier-17181346.

Parent, Anthony S., Jr PhD. "Weathering Wake: The African American Experience." *Wake forest University.* February 26, 2009. Accessed March 3, 2011. www.wfu.edu/wowf/2009/20090226.parentspeech.html.

"Park Begun by Philanthropist." *The Chronicle* (Winston-Salem, NC), February 24, 1979,14-16.

Parker, Karen. "I raised my hand to volunteer." https://exhibits.lib.unc.edu/exhibits/show/protest/biographies/karen-parker.

Penry, Albert Pomp. *Turner & Co.'s Winston and Salem City Directory for the Years 1889-1890.* Yonkers, NY : E.F. Turner and Publishers, 1889. 107.

Penry, Albert Pomp. *Walsh's Directory of the Cities of Winston and Salem, NC for 1902-1903* Charleston, SC: The W. H. Walsh Directory Company, 1902. 278.

Penn, William K. prop Forsyth Employment Office. *Winston-Salem, N.C. City Directory.* Asheville, NC : Commercial Service Company Publishers, 1918,:532,417.

People's Printing Advertising. The *Winston-Salem, NC City Directory.* Asheville, NC: Piedmont Directory Company Publishers, Inc., 1912.

People's Printing Company. *The Winston-Salem, NC City Directory.* Asheville, NC : Piedmont Directory Company Publishers, Inc., 1912.

People's Printing Company. *The Winston-Salem, N.C. City and Suburban Directory.* Asheville, NC: Piedmont Directory Company Publishers, Inc., 1911.

People's Printing Company. *The Winston-Salem, NC City Directory.* Asheville, NC: Piedmont Directory Company Publishers, Inc., 1913.

Peterson, Audrey. "Northern Exposure." *American Legacy,* Fall 2005, 50-60.

Pharr, Malcolm A. "Black business Community has long History." *The Phoenix* (Winston-Salem, NC), January-February ca. 1998, 17.

"Phyllis Wheatly Home is the Answer to Prayers of 23 Twin City Negro Women." *Winston-Salem Journal* (Winston-Salem, NC), January 2,1927, 4A.

"Picketing Begins here at two Stores." *Winston-Salem Journal* (Winston-Salem, NC), May 7, 1960,1.

Poag, Mollie. *Hill's Winston-Salem (North Carolina) City Directory.* Richmond, VA.: Hill Directory Co., Inc., Publishers,1933.

Poag, Mollie A. *Hill's Winston-Salem(Forsyth County, NC) City Directory.* Richmond, VA : Hill Directory Co., Inc., Publishers,1934.

Poag, Mollie A. *Hill's Winston-Salem (Forsyth County, NC) City Directory.* Richmond, VA :Hill Directory Co., Inc., Publishers, 1945.

Poindexter, Jesse. "Bar Admits Negro Attorneys." *Winston- Salem Journal* (Winston-Salem, NC), July 18, 1963.

"Police Chief Asks Public to Co-operate with New Men." *Winston-Salem Journal* (Winston-Salem, NC), February 4, 1945 Accessed July 24, 2015.http://www.cityofws.org

"Police Review Board". City of Winston-Salem, NC. *Police Review Board*. http://www.cityofws.org/Department/City-Secretary/Police-Review-Board.

"Police Women Learn Duties in Twin City." *Winston-Salem Journal*, (Winston-Salem, NC), October 3, 1952.

POPE, IV, JONAS. " After 7 halls of fame, Bill Hayes joins another - one he aspired to be part of for 30 years." The News and Observer (Greensboro, NC), May 10, 2018. https://www.newsobserver.com/sports/article210794164.html.

Powell, William S. "Shober, James Francis." *NCPEDIA*. 1994 Accessed March 2, 2011. http://ncpedia.org/biography/shober-james-francis.

"Press Release: Appointment of Judge Roland H. Hayes." January 21, 2010. http://www.aoc.state.nc.us/www/public/aoc/pr/hayes.html.

Prichard, Robert W. MD. "Medicine in Winston-Salem: 1700's-1976 Winston-Salem's Black Hospitals prior to 1930." Reprinted from *Journal of the National Medical Association* Vol. 68, no.3. May 1976:240-249.

Prichard, Richard W.,MD. *Winston-Salem in History: Medical* VOL. II. Winston-Salem: Historic Winston-Salem, 1976.

Prichard, Dr. "Rays Hospital and Dr. Williamson Hospital. Medicine in Winston-Salem 1700's-1976." Vertical File: *Winston-Salem Medicine*. North Carolina Room Winston-Salem Central Library.

"Profiles of Black City officials". *Winston-Salem Chronicle* (Winston-Salem, NC), November 24, 1988,A3.

"Public, Private, Welfare Agencies Provide Relief for Needy Among Negroes." *Winston-Salem Journal and Sentinel* (Winston-Salem, NC), April 24,1938,14, Section 8.

"Race Riot in Winston." *The San Francisco Call* (San Francisco), August 13, 1895,1.

Railey, John. "In Winston: Sit-In's help end segregation." *Winston-Salem Journal* (Winston-Salem, NC), February 2, 2000, B1+.

Railey, John. "Clark S. Brown, Sr. Owner of Local Funeral Home Dead." *Winston-Salem Journal* (Winston-Salem, NC), September 7, 2001.

Ram Ramblings: Hayes fulfills dream with induction into N.C. Sports Hall of Fame. https://www.journalnow.com/sports/college/wssu/ram-ramblings-hayes-fulfills-dream-with-induction-into-n-c/article_331b6944-4eda-11e8-8557-034b056aeb57.html

Rankin, David R. "Brown: A Quiet Pioneer Who Simply Paid His Dues." *Winston-Salem Chronicle* (Winston-Salem, NC), August 8, 1985, A1+.

Rawls, Mollie Grogan. *Winston-Salem in Vintage Postcards*. Charleston, South Carolina: Arcadia Publishing, 2004.

Rawls, Molly Grogan. "June 13, 1970: Fries Auditorium Roof Collapses." *Winston-Salem Time Traveler*. June 13, 2014. Accessed October 18, 2015. http://winstonsalemtimetraveler.com/2014/06/13/June-131970.

Reed, Betty J. *The Brevard Rosenwald School*. Jefferson NC: McFarland and Company, INC Publishers, 2004.

Reed, Elizabeth. "Dr. James Shober." November 24, 2007. http://www.findagrave.com/cgi_bin/fg.cgi?page=g&Grid=23080615

Rice, Dr. William. "Earl the Pearl Monroe, wins national scoring Championship." Prepared paper. Vertical File: Winston–Salem African American Archive, Winston-Salem, NC.

Richard C. Erwin "210 Years of Progress in Winston-Salem." *The Chronicle* (Winston-Salem, NC), May 31, 1979, 5

Robinson, Louie. "Gridiron color bars topple at white southern Colleges." Ebony, December 1967. https://books.google.com/books?id=PtsDAAAAMBAJ&pg=PA25&lpg=PA25&dq=Gridiron+color+bars+topple+at+white+southern+colleges&source=bl&ots=2Pbejxe1V4&sig=ACfU3UoYt8CHBJrGImO56ygtxstQ7DeFoQ&hl=en&sa=X&ved=2.

Rodgers, Joan S. "Salem Blacks Built Schoolhouse in 1867." *Winston-Salem Journal* (Winston-Salem, NC), April 19, 1992, B1.

"Rolonda Watts." IMDb.com Accessed February 15, 2014. http://www.imdb.com/name/nm0005539/.

Roots of Black Winston-Salem - 1870-1900. Years of
 Transition." *The Chronicle* (Winston-Salem, NC), February 3, 1979,
 13-16.
"Roots of Black Winston-Salem - 1950-1960: A decade of
 Reckoning." *Winston-Salem Chronicle* (Winston-Salem, NC), March
 17, 1979, 17-18.
"Roots of Black Winston-Salem: The Early 20th
 Century." *The Chronicle* (Winston-Salem, NC), February 10,1979, 15-
 7.
Ruffin, Chris. "Former Winston-Salem bishop will preach homily
 at royal wedding ceremony."
 https://www.wxii12.com/article/former-winston-salem-bishop-will-
 preach-homily-at-royal-wedding-ceremony/20671599. May 12, 2018.
"Rupert Bell." Winston-Salem Sportsman Club, Inc. *Winston-
 Salem/Forsyth County High School Sports Hall Of Fame*.
 http://www.wssportsmenclub.org/w-s_sportsmenclub_058.htm.
Russell, Joi-Anissa. "Lorraine Hairston Morton: I Am More Than
 My Smile." *Profile, Shorefront*. Shorefront Journal: Shorefront
 Legacy Center (Evanston, Illinois), July 1, 2013. Accessed September 4,
 2014. https://shorefrontjournal.wordpress.com/2013/07/01/lorraine-
 hairston-morton-i-am-more-than-my-smile/.
Rutledge Jeanna D. "9-year-old Opens Candy Store." *Black Business,
 INK*. June 2013.
"Salem Academy and College." *History*.
 https://www.salemacademyandcollege.org/history.
"Salem Academy and College (Winston-Salem, North Carolina) Joins
 Universities Studying Slavery." University of Virginia Presidents
 Commission on Slavery and the University. University of Virginia
 Scholar's Lab, 2013.
 https://slavery.virginia.edu/salem-college-winston-salem-north
 carolina-joins-universities-studying-slavery/
Sandra Miller Jones. *The HistoryMakers*. August 14, 2014.
 Accessed May 6, 2015.
 https://www.thehistorymakers.org/biography/sandra-miller-jones.

Scales Cement Block Co. *Winston-Salem, NC City Directory* 1925 Asheville, NC: The Miller Press, September 1924.

Schilken, Chuck. "Happy Hairston-All Things Lakers." *Los Angeles Times* February 12,2011. Accessed March 6, 2012. http://projects.latimes.com/lakers/player/happy-hairston/.

Schofield, Rob. "Obama appoints former state judge from Winston-Salem to federal bench." *NC POLICY WATCH*. September 19, 2014. Accessed October 12, 2015. http://pulse.ncpolicywatch.org/2014/09/19/ obama-appoints-former-state-judge-from-winston-salem-to-federal-bench/#sthash.LagwjDpU.dpuf.

"Scholarship Established at WSSU to Honor Retired Mayor Lorraine Morton of Evanston, Ill." WSSU Rampages. https://rampages.wssu.edu/?p=4614.

Searcy, Herbert. *Turner's Winston and Salem City Directory for the Years 1894 and 1895.* Yonkers, NY : Turner and Company Publishers, 1894.

Segmented Marketing, Inc.
https://www.segmentedmarketing.com/aboutus.html. 14 Jul. 2014.

Segmented Marketing, Inc.
https://www.facebook.com/pages/category/Marketing Agency/Segmented-Marketing-Services-Inc-140742369364476/

Sensbach, Jon F. *A Separate Canaan: The Making of An Afro-Moravian World in North Carolina 1763-1840.* Chapel Hill: University of North Carolina Press, 1998.

Sensbach, Jon F. "The Afro American Experience in Early Salem." *Winston-Salem Journal* (Winston-Salem, NC), February 12,1990,A9.

Sexton, Scott. "Fullfillment of Promises?" *Winston-Salem Journal* (Winston-Salem, NC), June 29, 2014,A1+.

"Shaw was first in training African-American doctors." Health Team. WRAL.Com. February 28, 2013. Updated March 6, 2013. https://www.wral.com/shaw-was-first-in-training-african-american-doctors/12166574/.

"She Still Seeks to Educate." *The Chronicle* (Winston-Salem, NC), November 8, 1980.

Shirley, Michael. The Industrial Community: Drawing the Lines of Class and Race. In *From Congregation Town to Industrial City: Culture and Change in a Southern Community.* New York: New York University Press, 1994.
Accessed October 8, 2015. https://www.amazon.com/Congregation-Town-Industrial-City-Experience-ebook/dp/B004DTT4R4.

Simpson-Vos, Mark. "Basketball. Part IV: Basketball and Civil Rights." *NCPEDIA*, 2006. Accessed September 6, 2014. http://ncpedia.org/basketball/civil-rights.

Single Sisters' House. Salem College Old Salem, Winston-Salem, NC. February 15, 2010.

"Sit Down Strike Spreads to Twin City and Durham." *Winston-Salem Journal* (Winston-Salem, NC), February 9,1960,21.

Smith, Bonnie G., ed. "Xuma, Madie Hall (1894–1982)". *The Oxford Encyclopedia of Women in World History.* Oxford University Press. Published online January 2008
https://www.oxfordreference.com/view/10.1093/acref/9780195148909.001.0001/acref-9780195148909-e-1174?rskey=H65rmD&result=1169.

Smith-Deering, Patricia. "50th ANNIVERSARY: St. Benedict still going strong." *Winston-Salem Chronicle (*Winston-Salem, NC), November 1, 1990, B4.

Smith, Donald B. "Long Lance, Buffalo Child." *NCPedia.* January 1, 1991. Accessed May 10, 2015. http://www.ncpedia.org/biography/long-lance-buffalo-child.

Smith, Gerald L., Karen Cotton McDaniel and John A. Hardin, ed. Eliza Atkins Gleason, In *The Kentucky African American Encyclopedia. Lexington, KY: The University Press of Kentucky,* 2015. https://books.google.com/books?id=-0AoCgAAQBAJ&pg=PA208&lpg=PA208&dq=eliza+atkins+gleason+.+In+The+Kentucky+African+American+Encyclopedia&source=bl&ots=ALRSa052s1&sig=ACfU3U3y1DUrSgb1WAcPkNgoyAYWEysog&hl=en&sa=X&ved=2ahUKEwi955LJtYrkAhUOtlkKHQDvAo4Q6AEwD3oECAkQAQ#v=onepage&q=eliza%20atkins%20gleason%20.%20In%20The%20Kentucky%20African%20American%20Encyclopedia&f=false

Smith, James. "Black Lady Is Bank Manager." *The Winston-Salem Chronicle* (Winston-Salem, NC), January 24,1976, 7. Accessed May 6,2015. http://newspapers.digitalnc.org/lccn/sn85042324/1976-01-24/ed-1/seq-7/.

Smith, Jessie Carney. *Black Firsts:2,000 Years of Extraordinary Achievement*. Canton, MI: Visible Ink Press, 1994.

Smith, Margaret Supplee and Emily Herring Wilson. *North Carolina Women Making History*. Chapel Hill and London: The University of North Carolina Press, 1999.

Smith, Tonya V. "Legacy for Posterity: The History of Politicians in Winston-Salem." *The Chronicle* (Winston-Salem, NC), May 11, 1989,A1+.

Sparks, Jim. "New exhibit at transportation museum to feature black-owned bus company." *SCNow,* February 8,2008. Accessed April 4, 2013. http://www.scnow.com/living/article_411d2ffb-4910-5649-b32b-01f87cc8f197.html.

Sprague-Smith, Marilyn, M.Ed. *The Journal for Women*. July 2004. Accessed February 2, 2010. http://www.ncjournalforwomen.com/months/july04/july04smith2.htm.

"Sprinkle-Hamlin named to Commission by McCrory." *Winston-Salem Chronicle* (Winston-Salem, NC), January 9,2014. Accessed March 12, 2014. http://www.wschronicle.com/2014/01/sprinkle-hamlin-named-to-commission-by-mccrory/.

"Spurgeon Neal Ellington". *American Air Museum In Britain.* http://www.americanairmuseum.com/person/241749. Revised 3 Dec. 2016.

Statistical Profile Winston-Salem Forsyth County Schools Facilities Management Divisions. Winston-Salem, North Carolina: Winston-Salem Forsyth County Schools Facilities Management Division

Steelman, Ben. "State's First black doctor hung shingle in Port City." *Star News Online (*Wilmington, NC), February 28, 2008. Accessed May 5, 2010. http://www.starnewsonline.com/lifestyle/20080228/states-first-black-doctor-hung-shingle-in-port-city.

Steelman, Ben. "James Shober: A Carolina Healer."
    African American Registry, 2003. Accessed February 2, 2012.
    http://www.aaregistry.org/historicevents/view/james-shober-North-carolina-doctor.

Steele, Jane. *Key Events in the African American Community*
    of Winston-Salem, North Carolina 1870-1950. Old Salem, Inc., 1992.

Stinson, Tevin. "Lambson is first female football coach in N.C."
    *The Chronicle (*Winston-Salem, NC), October 1, 2015.
    Accessed December 14, 2015.
    http://www.wschronicle.com/2015/10/lambson-first-female-football- coach-n-c/.

Stinson, Tevin. "New Forsyth sheriff takes reins." Winston-Salem Chronicle
    (Winston-Salem, NC), December 7, 2018. Accessed December 21,
    2018. http://www.wschronicle.com/2018/12/new-forsyth-sheriff-takes-reins/.

Stinson, Tevin. "New police chief launches High Five Fridays."
    Winston-Salem Chronicle (Winston-Salem, NC), September 9, 2017.
    https:www.wschronicle.com/2017/09/new-police-chief-launches-High-five-Fridays/.

Stinson, Tevin. "Parkland auditorium renamed to honor Anderson."
    The Chronicle (Winston-Salem, NC), March 10, 2016.
    October 9, 2016.
    http://www.wschronicle.com/2016/03/parkland-auditorium-renamed- honor-anderson/.

Stinson Tevin. "Phi Delta Kappa honors Flonnie Anderson during
    talent show". Winston-Salem Chronicle (Winston-Salem, NC),
    January 14, 2016. Accessed October 9, 2016.
    http://www.wschronicle.com/2016/01/phi-delta-kappa-honors-flonnie-anderson-talent-show/.

Stinson, Tevin. "Teachers, Students Discuss History of Integration
    in Winston-Salem/Forsyth County." *Winston-Salem Chronicle*
    (Winston-Salem, NC), June 2, 2016, A1+. Accessed August 8,
    2016. http://www.wschronicle.com/2016/06/teachers-students-discuss-history-integration-wsfcs/.

Stracton, Eleonor. "Development of Education." *African American schools*. 1:1929 Vertical File W-S School History. North Carolina Room Winston-Salem Central Library.

"St. Benedict the Moor: United as a parish family." Catholic News Herald. October 28, 2016. Accessed December 8, 2016. http://catholicnewsherald.com/ news/144-news/local-header/960-st-benedict-the-moor-united-as-a-parish-family#sthash.KrhU3LxB.dpuf.

"Suffrage Amendment- NC Democrats won political control from blacks, Republicans with 1900's White Supremacy Campaign." *Winston-Salem Journal* (Winston-Salem, NC), August 2000.

Swinson, Angela P. Staff Writer. "TAKING THE LEAD: SHE'S USED TO IT\ MAKING HISTORY." *News and Record* (Greensboro, NC). December 7, 1994. Accessed May 5, 2015. https://www.greensboro.com/taking-the-lead-she-s-used-to-it-making-history/article_94e75e4c-3693-5977-9541-b8e2397f8937.html.

"Sylvia Sprinkle-Hamlin appears in 2016 Heritage Calendar." *Winston-Salem Chronicle* (Winston-Salem, NC), October 29,2015. Accessed February 10, 2016. http://www.wschronicle.com/2015/10/sylvia-sprinkle-hamlin-appears-2016-heritage-calendar/.

Taylor, C. B. "Professor Charles Calvin Nelson, Veteran Negro Teacher, Molding Characters at Clemmons School." *Winston-Salem Journal* (Winston-Salem, NC), December 26, 1926.

Temple, Bob. "Carl Eller is enshrined in the Hall of Fame." *Pro Football Hall of Fame*. August 8,2004. Accessed July 6, 2012. http://www.profootballhof.com/news/carl-eller-is-enshrined-in-the-hall-of-fame/.

"The Battle of Henry Johnson Albany in Albany County, New York." The American Northeast (Mid-Atlantic). 2012 http://www.oldmagazinearticles.com/WWI Battle Of Henry Johnson Pdf.

"The Black Community through Its Own Eyes." *The Chronicle* (Winston-Salem, NC), March 3, 1979, 5.

The Black Six. Directed by Matt Cimber. 1973; Cinemation Industries, VHS. http://www.imdb.com/title/tt0071227/.

The Chronicle (Winston-Salem, NC), January 27,1979,12.

The Churches. Calendar- Society for the Study of Afro-American History in Winston-Salem Forsyth County. Winston-Salem, NC.

"The Cleo Hill Story: He was Michael Jordan before there was Michael Jordan." *Ken Suskin Report* 22 Feb 2010. Accessed July 5, 2011. http://kennethsuskin.blogspot.com/2010/02/cleo-hill-story-he-was-michael-jordan.html.

"The Colored Fair". *The Union Republican* (Winston-Salem, NC), Aug.1900.

"The Colored Fair Not a Financial Success." Editorial by J.S. Fitts, Secretary of the Piedmont Colored Industrial Fair. *The Union Republican* (Winston-Salem, NC), Aug. 1900.

The Educators. Calendar-Society for the Study of Afro-American History in Winston-Salem Forsyth County. Winston-Salem, NC.

"The First Lieutenant of Spanish American War in Winston" *Twin City Journal* (Winston-Salem, NC), 1935.

"The Flamboyant Will Scales." *The Chronicle* (Winston-Salem, NC), February 17,1979,13-14.

"The Harlem Hell fighters and Henry Johnson Fighting in WWI." *For The Love of Liberty: The Story Of America's Black Patriots*. Directed by Frank Martin. 2010.United States:PBS. https://www.forloveofliberty.org/overview/Harlem_Hellfighters.html.

The Howler Yearbook. Winston-Salem, NC: Wake Forest College, 1964.

The Howler Yearbook. Winston-Salem, NC: Wake Forest College,1970.

"The Legacy Continues. Gaining Acceptance, Expanding Scope." *WSSU Archway Magazine*, October 28, 2012. https://issuu.com/wssuarchway/docs/archway_summer2012_now/9

"The Magnificent 7: Haywood Oubre's Students: Anderson, Bailey, Britt, Coleman, Feagan, Gary, Phillips." *University of Delaware Messenger,* Spring 2003. http://www1.udel.edu/PaulRJonesCollection/album.html.

"THE MEMOIRS OF FLONNIE ANDERSON." *Memorable Memoirs: Ghostwriting unforgettable stories of artists and their supporters.* Accessed May 16, 2015. https://docs.wixstatic.com/ugd/9acce2_73ea952a9ca74411a35b89ddb7e52eec.pdf

"The Story of North Carolina: New Ways to Move at the Turn of the 20th Century." *North Carolina Museum of History Revised* July 2013. https://www.ncmuseumofhistory.org/story-north-carolina-new-ways-move-turn-20th-century.

"The Tuskegee Flyers - The Black American Becomes A Fighting Airman." *Black Americans In Defense of Our Nation.* Dianne Publishing Company (Darby PA), 1990. https://books.google.com/books?id=ZIXqO-b-ReoC&pg=PA90-IA1&lpg=PA90-IA1&dq=diane+publishing+The+Tuskegee+Flyers+%E2%80%94+The+Black+American+Becomes+A+Fighting+Airman.&source=bl&ots=9GNUHNPQyO&sig=ACfU3U1lhoKpCzyoOmUks4A0gKuE9ncgA&hl=en&sa=X&ved=2ahUKEwiB3KHj4ofkAhUotlkKHdKhAJ4Q6AEwHHoECAgQAQ#v=onepage&q=diane%20publishing%20The%20Tuskegee%20Flyers%20%E2%80%94%20The%20Black%20American%20Becomes%20A%20Fighting%20Airman.&f=false

"They're Big Trees Now*.*" *Winston-Salem Sentinel* (Winston-Salem, NC), October 13, 1981.

Tilley, Keith. "So You think you know Lawrence Joel." Forsyth Family Magazine. May 2009,6.

Tise, Larry Edward. *Winston-Salem in History: The Churches* Vol.10, Winston-Salem, NC: Historic Winston, 1976.

Todd, Dee. First African-American Woman to Appear on Kellogg's Corn Flakes Box. Personal Interview with Chenita Johnson. Winston-Salem, NC, November 3, 2017.

"Hon. Togo D. West, Jr." The History Makers. Biography 8 February 8,2007 The History Makers (Chicago, Ill). Accessed July 5,2010. https://www.thehistorymakers.org/biography/honorable-togo-d-west-jr

Torian, Dr. Luke E. *First Mt. Zion Baptist Church.* Dumfries, VA. http://firstmountzionbc.org/fmzbc-history/pastor/.

Town of Winston Directing Board. City of Winston Government Meetings Notes. Town of Winston: 1907-1913. *Segregation Ordinance Enacted.* Winston-Salem, NC: Winston-Salem Marketing and Communications Department. http://www.cityofws.org/Portals/0/pdf/marketing-and-communications/history/Winston/Winston%201907-1913.pdf

Trawick, Jack. "Pools Called Biggest Recreation Attraction." *Winston-Salem Journal* (Winston-Salem, NC), 7 September 7, 2010, 1964, 17.

Tucker, Chad. "Winston-Salem female high school football coach is first in NC." WGHP: High Point, NC, September 3, 2015. Accessed November 7, 2015. http://myfox8.com/2015/09/03/winston-salem-female-high-school-football-coach-is-first-in-nc/.

Turner & Co.'s Winston and Salem City Directory for the Years 1889 and 1890. Yonkers, NY : E.F. Turner and Publishers, 1889.

Tursi, Frank. "Archeologists working to trace History of Salem's Black Church." *Winston-Salem Journal* (Winston-Salem, NC),July 28, 1991,E1.

Tursi, Frank. "History's Tracks: From the mid 1700's to the late 1980's." *Winston-Salem Journal* (Winston-Salem, NC), February 25,1988.

Tursi, Frank V. *Winston-Salem: A History.* Winston-Salem, NC: John F. Blair Publishers, 1994.

Tursi, Frank. "The Man Who Collected Bits of Black History Dies Here." *Winston-Salem Journal* (Winston-Salem, NC), June 23, 1988, 13+.

Tursi, Frank. "The People who wrote The Story." *Winston-Salem Journal* (Winston-Salem, NC), February 25,1988,20.

"20th Century Opens with Black Business Surge." *Winston-Salem Chronicle* (Winston-Salem, NC), February 10, 1979,5.

"29 Years Pays Off." *The Chronicle* (Winston-Salem, NC), August 16, 1980, 1.

"210 Years of Progress in Winston-Salem: 1970 to Present Blacks Still Achieving." *Winston-Salem Chronicle* (Winston-Salem, NC), 31 March 31, 1979,5.

"Twenty Years Advancement of Colored People In City." *Winston-Salem-Journal* (Winston-Salem, NC), October 7, 1923, sect. D

"Two 19th Century Men were Pioneers in Education." *Discover Winston-Salem* (Winston-Salem, NC), September 27,1990,20.

Upperman Hair School of Hair Dressing and Beauty Parlors. *Winston-Salem City directory.* Ashville, NC: Commercial Service Company, Inc. publisher, 1915.

Urban League of Greater Miami, INC. "Black Alliance for Educational Options Honors T. Willard Fair." March 2, 2015. Accessed March 6, 2015. http://www.miamiurbanleague.org/black-alliance-for-educational-options-honors-t-willard-fair.

"Victory Credit Union Helped to Open Doors." *The Chronicle* (Winston-Salem, NC) March 10, 1979,17—18.

"Victory Credit Union is now part of Truliant." *Winston-Salem Journal (Winston-Salem, NC),* December 12, 2003, D1+.

Wadelington, Charles W. "Wheeler Airlines: An American First." North Carolina Museum of History. 2005. http://avstop.com/history/F03.wheeler.airlines.pdf.

"Wake Forest's Kevin Johnson Drafted By Houston In First Round." *Wake Forest University Athletic Department* April 30,2015 http://www.wfmynews2.com/story/sports/2015/04/30/wfu-kevin-Johnson-houston/26681761/.

Walker, Shavonne. "East Spencer officially names Sharon Hovis as police chief." Salisbury Post(Salisbury NC), June 13, 2015. Accessed September 14, 2017. http://www.salisburypost.com/2015/06/13/east-spencer-officially-names-sharon-hovis-as-police-chief/.

Wallace, W.D. "A Negro Bus line of 42 busses". *Winston - Salem Journal* (Winston-Salem, NC.), June 29, 1935, 7.

"Walter L. Long Widely Known Negro Is Dead." *Winston-Salem Journal* (Winston-Salem, NC), March 28, 1941, 4.

Warren Wheeler: The 1st African American To Own An Airline. *Black History Special Delivery.* December 17, 2015. https://blackmail4u.com/2015/12/17/warren-wheeler-the-1st-african-american-to-own-an-airline/.

Washington, Mathew G. Wheeler. Warren H. (1943) Black Past. December 6, 2015. https://www.blackpast.org/african-american-history/wheeler-warren-h-1943/.

"Waughtown-Belview Historic District." *The Gombach Group.* June 2012. http://www.livingplaces.com/NC/Forsyth County/Winston-Salem_City/Waughtown. September 15, 2014.

"We Haven't Made It Yet." *The Chronicle* (Winston-Salem, NC), March 31,1979, 6-7.

Wellman, Manly Wadel and James Howell Smith. *Winston-Salem in History: Industry and Commerce 1896-1975* Vol. 8. Winston-Salem, NC: Historic Winston, 1977.

Wells, Grady. "Rear Admiral Walter J. Davis , Jr. Commandant Naval District Washington." *US Black Engineer and IT-Winter,* 1989:26 Accessed February 12, 2016. https://books.google.com/books?id=9WG85c15IlQC&pg=PA26&lpg=PA26&dq=Profiles+In+Leadership-Rear+Admiral+Walter+J.+Davis+Jr.+Commandant+Naval+District+Washington&source=bl&ots=PQ7j4BM6Nc&sig=ACfU3U0orJJiOky8iCI809pnsT02UcmhLw&hl=en&sa=X&ved=2ahUKEwiH30W790fkAhXptlkKHSkhAHYQ6AEwAH0ECAkQAQ#v=onepage&q=Profiles%20In%20Leadership%20Rear%20Admiral%20Walter%20J.%20Davis%20Jr.%20Commandant%20Naval%20District%20Washington&f=false.

"Wentz Memorial to Celebrate 73rd Anniversary with Concert." *Winston-Salem Chronicle (*Winston-Salem, NC), October 13, 1994,28.

"Wentz Evolves with Demolitions." *The Chronicle (*Winston-Salem, NC), March 29,1980,18.

"White, George Henry (1852-1918)." *History, Art & Archives: United States House of Representatives.* http://history.house.gov/People/Detail/23657.

Wilamena Lash. Personal Interview with Chenita Johnson. September 5, 2013.

Wilcox, Michael C. "Safe Bus Company." THE HISTORICAL MARKER DATABASE. *Winston-Salem in Forsyth County, North Carolina -The American South (South Atlantic)* January 25, 2012. Revised on January 24, 2018. http://www.hmdb.org/marker.asp?marker=51971.

Wilson, Emily Hearing. "Hope and Dignity-Older Black Women of
the South." Philadelphia, PA: *Temple University Press,* 1983.
Accessed November 8, 2015.
https://books.google.com/books?id=jCo3rUUcDsYC&pg=PR1&lpg
=PR1&dq=Hope+and+Dignity-
Older+Black+Women+of+the+South.&source=bl&ots=X4ffOBhz
n9&sig=fhRWUTQhVgt3YCeOJvXr4_bUEp4&hl=en&sa=X&ved
=0ahUKEwijicDPyq_WAhXDhFQKHQL9AWkQ6AEIVjAO#v=
onepage&q=Hope%20and%20Dignity-
Older%20Black%20Women%20of%20the%20South.&f=false.

Williams Audrey L. "Broadcaster tries to lift her audience's
spirits." *The Chronicle* (Winston-Salem, NC), October 1983, B5.

William, Audrey L. "Pioneer dealer wants to be No. 1 in the
State." *The Chronicle* (Winston-Salem, NC), July 26,1984, A7.

Williams, Cheryl. "Oubre creates miracles with art" *The
Chronicle* (Winston-Salem, NC), November 20,1986,B10+.

Williams, L.A.A.. "Board of Aldermen approve Proposal
naming Coliseum for Lawrence Joel." *Winston-Salem Chronicle*
(Winston-Salem, NC), February 20,1986.

William Oates Employment Agency. *Winston-Salem, NC City
Directory.* Asheville, NC: Commercial Service Co. Publishers. 1916.

Willis, Alan. "Blacks in Winston - A History Emerging from
Obscurity." *Winston-Salem Sentinel* (Winston-Salem, NC), February
10,1983,21.

Wingate University Athletics. "Bulldog men's tennis players
return for reunion." October 18, 2012. Accessed October 3, 2014.
http://www.wingatebulldogs.com/news/2012/10/18/MTEN_1018125
323.aspx.spec-rel/042005aab.html.

Winston Lake Golf Club
Information at Winston Lake Golf Course. Winston-Salem, North
Carolina.

Winston-Salem African American Historical and Cultural Guide: *Rich in
History Alive with Culture.* Winston-Salem, North Carolina: Winston-
Salem Visitors Center.

"Winston-Salem Honors a Hero." Journal and Sentinel (Winston-Salem, NC),
April 9,1967, A2.

Winston-Salem Journal Ask Sam: "Who was the first African-American news reporter for the Winston-Salem Journal?" *Winston-Salem Journal* (Winston-Salem, NC), February 24, 2013. Accessed July 3, 2013. http://www.journalnow.com/news/ask_sam/article_6df3d57a-7e1e-11e2-b7a2-0014bcf6878.html.

Winston-Salem Marketing and Communications Department. *Beaty Public Safety Training and Support Center Opens*. Winston-Salem, NC: Winston-Salem City Line, Fall 2009, 1.

Winston-Salem N.C. City Directory
Hackney and Moale Co. Printers. Asheville, NC: Hackney and Moale Co. Printers. 1918.

"Winston-Salem State started at Academy." *News and Observer (Greensboro, NC)* May 16, 1964.

"Winston-Salem State started at Academy." *News and Observer (Greensboro, NC)*. April 10, 1966.

"Winston-Salem State University Police Chief Named Association President." Winston-Salem State University. Nov. 2012. http://www.wssu.edu/about/news/2011/chief-named-president.aspx.

Winston-Salem State University (1892-). BLAST PAST. January 4, 2011. https://www.blackpast.org/african-american-history/winston-salem-state-university-1892/.

Wiseman, H.A. "Chestnut St. YWCA." News of Colored People In the City and County. *Winston-Salem Journal* (Winston-Salem, NC), October 7, 1925, 14.

"With focus on immigration, voters in NC's seven largest counties elected black sheriffs." https://www.newsobserver.com/news/politics-government/article221343255.html.

Wong, Edward. " 'Happy' Hairston", 58, Forward On Champion Lakers Team." *The New York Times*. May 2, 2001. Accessed October 10, 2010. https://www.nytimes.com/2001/05/02/sports/happy-hairston-58-forward-on-champion-lakers-team.html.

WSMX. *World Heritage Encyclopedia Edition*. Accessed February 7, 2010. http://www.worldlibrary.org/articles/wsmx.

WSSU Archway Magazine. Winston-Salem State University
Archway Magazine, 28 Oct. 2012
https://issuu.com/wssuarchway/docs/archway_summer2012_now
2014.

WSSU Department of Athletics. "WSSU Basketball Legend Cleo Hill
Passes Away." Men's Basketball. Winston-Salem State University.
August 11, 2015.
http://www.wssurams.com/sports/m-baskbl/2014-
15/releases/201508110nyeda.

WSSU Department of Athletics. "Clarence Gains. Profile." *Athletic News.*
Accessed April 2, 2015.
http://www.wssurams.com/about/clarence_gaines/index.

WSSU Department of Athletics. "Dr. Clarence Jones. *WSSU C.E.
'Big House' Gaines Athletic Hall of Fame." Winston-Salem State
University.* Accessed February 12, 2015.
https://www.wssurams.com/about/hall_of_fame/Hall_of_Fame_Bi
os/Dr._Clarence_-Jeep-_Jones_Bio?view=bio.

"WSSU Celebrates 50 Years of Excellence in Nursing Education with Yearlong
Observance." Winston-Salem State University
Archway Magazine: 50th Anniversary of Nursing Education
November 2003:4-5.
https://www.wssu.edu/about/news/_files/Documents/archway-
november-2003.pdf.

WSSU Department of Athletics. "Biography Of A Legend:
Clarence 'Big House' Gaines." April 20, 2005. Accessed February
10, 2017.http://www.wssurams.com/sports/m-baskbl/
spec-rel/042005aab.html.

WSSU Department of Athletics. "Clarence Gains. Profile."
Winston-Salem State University. Accessed April 2, 2015.
http://www.wssurams.com/about/clarence_gaines/index.

WSSU Department of Athletics. "Earl The Pearl Monroe Bio."
Athletic News. Accessed October 15, 2015.
http://www.wssurams.com/about/hall_of_fame/Hall_of_Fame_Bio
s/Earl_Monroe_Bio?view=bio.

WSSU Department of Athletics. "Elias Gilbert." *Winston-Salem State University.* Accessed November 9, 2015. https://www.wssurams.com/about/hall_of_fame/Hall_of_Fame_Bios/Elias_Gilbert_Bio?view=bio

WSSU Department of Athletics. "Todd, Delores." 2001. Accessed June 5, 2016. https://www.wssurams.com/about/hall_of_fame/Hall_of_Fame_Bios/Delores_-Dee-_Todd_Bio?view=bio.

"WSSU Graduate First in Country to Finish" *The Chronicle* (Winston-Salem, NC), January 22, 1977, 9A.

Young, Monica. "Diggs Gallery at WSSU continues its role as A center for Community." *Winston-Salem Journal* (Winston-Salem, NC), October 11, 2010. https://www.journalnow.com/news/state/diggs-gallery-at-wssu-continues-its-role-as-a-center/article_a376710a-cf90-574f-9b09-0104a9cfbdbb.html.

Young, W.E. *Winston-Salem NC City Directory.* Ashville, NC: Commercial Service Company, Inc., 1921.

Young, Wesley. "Former County Election Official Dies at age 73." *Winston-Salem Journal* (Winston-Salem, NC), May 19, 2009, A7+.

Zerwick, Phoebe. "Kennedy Decides to Leave the Legislature in '94." *Winston-Salem Journal* (Winston-Salem, NC), December 17, 1993, 1.

INDEX

A

"*A Giant of His Race,*" 316
Abbitt, Royal Joe, 81
ACC (Atlantic Coast Conference), 345-346
Adams, DeeDee, 86,90
Adams, John (J.M. Adams),272
Adelphia Ice Cream Company, 165
African American business District, 160
African American Caucus of the Forsyth County Democratic Party,85-88
African American Chapter of the National Retail Merchants Association, 160
African American Fire Company,126-126-127
African American High School,45
African American Physician, 212
African American Policemen,132-134
African Moravian church,3
African National Congress(ANC),89
African National Congress(ANC) Women's League,89
Agricultural and Mechanical College for the Colored Race, 22
Alexander Hamilton Ray Hospital,211
Alexander, Oscar, 260
Alexander R. Beaty Public Safety Training and Support Center,148
American Hotel and Barbershop,167
Amson, Robert, 287
Anderson Junior High School,26,61
Anderson, Albert (Albert H.),61,197
Anderson, Flonnie, 329
Anderson, William Roscoe, 237
Andrews, Mrs. Gwendolyn, 226
Angelou, Dr. Maya, 179,332-333
Ashely, J.D., 61
Ashley, S. S., 21
Atkins, Hannah Diggs, 124-125
Atkins High School, 5-57, 60-61,286 290-291
Atkins, Jasper, 206-207
Atkins, Simon Green ,23-24,45,62-63,195-196,206,233,281
Attorneys: (Black lawyers:):
Bright, H.O., 203-204;Davis, H Glenn, 203; Denning, Oliver T., 203-204; Fitts, Atty. J. S(John Shepherd), 182,205-206,311; Jones, Attorney W. Avery,197,203-204,287 ;Kennedy, Annie Brown, 207-208;Kennedy, Harold,89,203 292; Lanier, Atty. James S., 159, 182,202,205-206; Price, Hosea V., 17,203-204; Todd Curtiss, 185,203-204
Austin, Eldridge, 140
Austin, John, 162
Aycock, Charles B.,101

B

B. F. Goodrich franchise, 172-173
B. F. Goodrich Rubber Company,257
Bahnson, Dr. 227
Bailey, Beaufort, 118-119
Bailey, Don F., 81
Bailey, Gwendolyn,32-33

INDEX

Baker, Webster Bernard, 260,264-265
Baker, Gerald, 116
Baker, Matt, 325-327
Baker Caree (Wilson), Nancy, 262-263
Banks, Gloria Diggs, 291-292
Banks, James, 145
Barber, Jacquelyne (Jackie), 86-87, 286
Barnes, David C., 144
Barr, Robert, 119
Barrett, Emma, 224
Barringer, General, 43,167
Base Relief of Roosevelt, 321
Bass, Marshall B, 192
Beaty, Alexander, 148-149
Bell, Audley, 364-365
Bell, Marilyn L., 221-222
Bell, Rupert, 146
Belo's Pond, 15, 243
Belview, 73
Benjamin, Hannah Mae, 55
Best Choice Center, 75
Bethabara/Bethabara Tavern, 2,37
Bethania (Negro) A.M.E.Zion Church, 5
Bethell/Bethel, Nannie, 159
Bethell/Bethel, (W.L.), 159
Bethlehem House, 288
Big Four, 60
Biggs, Judge Loretta Copeland, 153-155
Bines, Doris, 86
Birkhead, Clarence, 116
Bitting, Wade, 245, 287
Black Chamber of Commerce, 197
Black Hollywood in the Twin City, 316
Black Hook and Ladder Company #2, 126
Black Moravians, 5,8,279
Black, Mr. George Henry, 200, 248-250
Black Panther Party, 82-84
Black-Phillips-Smith Government Center, 249
Black, Raphael O., 128-129

Black Senior High Schools, 70-72
Black soldiers, 294/WWI, 160,294,297
Blair, John J., 23
Blair, W.A., 63
Blume, John A., 182,196
Blunt, Theodore (Ted), 64
Board of Alderman/City Council, 112-114
Board of Commissioners, 122
Bond, III, John P. "Jack," 147-148
Bonner, Lillian, 137-135
Booie, George, 313
Boston Cottage Company (Boston Cottages), 235
Boston Redevelopment Authority (B.R.A.), 111-112
Boweaver, Frank, 340
Bowen, Jemmise, 87
Bowman Gray School of Medicine, 220-221
Bowman Gray Stadium, 132
Bowman, Mr., 246
Boy Scout Troop No. 68, 286-287
Bradley, Donald C., 81
Bradley, Eli, 179-180
Bradshaw, Joseph Elton, 290-292
Brandon, William, 176-177
Bright, William Andrew, 81
Bright, H.O., 203-204
Brim. J. H., 195
Brooks, Mrs. Annie, 224,240
Brown, A. J., 195
Brown, R.W. (Robert Washington, Sr.) 22,182,185,195,281,311
Brown, Mrs. Annie K., 224
Brown, Carl, 365-366
Brown, Sr. Clark S. Brown, 93, 287
"Brown Decision," 33, 34, 60
Brown Derby Hat Works, 186
Brown, Dorothy, 86
Brown Elementary School, 23, 27,28

INDEX

Brown, Ernest, 356
Brown, Jr., Frank O., 287
Brown Geneva, 119
Brown, Rev. Henry A., 13
Brown-Hiltz, Jill E., 191
Brown, John N., 174
Brown, O.S., 164
Brownlee, Fam, 131
Bruce, Dr. William H.(W.H.),169,181
Bruce, Jr., Dr. W. H., 170
Bryce, Mother (Mary), 263
Budney and Phoebe, 8, 279
Burke, Judge Todd, 116
Burke, Mrs. Vivian, 112-114,292
Burke, Selma, 321-322
Burns, Mary (Mrs. Mary M.),272-273
Butler, Alton, 287

C

C.B. Cash Barbershop, 162
Caldwell, Jim, 346
Calloway, Leonard "Tippy," 263
Camel City Clothing Company,188
Camp Meeting Choir, 252,261
Campbell, Clark , 274-275
Campbell, Dave, 341
Campbell, Nathaniel, 341
Cannery Agricultural Packinghouse and Allied Workers of America, 77
Carbogin, 169-170
Cardwell, Joan, 150,154
Carmon, Angela I., 151
Carpenter, Jasper, 241-242
Carter G. Woodson Charter School,101
Carter, J. A.(John A), 55, 242
Carter, Josephus, 299
Carter, Obadiah, 335
Carter, Phillip, 86
Carter, Willie "Chick," 341
Carter, Willie J., 128
Carver Consolidated School/ Carver High School,58-59,61
Cash, Crawford B. (C.B), 63,162
Cash, Mrs. C. B., 334
census takers, 145
Central Intercollegiate Athletic Association (CIAA) Hall of Fame, 348
Chambers, Daisy, 26-27
Chandler, Joe, 81
Chaplain of the 10th Ohio Cavalry, 10
Chestnut, Thomas, 174
Chicago Invitational Tournament Champions, 352
Chief Buffalo Child Long Lance,255-259
Chiropodist, 215
Chiropractor, 217
church on the railroad, 11
Churches :
African Moravian church,9;
Bethania A.M.E. Zion Church, 5;
Bethania Negro Church, 5;
Capernaum Church of Christ in Clemmons 50;First Baptist Church,13;First Waughtown Baptist Church, 73; Goler AME Zion Church, 17,246; Lloyd Presbyterian Church,44; Methodist Episcopal Church/ Methodist Episcopal Church North, 11;Mt. Zion Baptist Church, 15;New Bethel Baptist Church,15;People's Congregational Church, 16; Shiloh Baptist Church, 77; St. Benedict's Catholic Church, 17; St. Paul Methodist Episcopal Church,12; St. Phillip's Church, 11; Union Baptist Church, 13;Wentz Memorial United Church of Christ, 16;West End Baptist, 15

INDEX

CIAA (Central Intercollegiate Athletic Association),111,343,345,348,352, 355
Citizens Bank and Trust,196
Citizens Police Review Board, 292,
City Hospital/ City Memorial Hospital,241
City Hospital Commission, 218
Civil Rights Act of 1875, 68
Clanton, Harvey, 126
Clanton, Odell, 126
Clark Brown and Sons Funeral Home, 93-94
Clark Campbell Transportation Center, 275-276
Clark, Sam. 340
Clayton, Eli , 248
Clement, Israel, 5, 103-105,132
Clement, Rufus, 103,106
Clemmons School, 26
Clinton, President Bill, 332
Clyburn, Mr. James, 280
Coach Clarence "Big House" Gains, 61,64,342-344
Cobb, Mrs. Thelma, 335
Cohen, Linda G., 81
Coleman, Slick, 341
Colored Baptist Orphanage, 73-74
Colored Branch City Employment, 144
Colored Educational Association of North Carolina, 21
Colored Fair/ Piedmont Colored Industrial Fair, 311-312
Colored Fire Company/ Colored Hook and Ladder and Hose Co, 126,127-128
Colored Men's Ticket, 106
Colored Salem Moravian Church, ,9
Columbian Heights,62-63,126,234-235,271
Columbian Heights High School/Jr High,30,55,60-61,107,146,156,195, 242
Columbian Heights Primary School,24
Congressional Medal of Honor,302
Contract Office Furnishings, 175-176
Cook Jr., Lafayette A., 81
Cooper, Kenneth Richard and Roslyn Dianne, 34
Corley, Norma Ernestine, 34
county school board, 117
Covington, Dr. H. Douglas, 29-30
Crawford, William R/ *Crawford Park.* 156
Croix de Guerre with Star and Golden Palm Leaf, 295
Crosby, Doris , 280
Crump, James, 341
Cunningham, Dr. Isaac S., 214
Curry, Bishop Michael, 8
Cuthrell, Monroe, 143

D

Dalton, Dr.,227
Dance, Paula, 116
Davenport, Mr.,159
Davis, Charlie, 353-354
Davis, Dr. Edward, 218
Davis, Elliot (E. A. Davis), 272
Davis, H. Glenn, 203
Davis, J.L, 263
Davis, Rev. LeRoy,(Rev.W. LeRoy),253-254
Davis, Dr. Lenwood, 291-292
Davis, Lester, 292
Davis, Tom, 173,190,249
Davis, Jr., Rear Admiral Walter Jackson, 305-307
Dean, H.H., 71
DeJournette, Laverne, 165
Delwatts Radio and Electronics Institute, 185-186
Denning, (O.T.)Oliver T.,203-204

Dent, Jim, 369
Department of Housing and Urban Development, 35
Department of Public Works Department-Utilities and Engineering, 147
Depot Street Colored Graded and Industrial School,/Depot Street High School, 22,-23,45-46,52-53
Diggs, Dr. Edward O., 219
Diggs Gallery, 328
Diggs, Jr., James T (Thackery), 124,291-292,328
Diggs, Sr., James T., 124
Diggs, Rev. Jefferson, (Jefferson Davis) 253
Diggs III, Jefferson Davis, 81
Dillahunt, George (G.L.Dillahunt), 133-134
Dixie Classic Fairgrounds, 279,312
Donoho, Mrs. E. O., 282
Douthit, Lucille, 360
Drew, Dr. Charles, 215
Dudley ,Everette L., 81
Durham, Dr. Cynthia, 217
Dutch, Ron, 331
Dutton, Margaret Ann, 81

E

1867 Convention, 21
E. E. Tanner's Gospel Program, 261
Easley, Governor Mike, 96
Easley, Pete, 143
East Winston Public Library/Malloy-Jordan Heritage Center,85,283,285 286
East Winston Press, 254
Easton Elementary, 34
EastWay Plaza Shopping Center,176-177
Edith Cavell Nurses Club, 224

Education:
Act of 1867 , 21;Agricultural and Mechanical College for the Colored Race (N.C. A&T State University), 80;Anderson Junior High School, 60; Brown Decision, 33;Clemmons School, 26;Livingstone College24; Mebane Intermediate School,25-Public School Law 1869, 21; Skyland Elem.,28; Slater Industrial Academy (Slater Industrial and Normal School),23; St. Augustine's Normal Collegiate Institute,23; Wake Forest College, 38; Winston Salem Teachers College (WSSU), 62; Woodland Avenue School, 22
Edwell, (J.S.), James S., 188
Elam, Henry, 126
Elasya B's Candy Tree, .180-181
Elder, Lee ,371
Electro-Magic Hair Grow Company, 163
Eli's Pack and Ship, 179
Elite Beauty Shoppe, 163
Eller, Carl, 357-358
Ellington, First Lt. Spurgeon Neal (Ellington, Spurgeon), 281,287, 300-302
Ellington, (J A), Jim ,182
Ellis, Ben, 159
employment of Negro firemen, 128
English, William, 356
Ervin, Jr, Lester, 128-129
Erwin, Jr., (Judge)Richard C.,203-204,208
ESR(Experiment in Self-Reliance),90
eugenics program, 95-96

INDEX

Evangelical United Brethren Church, 12
Evans, Mütter, 265
Evergreen Cemetery, 279

F

15th Amendment, 100
Fair, Talmadge Willard, *97-98*
Farrakhan, Louis, 64-65
Feemster, Dr. John, 229-230
Female Missionary Society in Salem, 8
File Family, 281
File, Mozelle E., 163
First Baptist Church, 11-15, 43-44, 167
First Waughtown Baptist Church, 73
Fisk University, 11, 207
Fitch, F. M., 134, 281
Fitts, Atty. J. S (John Shepherd), 182, 205-206, 311
(the)Five Royals, 335-336
Five Star Supermarket, 165
Ford, Johns H., 128
Forsyth County Bar Association, 203, 208
Forsyth County Extension Homemakers Council, 91
Forsyth County Seal, 31-32
Forsyth Savings and Trust Company, 167, 196
Forte, Ola Mae, 163-164
Fourteenth Street School, 46-47
Foy, James, 279
Franke, 2
Franklin, Denise, 266-267
Franklin, Nia, 320
Freedman's Bureau, 68
Friende, Palmer Gill, *26*
Friende, Velma Hayes, 260
Friends Association for the Relief of the Colored Freedmen, 72
Friends Freedmen Aid Association, 42
Fries Auditorium, 336-338

Fries, Francis, 233
Fries, George, 159
Fries, Harry, 10-11
Fries, Henry Elias, 337
Fries, John, 10-11
Fries Quarters, 233
Fulton, Bishop, Todd, 116
Funches, Lonzo, 363
Funches, Ralph, 356

G

Gadson, Charles and Irma, 238
Gaines, Clarence E. (Coach) "Big House," 342-344
Gaither, Bruce .81
Gambrell, Mrs. Lillian, 335
Gates, Alex Gates Barbershop 161
George Moses Horton Branch Library, 285
Gilbert, Elias, 365-368
Giles, Algemenia, 81
Gleason, Dr. Eliza Atkins, 41-42
Glenn, Clarence, 287
Glenn, County, 341
God's Acre Cemetery, 279
God's Acre in Bethabara, 37
Godfather of Gospel, 262
*Goler AME Zion Church (*Memorial), 214
Goler Daycare Nursery, 289
Goler, W.H., 245-246
Gordon, Dr. Joseph, 220, 223-224
Gorham, James R., 304-305
Gorrell, A. B., 72
Gospel Media Radio, 262
Grace, Attorney Michael, 116
Graham, Dorothy, 75
Graham, J.L., 126
Graham, Polly, 84
grand jury, 63
Grandson, L.N., 63
Grant, Robert, 357

INDEX

Grater, Abraham, 240
Greene, Alphonse, 287
Green, David, 356
Green, Rev. Lizzie, 86
Green, Ulysses Grant, 81
Gregory, Marjorie, 86-87
Grier, Clarence, 287
Grier, Pam, 319
Grier, Robert L., 128
Griffin, Arcenure, 140
Grimes Jr., Dr. William T., 221
Guy, Linda, 81
Gwyn, Gilbert "Rags," 341
Gwyn, (John)J.B., 103, 106

H

Hadley, Frank, 356
Haggler, Joseph, 287
Hairston, Thomas, 126
Hairston, Jefferson, 272
Hairston, Frederick W., 286
Hairston, Harold "Happy," 350-351
Hairston, Harold Lee, 86, 254
Hairston, MacKay, 286
Hairston, Miss Lula, 227
Hairston, Mrs. M. M. (Mary), 283-284
Hairston, Rufus, 181
Hall, Ed, 416
Hall, George, 9
Hall, Dr. Humphrey Henry (H.H.), 170, 181, 213-214, 227
Hall, Leroy, 170
Hamilton Scales Tobacco Company, 132
Hamlin, Larry Leon, 329-320, 330
Hankins, Harry, 165
Happy Hill/ Happy Hills Settlement, 232, 238, 288
Hardy, Claudette A., 221-222
Hargrave, S.H., 103
Hargraves, Dr., 227
Harlem Hell Fighters, 296-297

Hargraves, Dr., 227
Harlem Hell Fighters, 296-297
Harris, R., 340
Hartsfield, District Judge Denise, 116
Hauser, Marion, 287
Hauser, William, 247
Hawkins, Maria Antoinette, 302
Hawkins, Mrs. Louise, 91-92
Hayes, Bill, 345
Hayes, Mrs. Jessie, 271
Hayes, Roland H., 152-153
Heggie, Louis, 240
Henly, James, 131
Henry, John B., 286
Henry, Kenneth, 357
Hickerson, Coral, 334
Hickerson, Mrs., 240, 334
Hickerson, R. W., 143
Hicks, John, 340
Hill, Cleo, 343, 348
Hill, Edward Everett, 58-59
Hill family, 280
Hill, George W., 182
Hill, Gilbert, 64
Hill, J. S (James), 63, 195
Hill, Mrs. Leather, 335
Hobson, D.C. *61*
Hodson, Eloise, 335
Holiness Review, 253
Holland, Catherine, 134
Holland, Rev. G.W. (George Washington), 13, 15, 73
Holmes, Arthur Lee, 159
Holmes, Johnny, 335
Hood, Bishop James W. 21
Hooper, T. H., 195
Hopkins, Larry, 291, 360-361
Hopkins, Velma, 77, 291-292
Horton, George, 285
Howard Robinson Funeral Home, 167, 312

INDEX

Howard, Blackburn, Scales Funeral Home,171
Howard, K., 170
Howard-Robinson-Scales Funeral Home, 170-171
Hughes, J.F.(John), 103,143
Hughes, Langston, 285
Hughson, Mr. J. S., 196
Hyman, John Adams, 100

I
Ingram, Emma, 86-87
Integration, 21,33-38,60
Irvin, Clarence, 253

J
Jackson, Dr. F.W.,81
Jacquelyne B. Barber Excellence in CommunityLeadership Award, 87
James Strates Show, 312
James, Mrs. Laura E, 335
Jeffers, Horace, 131
Jeffries, Dr. Jasper, 30
Jeffries, Otto, 335
Jeffries, Sr., Phil W., 334
Jerry Watkins Cadillac-GMC,174
Jessup, Elasya,180-181
Jitney, 270-271
Joel, Sergeant First Class Lawrence, 302-304
Johansson, Patricia, 64
Johnson, Anthony Wayland, 81
Johnson, Braeden, 87
Johnson, C. B., 281
Johnson, Charles, 287
Johnson, Chenita, 86
Johnson, Ernest B., 188
Johnson, Henry, 295-298
Johnson, Joe , 369-370
Johnson, Joycelyn, 86
Johnson, L. L., .182

Johnson, Leroy, 260
Johnson, Mabel E., 86-87
Johnson, Paul Brandon, 86
Johnson, Paul S., 261-263
Johnson, Rev. Elijah, 253
Johnson, Sergeant Major Gilbert "Hashmark," 299
Johnson, Jr., Victor, 81,120,
Johnson, Jr, Willie H., 31
Joines, Mayor Allen, 90
Jones Toni L., 86
Jones, Alvan, 284
Jones, Attorney W. Avery, 197,203-204
Jones, Charles (C.H.),H ,182,195-196 246,281
Jones, Dr. Beverly, 181
Jones, Dr. Clarence "Jeep," 111-112
Jones, Dr. J.W.(Dr. John W),181-182 196,213,227
Jones, Dr. W. A., 181-182
Jones, Glenn, 77
Jones, Jerry, 368-369,372
Jones, Lafayette, 178
Jones, Sandra Miller, 178
Jordan, J. C., 284
Joseph, Lerla G., 221-222
Joyce, John, 132-134
Joyce, Pinckney, 73
Joyce,Wash, 247
Joyce., Rev. Pinckney, 15,73
Joyner, Claude "Pop," 33

K
Kate Bitting Reynolds Memorial Hospital, 215,227
Kennedy, Annie Brown,203, 207-208
Kennedy, Francis M. (Frank) (F. M.), 196,281
Kennedy, Jr Harold (Attorney Harold) 89,203,292
Kimberley Park Elementary School, 49-49

INDEX

Kimberley Park, 288
Kimbrough, Jr, Bobby F., 115-116
Kimbrough, Vaughn, 356
Knight, Mrs. Beverly W, 226
Knights of Labor Hall, 70
Kurfees, Marshall, 81
Kyles Heights Apartments, 51-52
Kyles, Bishop Lynwood
    Westinghouse, 17,51

L

Labor Bureau, 144
Lafayette Theater, 167-168,315-316
La-Mae Beauty College, 163-164
Lambson, Angela, 361-362
Landon, J. A., 135-136
Langson, Mary, 215
Lanier, Raphael O'Hara (R. O'Hara),
    28-29,254
Lanier, Atty. J.S. (James), 159,182, 202,
    205-206
Lark, James, 335
Larry D. Little Fitness Course, 84
Lathan, John, 356
Lattie, Justice G.(J.G.),103, 126
Lawrence Joel Veterans Memorial
    Coliseum, 280,303
Leak, Robert, 86-87
Lee, Dr. Cleon Oscar, 216
Lee, L.O., 281
Lemely, Mr., 253-234
Leonard Medical School, 213-214
Leonard, Lloyd, 174
Lesure, Percy, 356
Lewis, Dr. Lillian, 117-118
Lewis, J. W., 182
Lincoln Theater, 167-168
Lind, Alfred, 43
Little Theater of Winston-Salem,329
Little, Camille, 354-355
Little, Dr. Larry D., 85-84,113
Lloyd Presbyterian Church, 44,159

Long, Abe Miles,256
Long, Detective Walter Lee,141-142
    255,258
Long, Joseph Sylvester, 255-256
Long, Sylvester Clark, 255
Long, T.,340
Louis, Joe , 363
Lowe, Paul, 86
Lucas, Moses"Mo," 282
Lundlow, Howard, 340
Lyles, William, 287

M

MacDonald, Rev., 161
Macedonia True Vine Pentecostal
    Holiness Church of God, INC.
    262
Mack, Bishop Sir Walter, 116
Mack, Felicia, 86
Mack-Hilliard, Hazel, 83
Malloy, Sr., H. D. 284
Malloy, Dr. H. Rembert, 215-216, 284
    286,291-292
Malloy, Nelson, 83-84,292
Malone, Misses Odessa, 335
Manasseri, Benedict, 17-18
March, Russell, 287
Marshall, Mrs. Georgia Murray,289-290
Marshall, Walter, 123
Martin, Al, 262-263
Martin, Davida, 151
Martin, Joe, 371
Martin, Peter, 43
Mathews, Carl, 80-81
Mayfield, A. A.,254
Mayo, E.P., 63
Mayor Pro Tempore,108,113
McCall, Fred, 272
McCardell, James,76
McCarter, Ed and Miriam, 175
McClenny, Ruth, 134

INDEX

McConney, Dr. Christopher, 217
McCurry, Mary, 27-28
McFadden, Gary, 116
McFadden, Joe, 362-364
McGregor, Noble, 165
McGuinness, Bishop Eugene, 17
McKnight, J. C., 182
McLean, Charles, 143-144
McLean, Naomi, 184
McLean's Stenographic and Tutoring Service, 184-185
McLoyd, John, 340
McManus, Alan, 356
MEAC, 345
Mebane Intermediate School, 24-25
Mebane, Lillian McLesterHayes, 24
Mechanics and Farmers Bank, 199
Melton, Mrs. Janie, 282
Memorial Industrial Institute, 74
Men's Outdoor Track & Field National Championships, 366
Merchants Hotel, 161
Meredith, John F., 128
Meta's Restaurant, 166-167
Methodist Episcopal Church North(Methodist Episcopal Church), 5, 11
Middleton, Joe, 365-366
Miller, Bruce, 260
Miller, (E. H) Elijah., 270-272
Miller, Gaither, 335
Miller, Joseph, 272
Miller, Lee , 335
Miller, Quentin, 116
Miller Robert, 255
Ministers:
    Goslen, Rev. A.T., 5; Hall, Dr. George, 9; Holland, Rev. George W., 13, 15, 73; Joyce, Rev. Pinckney, 13, 73; Kyles, Bishop, 17, 51; Wells, Rev. Isaac, 12, 283;

Wentz, Dr. Samuel, 16
Mission House, 72
Monroe, Earl "the Pearl," 352-353, 355-356
Montford Point Marines, 299-300
Montgomery, Derwin, 114-115
Moore, Aaron, 126
Moore, James, 335
Moore, Sam, 340
Moore, Shirese, 130-131
Moore, Winston, 185
Moravian Church, 2-4, 8-10, 42, 233
Morgan and Scales Garage, 171-172
Morgan, D.L., 186
Morgan, Mrs. Delphine, 272-273
Morgan, Harvey(F.)Franklin, 171, 236, 272
Morgan-Hoffman (Dry) Cleaners, 186 187
Morgan, Ralph R. (R. R.), 272-273, 287
Morisey, A. Alexander, 254
Morris, Addie, *Annie(Addie)*, 72-73
Morrison, Lula, 225
Morton, Lorraine Hairston, 109-110
Morwell, 236
Mosby, C.R., 272
Motley, Willie "Chic," 186
Motorsports Management, 66
Mr. Hall, 159
Mt. Pleasant Methodist Church, 12
Mt. Zion Baptist Church, 17

N

NAACP of Winston-Salem, 75, 143
Naismith Basketball Hall of Fame, 342-343, 353, 356
Nat Turner Rebellion, 20
National Association of Black Journalists, 255
National Association of Intercollegiate Athletics (NAIA), 255

INDEX

National Black Theatre Festival, 330
National NCAA College Division II Basketball Championships, 356
National Retail Merchants Association, 160
NC Baptist Hospital, 249
NC Medical Society(NCMS), 223-224
Neal, Henry, 126
Neal, Lena B., 74
Neely, Cicero, 181
Neely, Tom, 186
(St. Phillips) Moravian Church, 4, 9-10
Negro Congregation, 6
Negro Knights of Labor, 70
Negro National League, 341
Negro Orphanage, 15, 73
Negro Quarter, 8, 233, 279
Nell Hunter Choral Society, 334
Nelson, Charles, 50-51
Nelson Preparatory and Industrial School, 50-51
Nesby, W. M., 197
Newell, Dr. Virginia, 112-113, 292
Newell, G. F., 286
"News of Colored People," 254
NFL Hall of Fame, 357
Nicholas Brothers, 317
Nicholas, Harold Lloyd, 317-318
Nixon, President Richard, 248
Norris, Patricia, 137
North Carolina A&T State University, 22, 80, 146, 345, 348
North Carolina Association of Chiefs of Police (NCACP), 137
North Carolina Black Repertory Theatre Company, 330
North Carolina Chapter of the PGA, 369
North Carolina Colored Volunteer Fireman's Association, 126
North Carolina General Assembly, 208
North Carolina Journalism Hall of Fame, 40
North Carolina State Association of Colored Graduates Nurses, Incorporated, 224
North Elementary school, 92
Northern Quakers Friends Association, 42
Northington, Robert, 292
Nurses:
    Andrews, Mrs. Gwendolyn, 226; Barrett, Emma, 224; Brown, Mrs. Annie K., 224; Knight, Beverly W., 226; Morrison, Lula, 225; Strickland, Girlie Jones, 224; Teer, Miss Daisy, 224;
Nursing Degree program at Winston-Salem Teachers College, 226

O

Oak Street Colored Grade School, 49
Oates, William, 144, 169
Obama, President Barack, *154, 298*
Odd Fellows Cemetery, 279, 281
Odd Fellows Lodge, 280
Old City Hospital, 90, 219
Old Hedgecock Brickyard, 249
Old North State Medical Society, 223 224
Old Salem, 18, 36
Oliver, Peter, 2
Otesha Creative Arts Ensemble, 331-332
Oubre, Hayward, 322-324
Overbea, Luix V., 255

P

Paisley High School, 49, 60-61
Paisley, John, 48, -49, 287
parish or stranger's graveyard, 9, 279
Parker, Karen L., 39-40

Parmon, Earlene, 34-35,84-86,125
Patterson, Dollie, 27
Pauling, Lomond, 335
Peace Paper and School Supply, 177
Peace, Jim, 177
Pearson, Mrs. William, 335
Pearson, Rev., 246
Peebles, Charlie R., 272
Pegram, Oleona Glenn, 41,206
Pender, Randon,86
Pendleton, Henry ,43, 103
Penn Relays, 365-366
Penn, Benjamin, 165
Penn, George W., 128
Penn, William K., 144
Penry, Albert "Pomp," 164
People's Printing Company, 174
People's Spokesman, 253
Peoples, Bryska, 145
Pershing , General Blackjack, 297
Pete, Geraldine, 324
Petree, Mr. Nelson, 341
Pfohl, Dr.,227
Phillips, Dr. Irene, 86
Phillips, Mr. Garret E."Roy,"200,249
Phyllis Wheatley Home (Institute), 74,184
Philson, Annie Bell, 145
Physicians:
>Bell, Marilyn L., 221-222;.Bruce, Sr Dr. William (W.H), 169,181; Davis,Dr. Edward, 218;Diggs, Edward O.,219; Durham , Cynthia, 217; Feemster, Dr. John, 229-230; Gordon, Dr. Joseph,220,223; Grimes Jr., Dr. William T., 221; Hall , Dr. H.H.(Henry)Humphrey Hall), 213;Hardy, Claudette A., 221-222; Jones, Dr.J.W., 181; Joseph, Lerla G., 221-222;Langson, Mary, 215;Lee,

>Cleon Oscar, 216; Malloy, Dr. H. Rembert, 215; *McConney, Dr., 217;* Ray, Dr.Alexander Hamilton,210 Richardson, B. Parthenia, 221-222; Shober, Dr. James,212; Walker, Joseph , 218-219; Weaver, Yvonne J., 221-222; Williamson, John (J.C.)C., 217; Young, William E., 214;

Piedmont Airlines, 188,190,249
Piedmont leaf strike (1944), 79
Piedmont Publishing, 253
Pitt, Ernie, 253
Pitts, Columbus and Alice, 234
Pitts, Rev. Robert, 77-78
Pleasants, Nancy, 292
Plyler, Dave, 116
Poag, Mollie, 144-145
Poag, T.F., 286
Policewomen, 134
Pond Giants, 341-342
Poole, Almeta ,167
Pope, James D.,287
Porter, Albert, 86, 147
Postal carriers, 145
Powell, W. H. T.,295
Price, Attorney Hosea V.,17, 203-204
Public-School Law in 1869, 21
Purple People Eaters defensive line, 358
Puryear, Royal, 281
Pyramid Barbershop, 171
Pythian Hall, 159

Q

Quakers, 21
Quick, Dr. J. D.(Jr., John D,197,287

R

R. J. Reynolds Tobacco Company, 76-77
R.J. Reynolds High School, 32
R.J. Reynolds Local #22, 68,76-77

INDEX

Ragsdale, George, 272,281
Ragsdale, Lillian, 254
Ralph and Harvey Morgan, 171-172
Randthaler, Bishop Edward, 9
Ray, Dr. Alexander, Hamilton, 210-211
Ray, Mrs. M. Y , 284
Ray's Hospital, 210
Raymond, H., 340
"Red Tails," 301
Redd, Oliver D., 135-136
Reeves, Deloris M.,81
Reid, James, 256
Relief of Colored Freedmen, 42
Resolution for Israel Clement, 105
Rev. A.T. Goslen, 5
Rex Theater, 167, 314-315
Reynolds Town (Cameron Park),242
Reynolds, A.B., 61
Reynolds, Charles, 86-87
Reynolds, Edward, 37-38
Reynolds, George, 196
Reynolds, Mr., 159
Reynolds, W. N., 227
Rice, Dr. William, 78,291-292
Rich, Billy, 292
Richardson, B. Parthenia, 221-222
Rising Ebenezer Baptist Church, 238
Roberts, Needham, 296-297
Robinhood Park, 312-314
Robinson (Aladine,), 167, 170,197,287, 313
Robinson Funeral Home, 17,
Rock N Roll Hall of Fame, 336
Rogers, Danny, 116
Rolanda, 268
Roosevelt, Eleanor, 321
Roosevelt, Franklin, 92,298,334
Roosevelt, President Theodore, 294
Rorie, Charles, 126
Ross, Wilbur, 366
Roundtree, Barry, 138

Roundtree, Robert "Bobcat," 261
Rucker, Wentz,182
Ruffin, Miss Adele, 282
Russell Funeral Home, 108
Russell, Carl (Carl H.), 253
Russell, Cedric, 116

S

S. H. Kress Company, 80
Sadler, Pete, 271
Safe Bus , (Safe Bus Company),271- 274
Saleem, Amatullah, 331
Salem Academy, 36-37,268
Salem Female Missionary Society, 8
Salem Tavern, 2
Sam, 9
Samuel, Anna Maria,36-37
Samuel, Jacob, 4
Samuel, Johann Christian, 4
Samuel, Johann, 8
Sanford, B.O.,186
Sanford, Governor Terry, 190
Sansom, Jr., James Joseph,198-199
Saxon, William R. ,253
Scales, Archie, 126
Scales Cement Block Manufacturing Company, 167
Scales, I.A.,340
Scales, Irving, 126
Scales, R. W.,167
Scales, William Samuel, 167-168,316
Schumann, Dr. Frederich, 233
Searcy, Herbert, 247
Searcy, Robert, 126
Segmented Marketing Service, Inc. (SMSI), 178
Segregation Ordinance, 239-238
Seward, H. S., 126
Shabazz, Ciat, 86
Sharpe, Linda, 292
Shaw Tire, 173

INDEX

Shaw University Leonard Medical School, 213
Shaw, James, 172-173
Shiloh Baptist Church, *15, 77*
Ship, Walter Lee ,299
Shirley, Josie , 86
Shoaf, Robert, 81, 166
Shober, Dr., James, 212-213
Shuler, Olin, 116
Siewers, Richard, 233
Simpson, Theodosia, 77
Single Sisters House in Salem,36-37
Sister Larretta Rivera-Williams, RSM,6
Sisters of Mercy of North Carolina, 6
Sit In Movement, 90
Skyland Elementary, 28,61
Slater Hospital, 226-227
Smith Reynolds Airport, 279
Smith, E. W.,281
Smith, James,161
Smith, John, 126
Smith, John H.,247
Smith, Louise, 25
Smith, Mrs. Georgia (Georgia M.), 199-200,248
Smith, Steven,356
Smith, Willie, 357
Smith., Mrs. Carrie M, 335
Southeastern Center for Contemporary Art (S.E.C.C.A.), 328
Southeastern Lawyers' Association, 203
South Pacific Heavyweight Championship,364
Spanish American War, 295
Special Occasions Bookstore, 175
Sprinkle-Hamlin, Sylvia, 149-150
St. Anne's Academy, 51-52

St. Augustine's Normal Collegiate Institute, 23
St. Benedict Elementary School, 52
St. Benedict the Moor Catholic Church,17-18
St. Home Methodist Episcopal Church, 235
St. Paul Methodist Ep. Church,11,94, 235, 253
St. Phillips Church Museum at Old Salem, 8
St. Phillips Moravian Church, 9-10
St. Stephen's Episcopal Church, 7
Star Stenographic School of Business, 184-185
Starbuck, H.R., 63
Starbuck, Judge Darius H 132
Steiner, Abraham, 9
Stemmers, 76,79
Stephens, Priscilla,274
Stevens, Bill, 81
Stinson, William, 335
Strickland, Mrs. Girlie Jones,224
Suffrage Amendment ,101
Sumler, Rodney J.,253
Summers, Freddie, 358-359
Sutton, Thomas H., 63

T

Tanner, John,335
Tatum, Ronda, 152
tavern in Bethabara, 2
Taylor, Deanna, 120
Teer, Miss Daisy, 224
Terry, Evelyn, 86
Texas State University for Negroes, 29
The A.C. Phoenix, 253
The Battle of Henry Johnson, 297
The Brown Derby, 186
The Carolina Times, 253

INDEX

The League Grocery Store, 164
The Mighty Rams of Winston-Salem State College (Winston-Salem State University), 355-356
The National Black Theater Festival, 330
The NC Black Repertory Company, 330
The North State Film Company, 316
The Old Prince Albert Pond Giants (Winston-Salem Pond Giants), 341-342
The People's Building and Loan Association, 195
the pond, 243, 341
The Post newspaper, 253
The Rosenwald Fund, 56
The Society for the Study of Afro American History in Winston-Salem/Forsyth County (SSAH), 291
The Upperman School, 163
The W Times, 254
The Winston-Salem Chronicle, 253
Third Street Bank, 199-200
Thomas, John R., 128
Thompson, Catrina A., 139
Thompson, Odert, 86
Thompson, Will, 341
Tillman, Patricia, 86
Timlic, James, 311
tobacco rollers, 70
Todd, Curtis(Curtiss), 185, 203
Todd, Delores, 346-348
Todman, Norwood, 351-352
Torian, Luke, 64
Trollinger, Tom, 175-176
Truliant Credit Union, 197
Tunstall, Spencer, 131
Turner J. H., 196, 281, 311
Turner, Mrs. Lillian B., 282

Turner, Mrs. Virginia, 335
Tuskegee Airman, 281
Tuttle, Arthur, 71
Twin City Building and Loan Association, 195
Twin City Chrysler Plymouth, 174
Twin City Glee Club, 334
Twin City Hospital, 210
Twin City Medical Society, 214

U

U.S. Employment Office (colored division), 144
UNC Medical School, 124, 219
Union Republic Newspaper, 72, 104, 243
United Tobacco Workers Union (Local #22), 76
University of North Carolina at Chapel Hill (UNC- Chapel Hill), 39, 124, 190, 219, 285, 355
Upperman School of Hair Dressing and Beauty Dressing and Beauty Parlors, 163
Upperman, Annie R., 163

V

Venable, Hazel, 134
Vickers, Michael M., 71
Victory Credit Union, 197
Victory Dry Cleaners, 187
village of Bethabara, 2

W

W. H. Bruce Building, 144, 169, 184
W.A. Jones drugstore, 181-182
W.L. Robinson building, 186
W.P.A *(W.P.A. Program)*, 92, 288
WAAA Radio, 260-261
Wachovia, 4
Wachovia Administration Farm, 8
Wachovia Bank and Trust Company, 198-200

INDEX

Wade, Frank,340
Wake Forest College (Wake Forest University), 6, 37,40,80,
Wake Forest University School of Law,84
Walker, Dicker, 354
Walker, Dr. Joseph, 219,197-198,223-224
Walker, Joseph, 299
Wallace, Chris, 165
Wallace, Raymond, 341
Washington, Francis, 365-366
Watkins, Jerry D., 174
Watkins, Johnny, 356
Watson, Jr., Joe, 253
Watson, Maggie, 83
Watson, Paul, 81
Watts, Rolanda, ,267-268
Waugh Plantation, 212
Waugh, Betsy Ann, 212
Waugh, Sallie, 45
Waugh, Samuel, 45
Waughtown, 10-11,21,43,73
Weaver, Yvonne J.,221-222
Wells, Ida B., 69
Wells, Reverend Isaac, 12,281
Wentz Memorial Congregational Church, 16
Wentz, Rev(Dr. Samuel)., 16
West End Baptist, ,15
West, Jr., Togo Dennis, 260,307-308
WFDD FM 88.5, 266
WFMY-TV2, 268
Wheeler Airlines, 188-191
Wheeler, John, 199 ,
Wheeler, Warren H., 188-191
White, George H., 69
White Jr., J.C., 287
Wilburn, Andrew, 11
Wiley, Dr. Calvin H., 44
Will Eisner Comic Book Hall of Fame, 327
William Oates Employment Agency, 144
Williams , Lt. L. C., 128
Williams, Donald, 356
Williams, Frank, 86
Williams, Jr., Irvin,287
Williams, Kenneth R.,78,107,121
Williams, Larry , 261
Williamson, Dr. J. C. ,181,210,217-218
Williamson Hospital, 218
Williamson, George, 81
Wilson, Bobby,286
Wilson, Charles B., 265
Wilson, Jerry, 81
Wilson, Louise, 90
Winston Industrial Association, 182
Winston Lake Family Y,281-282
Winston Lake Golf Course, 370-371
Winston Mutual Insurance Company (Winston Mutual Life Insurance Company),22,182-183
Winston-Salem African American Archive, 291
Winston-Salem Chapter of the Black Panther Party, 82-84
Winston-Salem Enterprise, 253
Winston-Salem Forsyth County Board of Education, 118
Winston-Salem Forsyth County Fire Department, 128-130
Winston-Salem Forsyth County School System, 24-25
Winston-Salem Negro High School, 53
Winston-Salem, North Carolina Chamber of Commerce, 180
Winston-Salem post office, 143
Winston-Salem Prep, 56
Winston-Salem State University (Winston-Salem State Teacher's

College(WSSU),22,25,28,63,143,
   184,207,225,234,242
Winston-Salem State University
   School of Health Sciences, 226
Winston Town Commissioners,103
Wiseman, Sr. ,Hoyt, 254
Womble, Larry,81,86-87,95-96,275,292
Wood, Mayor Martha,116,292,302
Woodbury, Malishai "Shai,"121
Woodland Avenue Colored Grade
      School (Woodland Avenue
      School),27,77
Woodland, (C. T) Clarence T.,272
Woodruff, Mazie, 122,292
Wooten, Mrs. Marian, 288-289
World War I, 160,256,294-295,297
Wright, Ennis , 116
Wright, Hugh, 292
WSMX, (WSMX Radio), 261
Wyfall, Willie, 363

X

Xuma, Alfred Bitini, 89
Xuma, Madie Hall , 88-89

Y

Yarbrough, Sally A. U, 163
YMCA, 281-283
Young Memorial Hospital, 210
Young, Gilbert, 331
Young, William E., 214
YWCA, 75,282-283

Z

Zinzendorf Hotel, 161

About the Author

Chenita Barber Johnson is Vice-President of the Winston-Salem African American Archive, an educational and history repository of local historical African American artifacts and documents. As part of the WSAAA she aids in the investigations and documentations of all aspects of African American history in Winston-Salem and Forsyth County, NC from the county's inception until present. She also works with the Friends of Oddfellows, INC. This organization works to preserve the historical African American Oddfellows Cemetery located in Winston-Salem, NC.
Johnson is also an advocate for public education and a community activist.

Born and raised in Winston-Salem, NC she attended the local public schools however, due to her mother's employment with the Federal Government she also attended school in Danville, VA, graduated from high school in Parkersburg, WV as well as attending Marshall University in Huntington, WV. When she returned to Winston-Salem, she attended and graduated from Winston-Salem State University with a degree in Political Science/Public Administration with a minor in History.

Johnson was inspired by her mother and maternal grandmother, to understand the empowerment of owning and telling *our history*. She was also taught that it is the responsibility of us all to understand the importance and impact of African American history in our local, state and national history. Recognizing that African American history is not only important to the growth of the entire community, it is a part of the community. She hopes the information within these pages will allow you, the reader, to feel the same inspiring empowerment of owning and telling y*our history* in your community.

Made in the USA
Middletown, DE
05 November 2023

41843977R00258